Coaching the Gap-Control Rover Defense

Coaching the Gap-Control Rover Defense

Tom Olivadotti

Parker Publishing Company, Inc.
West Nyack, N.Y.

PARKER PUBLISHING COMPANY, INC.

West Nyack, N.Y.

Library of Congress Cataloging in Publication Data

Olivadotti, Tom
Coaching the gap-control rover defense.

1. Football--Defense. I. Title.
GV951.18.O44 796.33'22 75-22341
ISBN 0-13-139311-1

Printed in the United States of America

In dedication to my dear wife without whose patience, understanding, and support I would not be permitted the opportunity and time to coach and prepare to the maximum.

How This Book Will Help You

The Gap-Control Rover Defense is easy to teach and easy to learn. It assigns definite gaps for the defensive front seven which they must control, and definite responsibilities to all defenders. Usually, every gap is controlled by two defenders on movement by the offense. The ball carrier is left with nowhere to run. The rover gives the defense the necessary flexibility, because the rover can make most of the common adjustments to the offense. The defense is constantly moving on the snap of the ball, yet there is little stunting and therefore there is no loss of depth. Since there is no loss of depth in the defense, seldom does the "big" play occur for the offense.

Included are the technical skills for each position, presented in such a way that they can easily be understood and organized to allow for proper teaching progression. However, the most important benefits to be derived from the book are the details and coaching points that can be used by any coach to fit into his defensive scheme. The whole defense need not be incorporated for success.

The defensive tackle movement in controlling his gap is unique, as demonstrated in Chapter 5. The coach can have much success in this position without having superior personnel, because of the constant movement of the tackles. Yet they are not penetrating, thereby losing pursuit or giving up the big play for the offense. The tackle technique will squeeze the internal running area shut, and also close the running alley on counter plays.

The techniques and quick flow of the linebackers illustrated in Chapter 8 show how linebackers are not held by internal fakes and are free to move to the ball. The coach need not worry about blockers constantly blocking the linebackers. From the base alignment only one blocker even has a chance at the linebacker, and that blocker is being hit on the line of scrimmage.

The great flexibility that comes with the movement of the rover gives the coach a weapon that is a continual problem for the offense, yet is a very simple maneuver for the defense. The rover can be used to create an 8-man front versus teams that tend to run a majority of the time, or it can be primarily a pass defender versus passing teams. The possibilities are endless. Some ideas are brought out in Chapter 10. The coach can expand on the ideas that are shown in the book. The rover theory can be used according to a coach's needs at a given time. Also, the rover can make all the adjustments to formation, field position and motion so that other defenders won't be tied down.

The multiple defensive fronts never change the basic defensive concepts of gap control, and the various fronts do not change the technical skills and responsibilities for the players. What does this mean for the coach? It means that you can have a simple and consistent defense that is still flexible enough to create problems for the offense and be in a good strategical alignment versus any offensive set-up. Also, because of various defensive fronts, the utilization of the best personnel in any given game or in any given year allows for long term consistency. This point is clearly brought out in Chapter 3. The players have a chance to build confidence in one system.

At the end of each chapter that deals with a particular position are discussed the common faults a coach may find at that position. Now the coach can work to avoid the errors before they occur. Many possible problems are tied together for the coach in Chapter 13. The remedies are given so the coach won't be hurt on the field of play.

This book presents to the coach a defense that has proven successful, not only on the blackboard, but also on the playing field against the best possible competition. This defense is not a hodge-podge defense but a coordinated and consistent defense that can be highly successful with players of average ability. We know that reading this book will make you a better coach. It will at least help stimulate the coach, especially the offensive-minded coach, into a plan of attack.

Tom Olivadotti

Table of Contents

Symbols

Center — ⊗

Offensive Man — ○

Defensive Man — △

Coverage Area —

Key and/or Pass —

Responsibility —

Ball —

Handoff —

Ball Carrier — ●

Offensive Man Being Referred to —

Collision Point — ✱

1

Defensive Attitude

All defenses must have some basic principles to follow in regard to non-technical aspects. These aspects are common to most defenses:

1. Playing Offense on Defense

A coach must make his defensive men conscious of getting the ball from the offense. He cannot take for granted that the defense will play offense on defense. For example, if there is a fumble in an open area, will the defender fall on the ball or will he pick it up and run with it? If he is thinking "offense" on defense he will pick it up and score. Every coach knows there are more ways to score on defense than on offense, but do the players know? Take nothing for granted! Remember, no matter how much knowledge the coach is giving out to his players, if his players aren't learning, then the coach is not teaching.

2. Defeating Offense Physically and Mentally

It is possible to work on defenders' minds; they must believe they can beat the offense. You, as a coach, may know that you are outmanned physically, but knowing your opponent is superior in talent cannot be an excuse for the defense. We try to sell our players the idea that they are in better condition and mentally more prepared than their opponent. We never think of winning the game. We only think of winning the play. Each play is a battle in the war. Looking at it mentally, a man who doesn't want to be beaten will not be beaten.

Naturally, working on the players' minds is only part of the battle to put together a great defense. We believe quickness is most important, along with strength, hitting intensity, and desire. These are common sense to any coach, but do the players know exactly what is expected of them? We sell the players on the fact that quickness and agility can be improved to a degree.

3. Defensive Challenge

Any defense should be able to stop an offense much of the time —that is, starting on the offense's own 20-yard line. The challenge comes to a defense when the defense has held the opponent on our 20-yard line. Our offense comes in and fumbles or the ball is intercepted. Now the defense must rise to the occasion. Assuming the defense holds again and the offense errors again, now is the true challenge of a defense.

Can the defense rise to this sudden change? This is the defensive challenge! The opponents will be thinking:

- What a great break.
- We have them going now.
- Their defense will be tired.
- Let's hit them quick.
- Our defense did a great job of getting the ball.

If the defensive thinking is along the following lines, the defender does not belong on defense:

- What a lousy break.
- I don't know whether I can hold again.
- Boy, I hope someone comes up with the big play.
- Our offense put us here. How could they do this.
- It just isn't fair.

If the defender has this immature, silly attitude, he had better get out of football. Mistakes occur and they will occur to everyone. Naturally, the team with fewer mistakes usually wins; however, all must play over mistakes and petty complaining. The defensive thoughts should be: "What a tough break, but now is the time for me to make the big play. Now is the time to show what defense really is. It was a tough break for the offense, but no one wants to make a mistake." Take this attitude and the defense will never falter.

4. Ground Time and Recovery

A player's value to the team is easily answered: how close he is to the ball and how long he was on the ground. No defender can stay blocked; they all may get blocked but can't stay blocked. They must accelerate away from the blocker. If a defender is blocked or beaten, he must recover. The secret to defense is recovery! There is no excuse for poor pursuit or poor movement to a ball in flight. Not moving to the ball is poor mental discipline, and most of all it is our fault in coaching if we allow it. On the way down to the ground the defender should be thinking of getting up off the ground and what he will do when he does. We feel pursuit and ground time must be overemphasized to the point of being almost absurd. (Note: Slipping is no excuse for an error!)

5. Goal Line Philosophy

If a coach plays any type of competitive schedule—when talent is equal to his talent—be assured that in the course of the season he will be in a goal line defense at least 25 times in a ten-game schedule. The players must be convinced that on the goal line the opponent will have to work to score—if they are "lucky" enough to score. We believe the defensive success of our team is based on our goal line defense. This is where defensive pride is a must, and it is also where defensive pride can be developed.

On the goal line, emphasis is placed on getting the ball and putting the "face" on the ball. Force the fumble.

6. Personnel Philosophy

This is my favorite topic. You, as a coach, will not see the ideal type of player for each position section in this book. Being realistic, on a high school level we don't have much choice. Ideally, to keep everyone happy this is what we would like at each position: a 6′4″ 250-pound Adonis with 4.6 forty time who has great agility and who runs through brick walls and jumps over the goal posts for a warm-up. Generally, we will get players who average 5′10″ and 170 pounds. The point is that we want the best people we can find on defense. Only the best will play without regard to personality. This will offend many people, but if a team is to be successful the best personnel must be used.

7. Scouting

We believe that for a defense to succeed, the opponent's offense must be scouted with a play-by-play breakdown. This is especially true if film exchange is not possible. We will get (if any) a formation tendency, down/distance tendency, hash tendency, field position tendency, sequence tendency, personnel tendency, after loss or penalty plays, etc. Then we want to know their primary plays. We feel it is important for the defense to know all of the opponent's plays, but we only practice stopping their primary plays. Most coaches do these things and it is nothing new, but what is important is who runs the opponent's plays in practice. We use the best football players we can possibly get on our scout teams. That means many offensive starters who are only playing offense. If the scout team is poor we all fail, and a coach who fails enough will have to go to another school to fail or retire.

If a coach has enough players he should try to get two offensive scout teams so the defense is constantly being drilled on the opponent's plays. "Correct repetition is the mother of learning!"

2

Getting to the Line in the Gap-Control Rover Defense

Many defensive signals are given from the sideline; therefore, a quick and disciplined huddle is of prime importance. The reason for giving signals from the sideline is that it relieves the players of having to think on the field. The coach does the thinking, while the players concentrate on playing to the best of their ability.

1. Huddle (Middle Man Sets Huddle)

After each play everyone must hustle back to the huddle. This huddle must look the same way in the fourth quarter as it did in the first quarter. When the huddle gets sloppy, so does the playing. The opponents, seeing our disciplined huddle, will realize that we came to play football and that we are a disciplined football team.

The front-line people will have their hands on their knees and heads up listening for the call. The players in the back will have their arms behind their back and stand tall. The signal caller or callers will call the defense or defenses. Before this, one signal caller will say "Brace" and all will come to their huddle position. After the "Brace" call, the defensive call(s) is made, the the "Ready" call and then "Break." On break, all will clap together. This clap will show our unity and discipline (see Diagram 2-1).

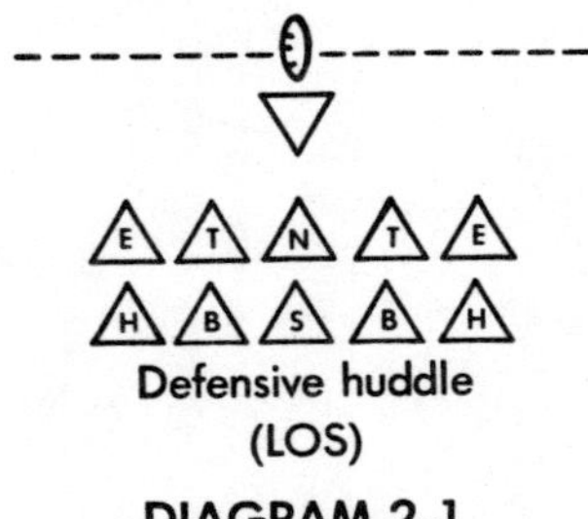

Defensive huddle
(LOS)

DIAGRAM 2-1

2. Call in the Huddle

Just before the defensive call is made or just after the call, the defensive signal caller should remind everyone in the huddle of the down and distance, the hash, field position, and special situations (time, etc.). Our scouting report is worthless unless we can identify the obvious situations. The call in the huddle will be the alignment of the front seven, any stunts or adjustments. Then the defensive secondary call is given, if any, and any adjustments, and then special situations that need to be mentioned.

3. Position After Huddle (Waiting Position) (Diagram 2-2)

We must be at the line before the offense, preparing ourselves mentally. The nutcracker will align on the ball. The tackles will align in their respective positions. All three will be on one knee. The ends and linebackers will be in the area of their respective positions with their hands on their hips. The rover will be in the middle, the halfbacks will align outside the linebackers, and the safety will align behind the rover. This is the time to prepare mentally for the play. We think of winning the play and of the scouting report.

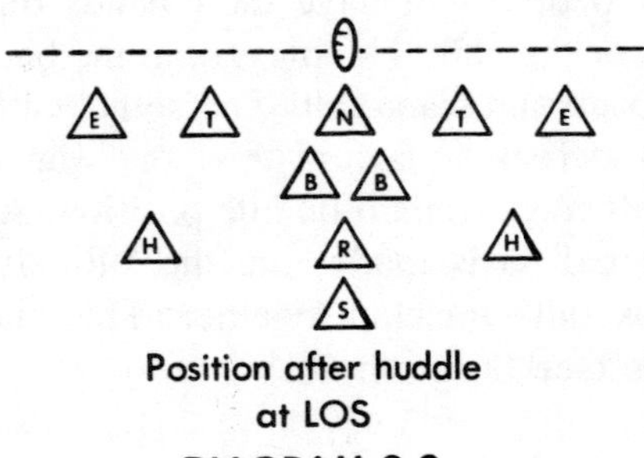

Position after huddle
at LOS

DIAGRAM 2-2

4. Offense Comes to the Ball

Once the center puts his hands on the ball, the nutcracker will immediately yell ''Ready!'' The nutcracker will do this no matter what alignment he is in at the time. All shifts will be made by the time the quarterback puts his hands under the center. We should be set by that time. The linebackers will call the backfield alignment examples —split backs, ''I,'' Delaware, etc. The rover may determine strength or any special circumstances that must be called.

5. Basic Preliminary Set-up and Alignment

Giving our basic defensive structure and alignment at this time will make things more understandable. Remember that our alignments do vary. Also, the quicker a defensive lineman is, the closer we like him to align to the ball; it is difficult to give vertical alignment (see Diagram 2-3).

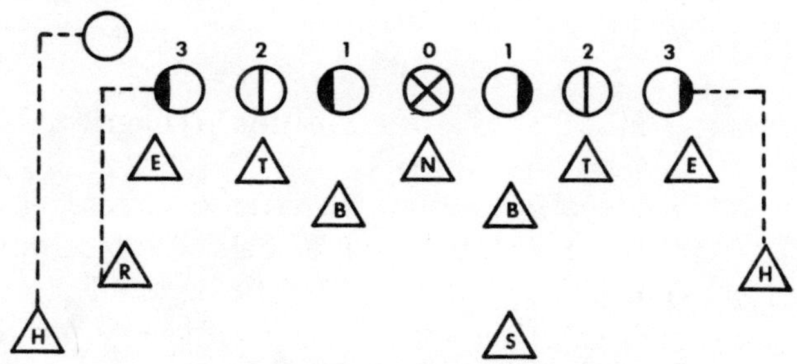

Basic defensive alignment

DIAGRAM 2-3

Nutcracker (N): Head on the man located on the center of the line.

Tackles (T): Head on the second man from the center of the line (provided splits allow it).

Ends (E): He aligns his inside eye on the outside eye of the third man from the center of the line (provided split allows it). On occasion, we let him move to outside shoulder alignment.

Linebackers (LBs): He aligns his inside eye on the outside eye of the first man from the center of the line. He should always have his toes behind and never even to heels of downmen. Always align deeper.

Rover (R): Align on the second ''quick'' receiver (receiver near line of scrimmage) from outside counting in; depth and width depend on scouting report and base plays of opponent.

Halfbacks (HBs): Align on the outside of the first outside man. (Exact alignment will vary—generally one yard outside and six to eight yards deep.)

Safety (S): Alignment will vary according to the scouting report, but usually align opposite the side the rover is on, about eight to ten yards deep. (*Note*: The center of the line may not be where the ball is placed. See the unbalanced line.)

6. After the Play

After the play it is of the utmost importance for the defensive team to quickly huddle again. We must make our calls quickly and be prepared well before the offensive team comes to the line of scrimmage.

3

Coaching Principles and Advantages of the Gap-Control Rover Defense

In order to understand the discussion that follows in the subsequent chapters, we must establish some general thoughts on the defense. This will clear up some of the more specific techniques and skills that must be understood.

1. Gap-Control Theory and Reading Philosophy

Controlling a gap does not mean the lack of reading by defenders. On the contrary, it is based on reading. The basic theory is that the defensive downmen are generally responsible for a gap before the snap of the ball, while the linebackers are responsible for a gap or an area depending on movement of their key.

The downmen read once they feel pressure of the blocker. It might be said that on some occasions they are sacrificed. However, this is not true. Their pursuit is enhanced and they become most proficient in fighting pressure of the offensive blockers.

Once we have controlled every gap along the line of scrimmage to the side of the ball, we can close to the ball. Theoretically, the ball carrier should have nowhere to go.

Our defense is not a standard penetrating defense, yet it is not a pure reading defense either. We want to control the line of scrimmage, reading on the move and pursuing to the ball. To get penetration, we will stunt and/or move our downmen to a gap. These are "called moves."

2. Pass/Run Ratio

We feel that the running game must be stopped first, then the opponent's long passing game, and finally, the short control passing game of the opponent. Our defense can accomplish all of the above. We have five defenders exclusively responsible for run in our base defense. These defenders have no dual responsibilities of pass and/or run. Naturally, the linebackers are responsible for both run and pass.

Since we have five defenders in our base defense responsible for run, it is obvious that we have a 6-to-5 ratio in regard to pass. Obviously, we must play some man-for-man pass defense (about 50%). Most defenses have a 7-to-4 ratio (7 defend, 4 rush) in regard to pass. However, versus sprint out or roll out this imbalance is quickly corrected. Also note that our ratio becomes standard or varies according to our defensive alignment. This adds a new dimension to the defense—a change of ratio to meet specific problems.

3. Force-Contain Principle

In order for any defense to be sound, the corner of the defense must be sound. If the perimeter of the defense is unsound, the entire defense will be unsuccessful. The corner should have one defender who will be primarily responsible for aggressive contain on run action his way. He throws caution to the wind and must attack aggressively from outside-in to close the running lane which can develop inside (see Diagram 3-1).

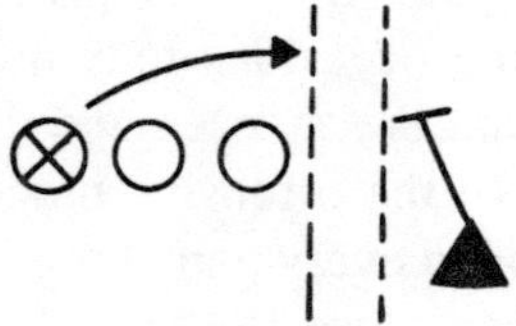

(Aggressive contain man closing running lane.)

DIAGRAM 3-1

The second contain defender is called the auxiliary contain man. He is the last resort in containment and must be absolutely sure of run before committing to contain. He usually is also responsible for the halfback pass to his side. The force defenders move to the football from inside-out (the tackles, nutcracker and linebackers).

The defensive end is the apex of our defense. He has definite responsibilities (which will be discussed later). Basically, he is neither force nor contain. He is the pressure fighter; he must move to the ball carrier or play his way (see Diagrams 3-2, 3-3, 3-4).

The force-contain principles presented are not new, but to understand the specifics of the defense it must be clear that aggressive contain will fall on the rover or defensive halfbacks and there will always be someone responsible for auxiliary contain. This principle will hold in all situations and regardless of alignments. If the principle isn't held up on every play, success on the corner is impossible with any consistency.

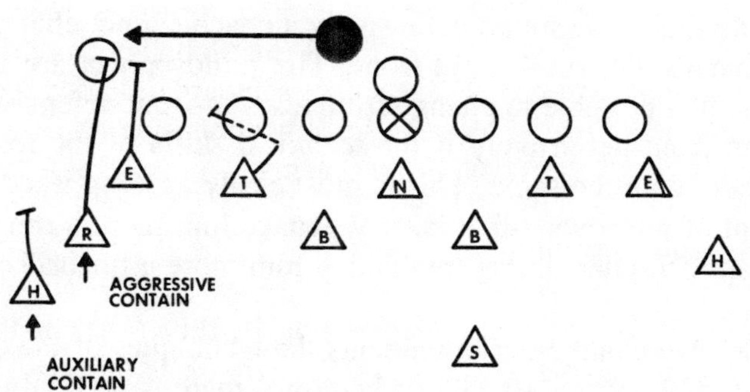

(One force-contain principle)

DIAGRAM 3-2

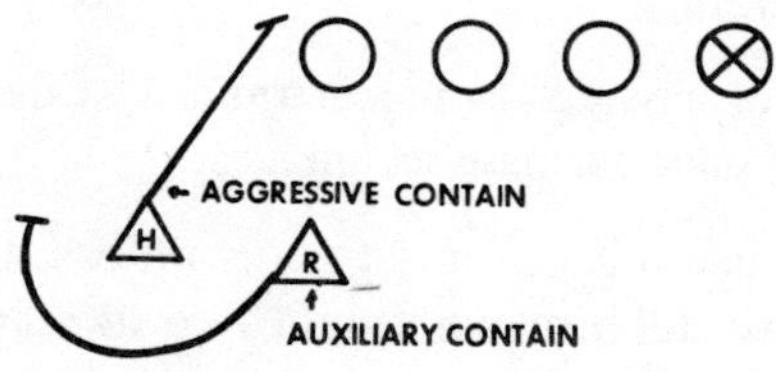

(Another type of corner force we use commonly.)

DIAGRAM 3-3

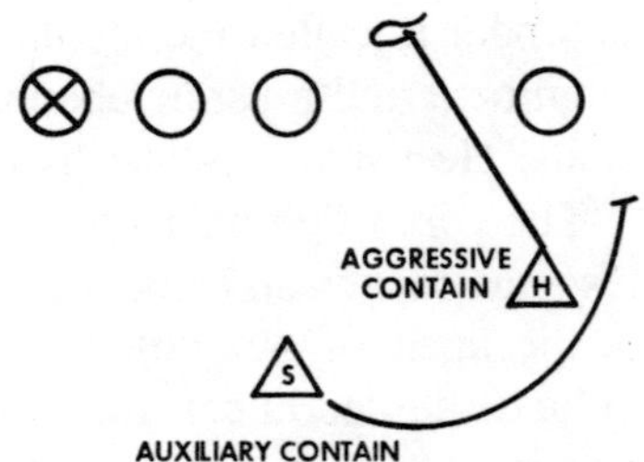

(Another type of contain: defensive HB to split end side who has aggressive contain.)

DIAGRAM 3-4

4. Different Alignments and Multiple Defenses

When we speak of multiple defenses there are certain basic principles we adhere to no matter what the alignment. We will always be in some form of a seven-man front with a rover (monster) secondary. It is our feeling that to be sound defensively a coach cannot change from a seven-front to a "true" eight-front. The philosophies are different. However, it is possible to change from a seven-front defensively to an eight-man front defensively if the technical skills of the front seven defenders remain the same. This is most easily accomplished with the placement of the rover—that is, if we make him more a run defender than a pass defender, therefore making him more a linebacker type of player.

When we change our alignments the techniques of the defenders being changed are not affected. Therefore, there is no confusion. For example, if our defensive tackle is asked to execute his base technique from head-up on the offensive No. 2 man (usually the offensive tackle), then he is asked to execute the exact technique if his alignment is changed to head-up on the offensive No. 1 man (usually the offensive guard). See Diagram 3-5.

(Note: We are not discussing any predetermined "called" moves. We are discussing only our base techniques.)

We don't like to use a lot of alignments unless it is necessary. If we can win in our base defense we would like to stay out of various alignments. But there are those times when you just can't sit in one

Tackle head-up on #2 Tackle head-up on #1

DIAGRAM 3-5

Note: Tackle uses same technique whether head-up on guard or tackle.

defense. Either adjustments in alignment must occur or more stunting must occur.

In reading this book you will see that the way a defender is blocked will remain the same, regardless of alignment. This is important because the more familiar a defender becomes with the type of blocks he will face, the better he will become at defeating the block. Remember, we are talking in generalities. We do have called moves that may change an alignment after the snap, or change a technique.

We like to use variation in our defensive front to take advantage not only of down and distance but also of the offense's formation. Most formations by their alignment have limitations. For example, some type of ''over'' shifted offensive formation may be better handled by our ''over'' defense (see Diagram 3-6).

Multiple defenses can also take advantage of an offensive team's tendencies. Of course, we will also stunt to take advantage of offensive tendencies since this is not as easy to recognize as a pure alignment change. However, we have been successful with both. One example of an alignment change to take advantage of a tendency is this: A team likes to run weakside on second down with 7 to 4 yards to go for a first down. We may make a shift to a gap stack weak but cheat the strong linebacker over (see Diagram 3-7).

I am sure that every coach, immediately upon seeing this, is saying that we just won't run there, but it is difficult to determine when we will do this and many coaches don't care what attempt you make to stop their best play; they are still going to run the ball until you stop their best play. An interesting point should be noted—with the teams we play against, the strongest and most obvious tendencies are the

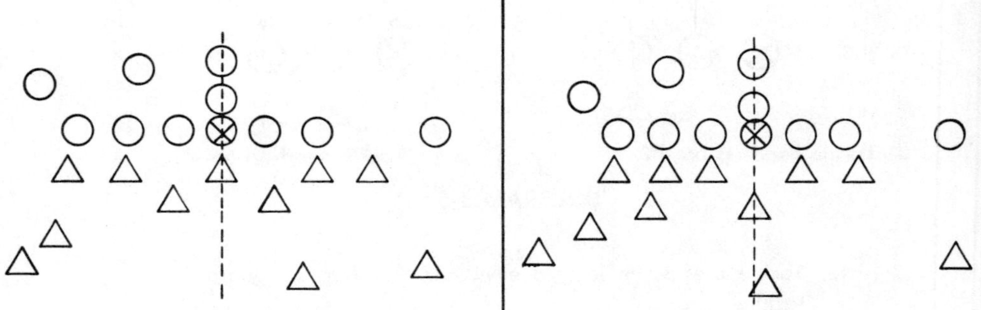

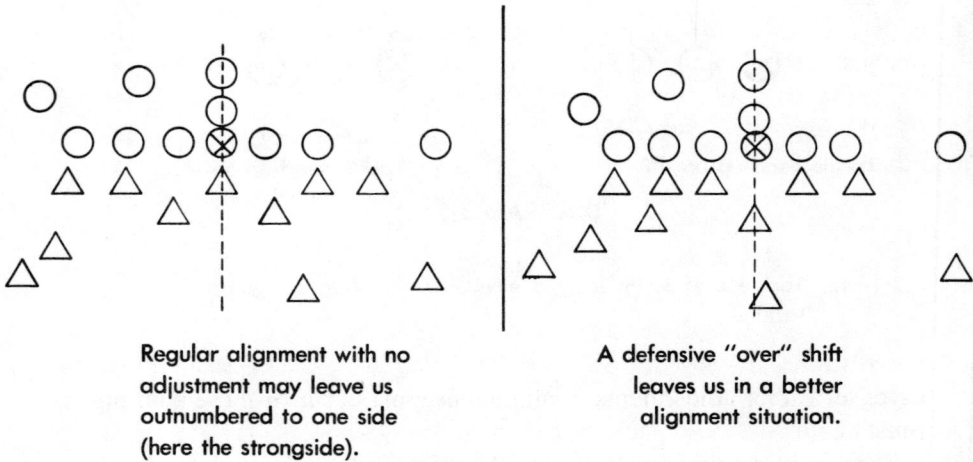

Regular alignment with no adjustment may leave us outnumbered to one side (here the strongside).

A defensive "over" shift leaves us in a better alignment situation.

DIAGRAM 3-6

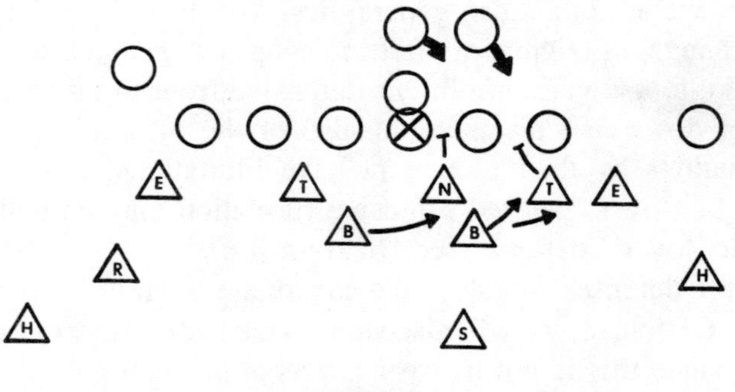

DIAGRAM 3-7

most difficult to stop. They usually execute the best. We know what play is coming; they know you know it is coming but dare you to stop the play. We have been fortunate thus far and have been able to stop many opponents.

A reminder to coaches: Don't give up on an alignment or stunt because it doesn't work once. To illustrate a point: We were playing our biggest rival in state. We knew that on particular down and distance situations this team would run bootleg to the tight end's side with the quarterback keeping the ball all the way. We eagled to the tight end's side, hoping to cut off the guard's block and hoping the linebacker could more easily read the play. The defensive end had worked every day from the beginning of the year on beating the hook (reach) block and was made especially aware of it for this game. Finally, the defensive halfback knew that when he saw motion, his key was the tight end and he should expect the bootleg. As was expected, they ran the bootleg, our defensive end beat the reach block, our tackle cut off one guard and our halfback was at the line waiting with our linebacker. Their quarterback cut up in an unexpected running lane (something he wasn't supposed to do) and gained 43 yards—one of the longest runs of the year against us (see Diagram 3-8.) We could have shied away from the defense, but the theory was sound—their quarterback just didn't know that. The point is this—we won't give up on an alignment or stunt because it didn't work once.

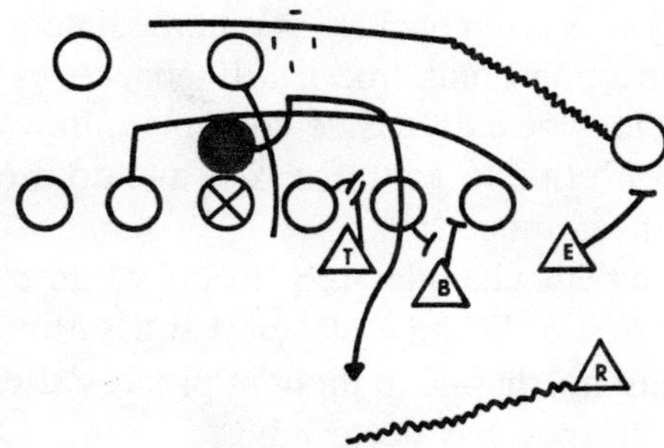

(Bootleg was stopped on the blackboard.)

DIAGRAM 3-8

Also, to take advantage of a situation, if the offensive team is in an obvious passing situation we take out our nutcracker and put in another linebacker. We play a college 4-3 using an extra linebacker (see Diagram 3-9).

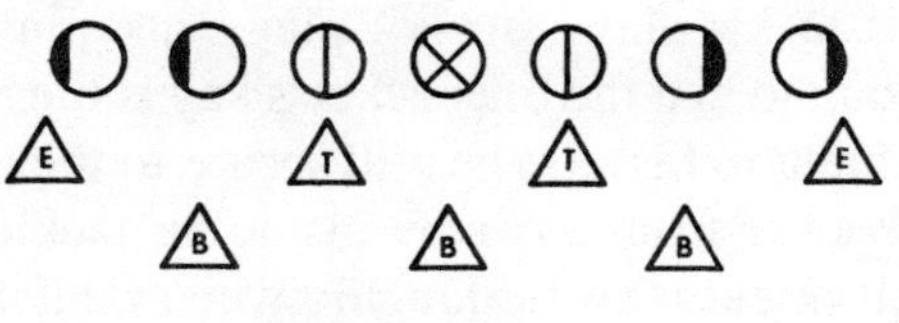

DIAGRAM 3-9

There are other possible alignments that may be used; we will discuss them later.

Another reason for using multiple defensive fronts is personnel. In regard to personnel, there are two reasons for using various fronts. First, it can disallow any physical mismatch that might occur. For example, if we find that a team is base-blocking (hitting straight out) and their tackle is cutting our defensive tackle off or their tackle is really doing a job on our man, we will make a coordinated call and move our defensive tackle to head on the offensive guard and move our linebacker to the offensive tackle position. Doing this frequently makes it difficult for an offensive blocker since the man the offensive tackle is now blocking is off the ball.

Second, and most important, if a coach has the philosophy that he wants his best defenders on the field, our defense is ideal. Let's assume that in our base defense one defensive downman gets injured. Our next best defensive player is a linebacker. We immediately go to a 4-3 (see Diagram 3-9). The same holds true if a linebacker is injured and our next best defender may be a defensive downman, in which case we can go to a 6-1. We don't like to go to the 6-1, and do it only when it is a must for personnel reasons.

We find alignment changes easy to do while creating blocking problems for the offense. When a player changes alignment it is a pre-snap move requiring no change in thought process after the snap—it is all reaction once the snap has occurred.

5. Advantages

What are the advantages of this defense? There are many, and we will give a few of them. The biggest advantage we have now is that we know most of the weak areas and we know how to correct most of the problems. It may take a lifetime, but knowing everything about the defense being run is essential to winning.

The Gap Control defense has the advantage of freeing the linebackers for off-tackle plays, outside plays, and plays away (pursuit). It is important to note that the linebacker's key is the near offensive back. On key movement to his side he will scrape to the off-tackle area. This frees the linebacker from any play inside his tackle area (see Diagram 3-10). We will discuss this thoroughly when we get to Chapter 8. Keys are always back(s), but they can vary in regard to who will be keyed in the backfield, depending on tendency, etc.

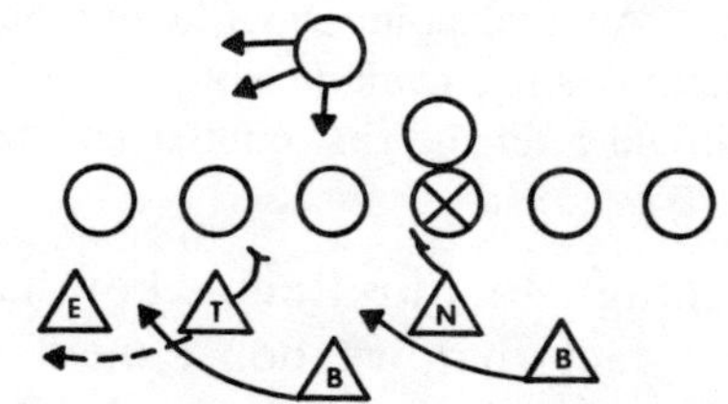

(LB is free to move off-tackle and outside.
He is not tied down by internal fake.)

DIAGRAM 3-10

This is especially effective versus option teams since the linebacker is free to play football and move to the pitchman. He is not generally responsible for the quarterback. If the option fake is outside the tackle, he may be forced to tackle the man being faked to, but, if he is able, he will read the fake and move to the pitchman.

We felt this technique was a must since many teams ran more than half their offense off-tackle or outside after an internal fake (for example, a buck drive series—see Diagram 3-11).

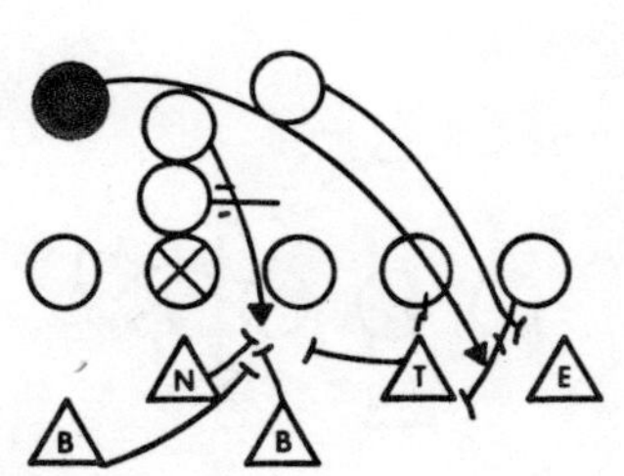

Buck drive—good fake was holding up our playside LB.

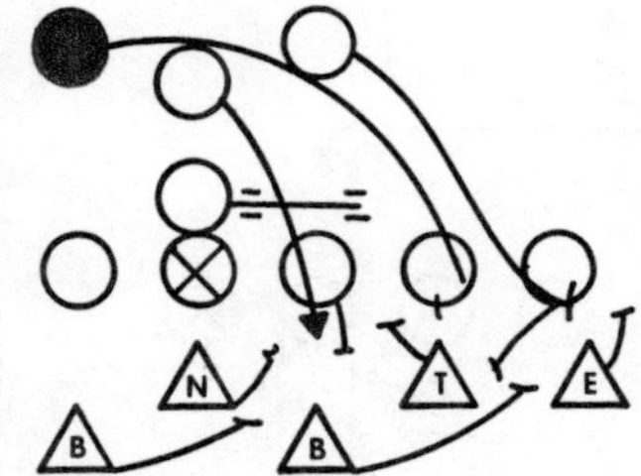

What occurs with our defense.

DIAGRAM 3-11

(Note: Earlier we said that we key backs. This fits in nicely with the overall scheme of the defense. There is no reason why a coach cannot key guards in a 5-2. However, this is not practical since the linebackers may be moved to various defensive alignments. It is much simpler to teach back keys—that is, if it fits into a coach's defensive scheme. Another point about keying backs is the fact that it is more natural since even disciplined linebackers tend to look in the backfield after the first quarter and really don't key guards.)

Another advantage to our linebacker having more freedom outside is the fact that we don't need big men for this position to take on their guards or to beat the isolation from the backs. By his movement he is not confronted straight on—one on one—by a block. Don't misunderstand us, we would like big, quick hitters in that position. In fact, we want that at every position. Every coach would like to have that type of player.

Another advantage this defense gives us is in the play of our defensive tackles. In any 5-2 defense the most common defender who is trapped is the defensive tackle. The initial movement of our tackle is a lateral movement to the inside gap. If the defender feels no pressure, he has an easy read and is generally being trapped. He is now in excellent position to meet the trapping offensive lineman. The defensive tackle is in good position to close the running lane for the ball carrier. In a regular 5-2 the running lane is larger (see Diagram 3-12), due to the tackle's alignment and technique.

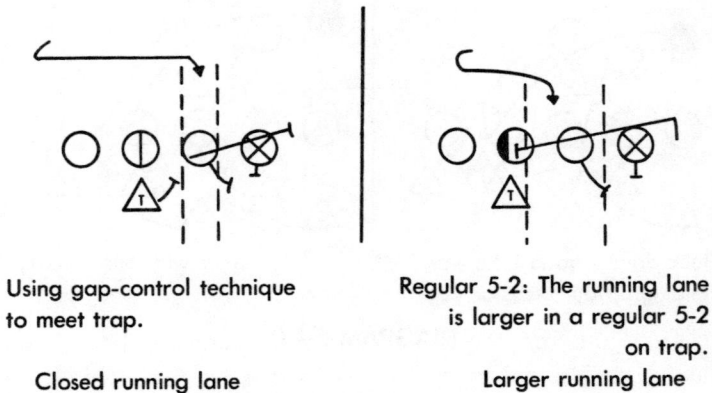

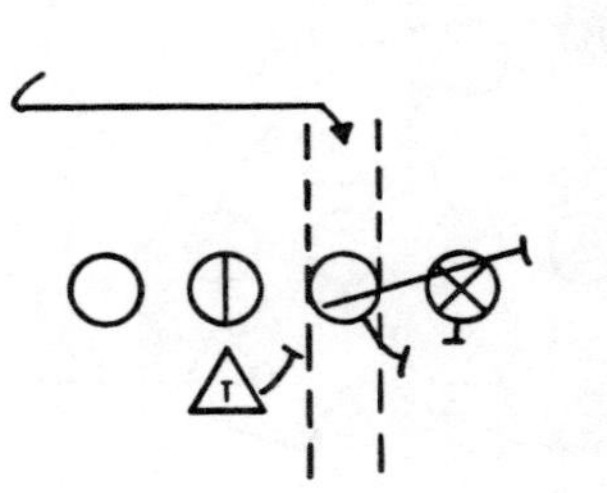

Using gap-control technique to meet trap.

Closed running lane

Regular 5-2: The running lane is larger in a regular 5-2 on trap.

Larger running lane

DIAGRAM 3-12

(Note: This technique, in many instances, protects the linebacker from the offensive tackle's block on counters or misdirection plays and enables the linebacker to recover to the play unblocked.)

The defensive tackle's technique also allows him a head start if the offensive tackle is attempting to trap. The defensive tackle is able to get "in the hip pocket" of trapping linemen and he usually can beat the fill block by an offensive back since our tackle usually has a great head start (see Diagram 3-13).

(Initial move by tackle gives him a great head start on tackle's trap.)

DIAGRAM 3-13

We were fortunate and actually had a tackle who executed so well that he was able to get on the hip of a pulling guard from his tackle position (see Diagram 3-14). Many teams don't use a fill block when they pull a guard versus a defense that doesn't have the guard covered by a downman.

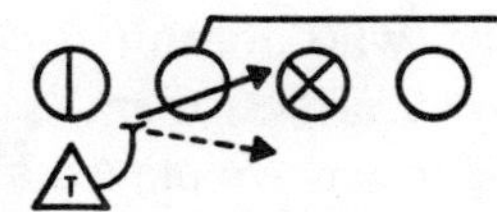

(Defender gets on hip of guard.)

DIAGRAM 3-14

It is obvious that the tackle also has a good head start on plays away and pursuit is enhanced since the offensive tackle has difficulty cutting off the defensive tackle from his pursuit angle.

The basic defensive scheme is not based on a predetermined penetrating slant. The wholesale slant can be costly to pursuit, and if one defender is cut off it can mean a large gain for the offense. Our defense has many of the advantages of slanting without a number of the disadvantages. We seldom slant our middle guard. We have discovered that slanting this man is very dangerous, especially against opponents who have a quick-hitting fullback offensive attack.

Another advantage we have with our defense is that we play a rover (monster) in the secondary. In itself this is not an advantage, but we use the rover to make most adjustments to motion, we put him to team tendency, or just put him where our opponent might be hurting us. This allows us to make adjustments with one defender. This simplifies things in the secondary, and seldom does the entire secondary have to make adjustments to unusual conditions. Being able to move one defender anywhere on the field, in a calculated procedure, can cause problems for the offense while keeping things unchanged for the defense. Why not do it to the offense—they have a number of weapons to foul up the defense!

Of course, every coach is now saying to himself that you need a super athlete to play the rover position. He doesn't have to be a super athlete. Maybe in theory he has to be super, but on the field we have discovered that coaches immediately base their offensive attack away from the rover. We have even considered putting our worst defender in the rover position against some teams. One team we played actually ran to the rover side only twice the entire game; whether he, the rover, went to field position or formation strength made no difference.

The interesting point is that most coaches, seeing a rover flip-flop to field position or formation strength, automatically seem to plan the offensive attack away from the rover. However, seeing a pre-rotated corner or an inverted safety (who doesn't flip-flop) doesn't seem to affect coaches the way a rover affects them (see Diagram 3-15).

Knowing this about the rover, we played a team with a secondary similar to ours. We began our plan of attack away from the rover. Now the defense was determining which way we should run. It certainly wasn't very intelligent on our part—that is, allowing our own defense to succeed against us for a good part of the game.

In the base defense there results a situation that we feel is very good. There can be no effective double team on the defensive tackle because of his initial movement (see Diagram 3-16). When teams do attempt to double team the tackle they usually waste a blocker and our linebacker is free (see Diagram 3-16). Needless to say, most coaches will attempt to have the tight end slide to the linebacker. This is a difficult block, especially since the tight end is getting hit by our

(Alignment same but coaches seem more affected by a rover flip-flopping.)

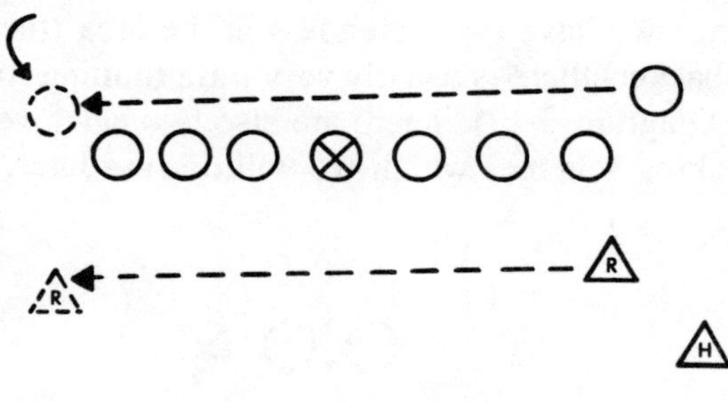

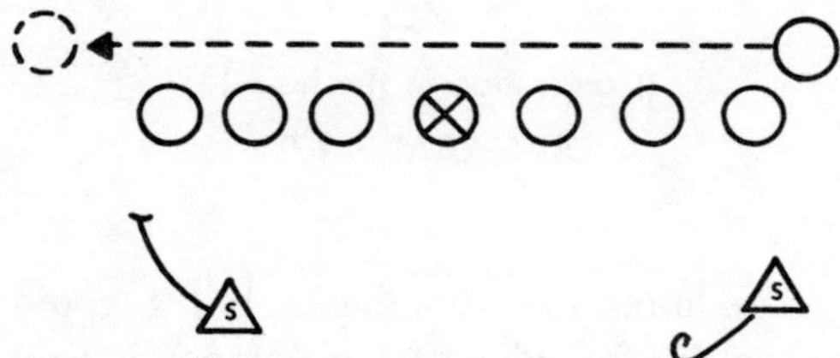

This has no effect.

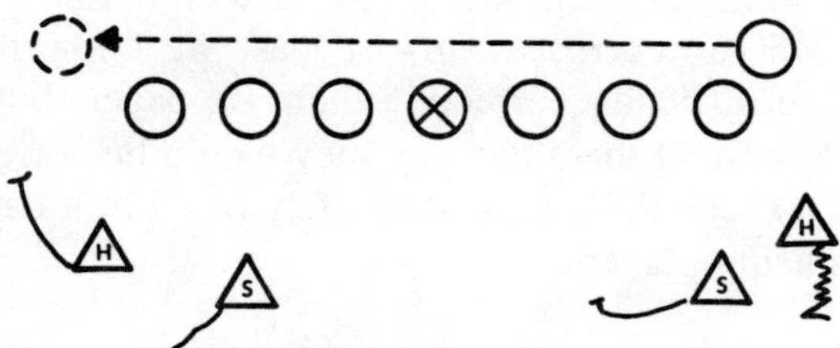

This has no effect.

DIAGRAM 3-15

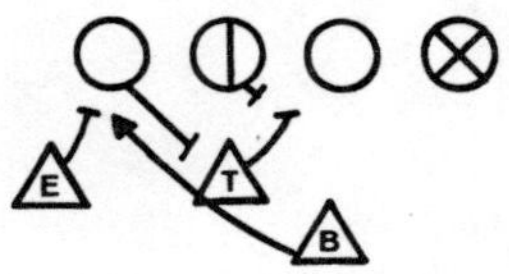

(No double team)

DIAGRAM 3-16

defensive end, which is really enough to stop an effective block on our linebacker. If the block is made, it is usually made in the off-tackle hole and since we have two defenders in the area (the defensive end and the linebacker) there is usually very little running room for the ball carrier (see Diagram 3-17). There are also two calls we make to combat this blocking scheme, which we will discuss later.

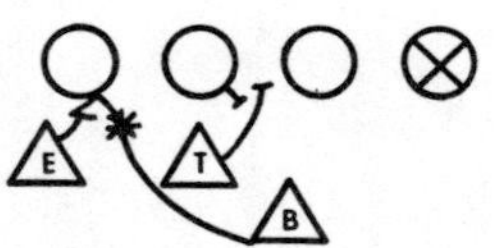

(Congestion in the hole.)

DIAGRAM 3-17

We could go on about the advantages, but it would be clinic talk. The best way to see the full idea of the defense is to read about it in total. We will devote a section to the problems of the defense. Yes, there are some problems we are faced with in our defense! Naturally, we feel we can correct them—at least we know the problems. We never have difficulty correcting them on paper, but there will be an attempt to correct them the way they would be corrected on the field. There is no such thing as a completely fool-proof defense as long as a coach is using players.

4

Teaching Gap-Control Defensive Skills

1. Breakdown Position (Also Called Hitting or Football Position)

The faster a player can move from this position and the longer he can stay in this position may determine his success as a football player. At some point in a game a player is in this position, whether playing offense or defense. It is most important on defense. The purpose of the position is to maintain good body control and balance. It facilitates movement in any direction while allowing a position that will make an explosion possible at any time it is desired by the defender. Finally, it lessens the blocking surface that will be exposed by the defender. It is not a difficult position. At first it may seem awkward, but with practice it will be just like walking.

a. *Feet*: Weight is almost evenly distributed over the feet, with more weight on the balls of the feet than anywhere else. The heels may be on the ground or just slightly off. Feet should be at least shoulder-width apart.

b. *Knees*: Should be flexed and ready to uncoil. They should be even with or just over the toes.

c. *Waist*: Should be bent.

d. *Hips*: Hips are set low (weight carried low). Hip rotation is most important on any contact.

e. *Back*: Is straight, not bowed forward.

f. *Shoulders*: They are slightly forward, just over knees.

g. *Head*: The head is up, neck is bulled, chin up and eyes open.

h. *Arms*: They are in front, elbows bent, fists clenched, ready to shed.

(Note: A player can't get in a breakdown position just before contact; that's too late—he must be in it before that time.)

2. Tackling

Tackling is 70% desire, 15% technique and 15% positioning. *Any tackle who gets a ball carrier down, without the ball carrier moving forward, is a good tackle.* Missing a tackle is one of the worst things that can happen to a defensive player.

a. Approach: If there is no angle for the defender, he must break down when he gets to the area of contact, eyes focused on the ball carrier's numbers; his feet should be moving but not high off the ground. If the defender has an angle, he must not lose it; the better the angle the less the defender must come under control. Feet must be under the tackler's body. Shoulders should face the ball carrier.

b. Contact: The forehead must be up, eyes open. When on the ball carrier's toes (about six inches from the ball carrier), an explosion must occur with the face mask on the numbers of the ball carrier. The hips, thighs, knees and arms must uncoil. The hips must rotate and extend; this is where the power will come from, along with good timing. Through the entire procedure the back remains straight. Be sure to get under the shoulder pads of the ball carrier.

(Note: If the head is down, chance of injury is a distinct possibility.)

c. Follow-through: The tackler should continue running through the ball carrier, lifting upward. Ideally, the attempt should be made to bend the ball carrier back with the tackler's arms which are pulling the ball carrier to the tackler. If this can't be done, he should at least grab somewhere and squeeze.

d. Angle tackling: Be sure not to lose the angle you have acquired. Tackling remains the same except that the target now becomes the ball instead of the numbers. This will get the tackler's head in front of the ball carrier and may cause a fumble besides maintaining the angle.

e. Open field tackling: An open field tackle must be accomplished any way possible. The tacklers should get into a position that will allow the ball carrier only one way to go, especially if he is pinned to the sideline. In the middle of the field, a tackling angle should be taken that will bring the ball carrier into the pursuit. The tackler should keep his feet as long as possible, and not expect a good shot in the open field. If the opponent is approaching the goal line, the defender must close the cushion on the ball carrier (see Diagrams 4-1 and 4-2).

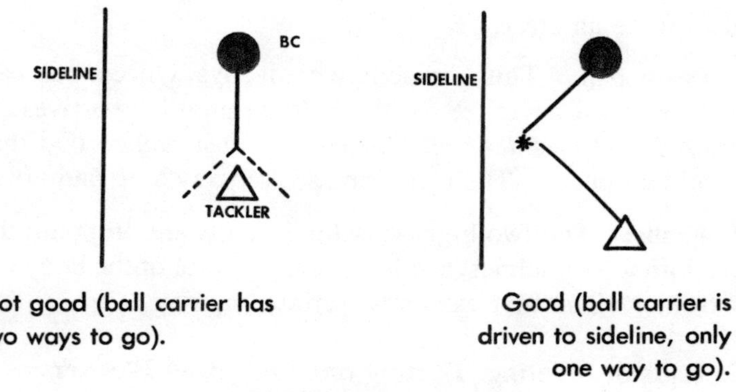

Not good (ball carrier has two ways to go).

Good (ball carrier is driven to sideline, only one way to go).

DIAGRAM 4-1

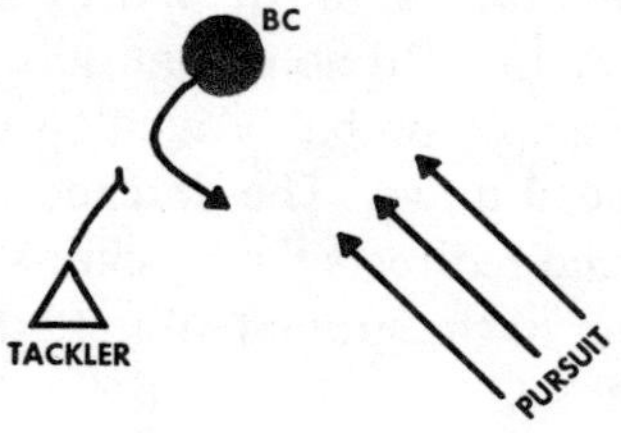

Bring him into pursuit.

DIAGRAM 4-2

f. Low-running ball carrier: A ball carrier who runs low to the ground presents no real problem. Keeping the same target, his numbers, the defender gets under his shoulder pads (this should be done on all tackles) and "sticks" him. It will wind up in a head-to-head confrontation which we want since we like to think we will win!

g. Gang tackling: One man should seldom have to make a tackle alone. He should have help; gang tackling is most important to our defensive success. The technique for gang tackling is very simple. Hit any area that is showing on the ball carrier—"*Don't hit your own man*!" We hit legally and do not "spear" the ball carrier. The first man tackles the ball carrier; other tackles must go for the football, putting their helmet on the ball—"*Force the fumble*!"

h. Tackling near goal line: The closer an opponent gets to our goal line, the more our target changes. The target becomes the ball. We must force an error.

i. Death grip: This is exactly what it says. Once a ball carrier is grabbed, we must never let go. We hold on until help arrives. This is emphasized—"*Never let go!*" Defenders must realize that the ideal "hit" seldom occurs. The tackler must grab anything and hold on.

j. Faults: The two biggest tackling faults are dropping the head (hitting with top of helmet) and not having control of the body (feet not under tackler). The first can cause serious injury.

3. Methods of Meeting, Beating and Defeating Blockers

(Note: These are brief general points made to the players.)

a. Controlling the head: If the defender can control the blocker's head, he will have very little trouble controlling the block. Versus a good blocker, this technique probably won't work. It works versus a blocker who has his head down. The defender puts his hands on the helmet of the blocker and redirects the blocker's helmet with his hands or he shoves the helmet to the ground. Where the head goes the body will follow.

b. Beating a low block: Blockers many times attempt a low block—below the waist. They must *never* get to the legs of the defender. To combat this, the technique involved is similar to the above: take the blocker's helmet, and the defender rolls his own hips and legs backwards and pushes the blocker's nose to the ground. This will keep the legs free. Lost ground must be regained.

c. Playing through the head: If the defender feels he is getting blocked, he should immediately attack the pressure at its weakest leverage point, if he can't "out-quick" the blocker. The defender should redirect all power and strength to the head and redirect the blocker's head.

d. Delivering the blow (forearm shiver): This method is especially good for plays coming straight at a defender. However, it does tend to tie up the defender if he doesn't shed quickly and free himself of the blocker. The technique involved is done from the breakdown position and the entire body is brought up and under the blocker, stepping (generally) with the same foot and arm. Once the step is made into the blocker, the hips of the defender are rolled and the last thing to come up is the forearm. We don't try to ward off a blocker with just the forearm. The final movement is to free the defender—roll the wrist back and use the free hand to throw off the blocker. Remember, the forearm is merely the end of the hammer. The rest of the body must be used, along with the forearm, to deliver a good blow. Be sure the feet are moving while the blow is delivered. Forearm shiver is excellent on short-yardage situations.

e. Hand shiver: This method is excellent when moving laterally. The arms are extended forward toward the blocker; if he is coming high it is a good idea to get under his shoulder pads. The elbows are locked and the heels of the hands make contact. If the play is moving away, it is a good idea for the defender to move his hips back slightly in order to free himself to get to the play. If the play is towards the defender, the hips may have to be used to get some power into the shiver. The shoulder pads of the blocker must be controlled and, if possible, the defender should be able to turn them any way he so desires. The feet of the defender must keep moving—a must in this type of technique because the tendency is to stop moving the feet on contact.

f. Drop step: This technique is excellent, especially versus an angle block or double team. The defender takes a step back and out

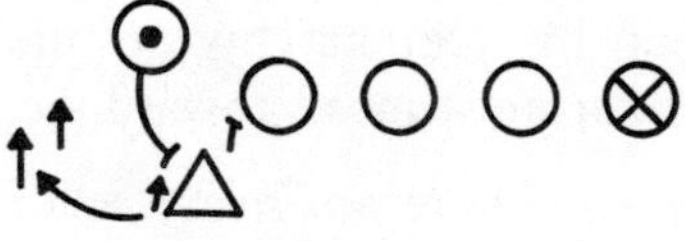

DIAGRAM 4-3

Drop step: Back and out then regains lost ground, using the defensive end as an example. Wing is making the block.

with the leg that is attempting to be hit by the blocker. While doing this, he shivers the blocker, and once free of the blocker, he regains the ground that was lost. He must also be sure to step out, as well as back, to be sure he is clear of the blocker. However, if he steps too far back he will interfere with other defenders in pursuit (see Diagram 4-3).

g. Beating the two-on-one: Whenever a defender is confronted by two blockers, either coming straight ahead or attempting to double team at an angle, the defender should redirect his attack and pick only one blocker and attack him! Generally, the blocker who is attempting to give direction, that is, applying pressure to the defender, should be attacked. Whatever occurs, he must get free and into pursuit. He can't be driven back; he must drop to a knee if necessary.

h. Splitting the seam: If anyone is trapped in a double team and the situation is difficult, just hold ground and drop to a knee; then drive through the leg of the blocker nearest the ball. We attempt to drive through the seam of the double team and get penetration if possible.

i. Spin-out: This is especially good if the ball is by the defender and he is still blocked. He whips the free leg and elbow around, taking a large lateral step. He stays low through pivot, attempts to sight the ball before the pivot and then whips his head around first during spin and finds the ball again. He doesn't step deep, because he will get in the way of pursuit.

(Note: If he is in a down position, he bends a leg and drops to buttocks and spins out. He doesn't get too much depth.)

j. Meeting the shield block: There will be times when a blocker won't block. He will just stand and shield the defender. The defender must immediately control him by putting his hands on the blocker's shoulders, and find the ball. He must not allow him to throw a block; possession of his shoulders will prevent a block. The defender may have to play "peek-a-boo," looking to the side of the blocker to find the ball. This block is especially prevalent downfield. The defender must be sure to keep his feet moving. If the block is being used downfield, our defender must move toward the line of scrimmage.

k. Other methods: There are many other theories of beating a block. Any theory is right if it allows a defender to get to the ball carrier the quickest way possible. Naturally, the best way would be to "out-quick" the blocker and not even be confronted by the blocker.

Whatever technique works fastest, consistently, is correct if it gets the defender to the ball.

4. Move on Movement (or Move on the Ball)

A defender, especially one of the front seven, must be like a time bomb ready to explode on movement of any offensive man (excluding a legal man in motion). We must be quicker than our opponents. This quickness on movement is especially important on a predetermined move by a defender; he cannot be cut off from his assignment. We must always move on movement, protect our area, read on the move and be redirected to the ball by the second or third step. If we find the offensive player extremely slow off the ball we will be forced to move on the ball.

5. Head Reading and Fighting Pressure

A defender who reads the blocker's head will seldom have to worry about fighting pressure (not including our defensive tackles). No one will get to him quick enough to block him. Naturally, reading the head of a potential blocker after the snap will tell us where the play is going. Of course, talking about reading the head is common knowledge to every coach, but this must be drilled constantly for a player to be successful. Our ends and nutcrackers most of all must be drilled in

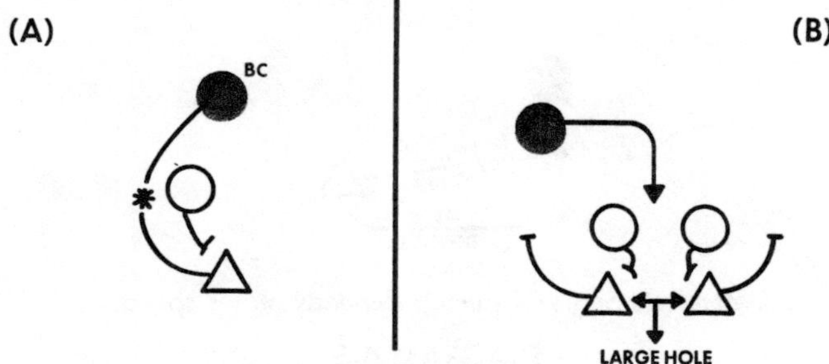

Head read by defender.

Defenders do poor job here and take a side or "run around" instead of fighting through head, and a large running alley results.

DIAGRAM 4-4

head reading. The defender must fight pressure if he can't beat the blocker. This, too, can be determined by the blocker's head. Whatever side the blocker's head goes on is, many times, the way the play is going; the defender fights through the head and/or pressure. If someone is trying to push the defender inside, he fights outside and vice versa. He should never take a side on the blocker (unless he is sure of a tackle); it leaves a large gap. The defender never runs around a block unless he is quick enough to do it and be successful with it consistently (see Diagram 4-4—A and B). It is very rare to have a player quick enough to use a run-around technique.

6. Acceleration Away from Blockers

The idea of a defender possibly getting blocked but not staying blocked is further enhanced by the fact that a defender must make a conscious effort to accelerate away from the blockers. The defender must get separation from the blocker. This will make the difference between a great defender and a fair defender. A defender must think of this constantly. The coach must constantly preach this to achieve the great pursuit, especially on wide plays.

7. Pursuit

Great defensive teams have great pursuit. An average defensive player can turn into a great one if he has great pursuit. When getting

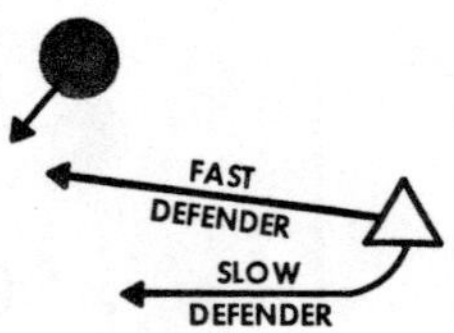

Defender's angle of pursuit depends on his speed.

DIAGRAM 4-5

into a pursuit pattern, never follow a teammate's jersey. Get to a point where the ball carrier will be, not where he was. The faster the defender, the less of an angle he will have to take to get to the ball carrier. We believe, to get proper and consistent pursuit, we must overemphasize it—almost "go crazy" about it! (See Diagram 4-5.)

There is a formula a defender could use to help him decide his pursuit lane. Naturally, players are not expected to memorize it, but it shows what is needed to establish a proper pursuit angle or pursuit lane.

Speed of ball carrier plus speed of defender plus distance from ball carrier plus proximity to goal line equals proper pursuit angle.

> Note: The closer a defender is to the goal line, the closer he must pursue to the line of scrimmage. A tough tackle over the goal line does us no good.
> Note: Pursuit lanes are the paths taken to the ball carrier by the defensive players to enable them to reach the ball carrier as quickly as possible. These paths vary with the play being run.

Shoulders parallel: It is most important when moving to the football that the defender keep his shoulders parallel to the line at all times, as long as the ball is between the ends of the line. Once the defender has the angle on the ball he must turn and sprint to a collision point.

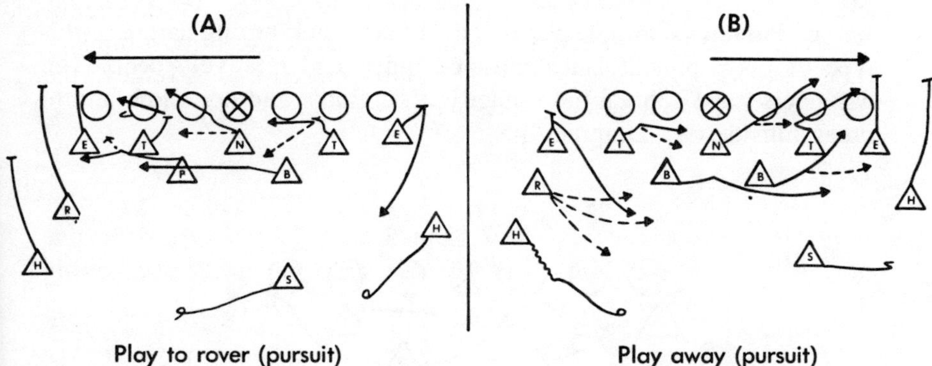

Play to rover (pursuit) Play away (pursuit)

Note: Notice the tackle away from the play may take a pursuit lane deep or a little shallower depending on his speed and that of the ball carrier. The same holds true of the rover. The tackle must work towards LOS and buttocks of blockers, he must not chase the play.

DIAGRAM 4-6

a. Pursuit vs. end run: Generally, pursuit versus end run requires a wide pursuit angle, keeping the ball carrier in front of pursuers (follow above formula). See Diagram 4-6 (A and B).

b. Pursuit vs. off-tackle play: Generally, the pursuit lane will not be as wide as pursuit lane versus end run. The offside pursuit men must prevent cut-back. Contain men do not move inside until they see the ball carrier and are sure of a tackle. Usually they wait until ball carrier is even with them before moving to him if they are responsible for contain (see Diagram 4-7).

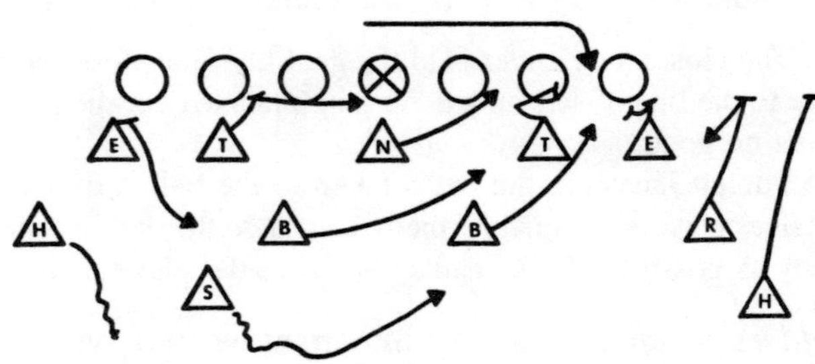

Position on off-tackle play

DIAGRAM 4-7

c. Pursuit vs. middle play: Due to the quick-hitting nature of this type of play, pursuit lanes must be quick and relatively deep. The defenders must contain the runner in the middle and not allow him to break outside (see Diagram 4-8).

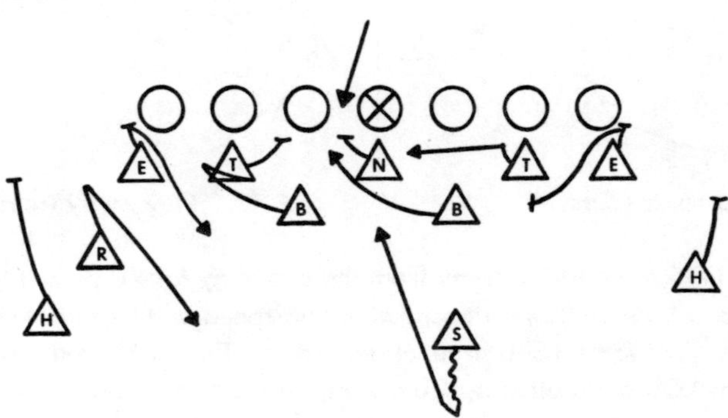

Pursuit vs. middle play

DIAGRAM 4-8

d. Moving to collision point: Situations may arise in which the ball carrier gets outside the containment, or the defender is confronted with an inside-out approach to the ball carrier somewhere on the field.

The defender must sprint downfield to an expected collision point downfield. This is especially true if the defender doesn't have speed—don't chase (see Diagram 4-9—A and B).

Reminder: When the ball carrier is between the offensive tackle areas, the defenders must be sure the shoulders are square to the line of scrimmage, especially in pursuit.

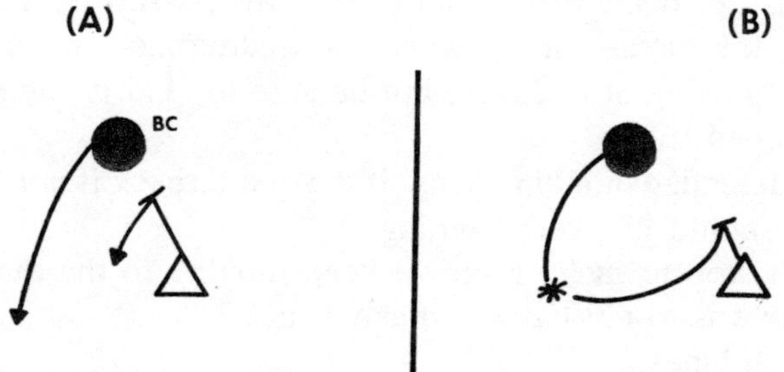

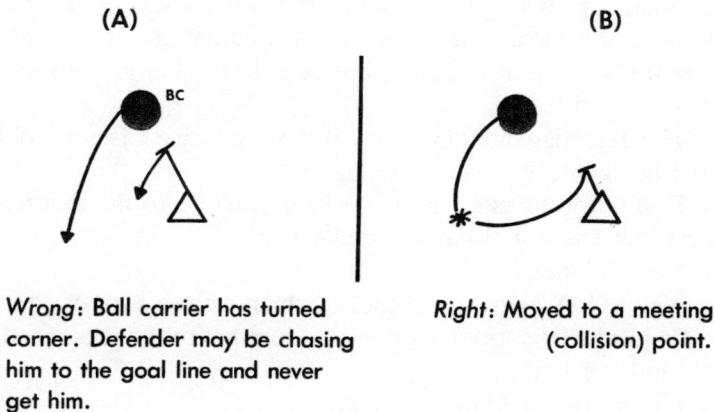

Wrong: Ball carrier has turned corner. Defender may be chasing him to the goal line and never get him.

Right: Moved to a meeting (collision) point.

Moving to collision point
DIAGRAM 4-9

e. Eyes on ball carrier: There will be times when the defender may get blocked or even knocked down. The defender must, at all costs, eye the ball carrier on the way down. Think of getting up, while on the way down, and immediately eye the ball carrier and move to him. These points given above can't be overemphasized; they will cut almost 2/10 of a second off of pursuit time. Look at the ball carrier and think of getting up!

8. Pass-Rushing Points and Techniques

We see a lot of play-action passing. There are some basic and important points the defender should know, especially vs. play-action passes, although these points could be applied against any type of pass.

a. Basic pass-rush principles:

- Accelerate on recognition. This is most important. As soon as the pass rusher discovers it is pass, he must explode from the initial contact of the blocker—and accelerate. He must close the distance between himself and the passer.

- The defenders attempt to turn the blocker's shoulders perpendicular to the line of scrimmage. He tries to "break the square" of the blocker while the defender tries to keep shoulders parallel.
- Hands up. If the rusher can't get to the passer, he must get his hands up in the air and jump when the quarterback moves the arm opposite the passing arm. Jump, but be sure to land in the same spot that was jumped from.
- The defender shouldn't jump if the quarterback is *not* looking to his side; he should just keep coming.
- Don't stop to make a move; keep moving to the quarterback. The best move is to not have to make a move.
- Stay in lanes.
- Versus low aggressive blocks (which we see a lot of), push the blocker's head to the ground—don't let him get to the legs—and keep moving to the passer.
- Hit the passer high.

(Note: If the blocker drops back to block for pass, the following techniques may be of assistance.)

b. Go-around technique: The rusher goes to the outside (or inside) of the blocker, then getting his leg between the blocker and himself, dips his shoulder and moves to the passer. He "out-quicks" the blocker.

c. Butt technique: The rusher should use this at least once a game (whether the rusher is a linebacker, end, or tackle). He charges straight ahead; butts his helmet into the blocker's chin, helmet or chest. He grabs the blocker's shoulder pads and turns him or pushes him back. He can go inside or outside, but he must be sure to punish the blocker.

d. Head and shoulder fake: The defender gives the blocker a head and shoulder move in one direction (turning the head and shoulder) and goes in the opposite direction. Then be sure that the defender gets the leg between the blocker and himself. Dip the near shoulder once the blocker is out of position; if necessary, the defender must use his hands to get the blocker out of position.

e. Grab and go: The rusher grabs the blocker's shoulder pads, steps in a direction, turns the blocker's shoulders in that same direction, then goes opposite. Control the blocker's shoulders and control him.

f. Spin: This is most effective if the rusher has been going outside continually or if the rusher is trapped and must move in the direction that he is being prevented from moving towards. The rusher makes usual contact, then whips a free leg and arm around, dips the shoulder and whips the head around and accelerates to the passer.

g. Play-action pass rush (see basic pass-rush principles): Among those things mentioned earlier, two points must be emphasized —acceleration after contact and staying on the feet. The defender must remember to keep leverage on the passer.

9. Stunting Technique

At some time almost all defenders will be asked to penetrate the line in order to get to the ball or anticipated point of attack. The move is usually made from one defensive alignment to another, penetrating the line of scrimmage on the snap or on key.

We want penetration; the defender must avoid contact with a blocker if he is the prime man in the stunt. If he isn't the prime man in the stunt, he will probably be asked to take out an offensive man —contact must be made.

The stunter must be reckless, but under control. Be sure that a wide arch is not made, it takes too much time. Be sure to pick up the feet; the defender can't be tripped. If the offense picks up the stunt, punish the blocker. The defender must be sure to disguise the stunt and stay in his normal alignment (unless told differently) until the snap of the ball. Once again, these are common-sense items that are sometimes overlooked.

We are very cautious in our stunting. Too much stunting can allow a loss in defensive depth and give up the big play for the offense. We don't like any "give-away" yards.

5

Coaching the Gap-Control Tackles

1. Stance

The defensive tackles will line up in a three-point stance, with the inside foot back and inside arm advanced. This position facilitates the easiest movement for successful execution of the required techniques. The weight is on the balls of the feet, the feet are about shoulder-width apart. Knees are bent, the back is straight, the neck is "bulled" and the buttocks even with the shoulders or slightly higher. There will be no leaning one way or the other; stay straight! The head is up, the arm is slightly in front of the shoulder, the fingers are spread. The inside leg is back, outside leg up.

There may be times when a four-point stance is necessary—gap alignment or goal line. The stance is about the same except that both arms are dropped even with each other but slightly in front of the shoulders. Feet alignment can remain the same as above. The four-point stance will facilitate the forward charge.

> *Note*: From the regular stance, *it is most important* that the inside leg is back, outside leg up.

2. Alignment

The defensive tackle will basically have two alignments.

a. Head-on: His regular alignment which is head up to the second man from the middle of the line (see also basic defensive set-up and alignment).

b. Gap alignment: This will be the second alignment and it will be in the gap between the first and second man from the middle of the line; generally, the tackle will align in the gap to his inside (from a regular alignment). This alignment will dictate a variation from the normal technique. Get as close to line of scrimmage as is legally possible.

Note: From head-up alignment, distance from the ball will depend on the ability of the tackle—the quicker he is the closer he can get to the line of scrimmage.

c. Split rule: If the man the tackle is aligned on tries to split an abnormal distance, the tackle will adjust and move to gap position. This is only done if the defensive tackle feels it is the only way he can protect his area.

d. "Cheat" alignment: This really cannot be considered another alignment. The tackles just align, before the snap of the ball, to the alignment they should be in after the snap of the ball. That is, the alignment should be our tackle's outside shoulder to the inside shoulder of the No. 2 man—usually the offensive tackle (see Diagram 5-1).

Note: We would use this if we were getting cut off from initial movement, or versus an unusual split by the offensive tackle.

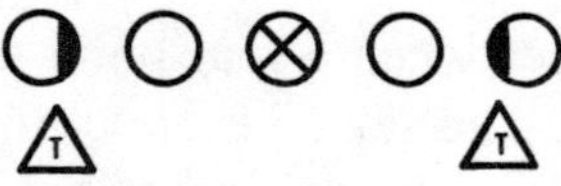

Cheat alignment

DIAGRAM 5-1

3. Basic Responsibilities

From a regular alignment the tackle is responsible for the gap to his inside. This means that whenever he is lined up in a head-up position on an offensive lineman he will execute his basic technique (which will be discussed). Therefore, if he is head up on the offensive guard in a particular defense he is still responsible for the gap to his immediate inside.

From his gap alignment, which is usually between the offensive guard and tackle (unless it is an unbalanced line), he is already in the gap that he is responsible to protect. He now has the duty of protection of the gap from a yard's penetration into the opponent's backfield. Naturally, once the initial responsibility is covered, the tackle is expected to move to the ball. If he does not pursue well, he will not play!

a. Play to him: He protects the inside gap and attacks from that position. He must not allow a ball carrier through his area. If the play is to his side, but is moving outside, the tackle has the responsibility of an inside-out approach to the ball carrier.

b. Play away from him: The tackle has the responsibility of taking the proper pursuit angle which, if a trap occurs, will put him in good position to beat it. If unblocked, he expects trap. Pursue on play away must be close to the line of scrimmage and close to the buttocks of the offensive line. He must not get penetration in pursuit. Remember, pursuit angle on plays away may be determined by the defender's speed.

c. Pass-action—play-action pass: He follows all techniques given previously (see pass-rush technique). He is responsible for moving directly to the quarterback without concern for a lane.

d. Drop back: If the offensive lineman sets to block (cup protection), the tackle follows pass rush technique and attempts to take an outside-in approach to the passer, *but* he can go inside anytime he feels there is a chance to get the quarterback.

4. Initial Movement and Technique

a. From basic alignment—head up: On movement (offensive blocker's down hand or ball), the defensive tackle will take a short lateral step inside, about six inches, with his inside leg, staying under the shoulder pads of the blocker. He brings the outside forearm up to the inside shoulder of the offensive blocker that he is aligned over. He is now in a low breakdown position, and must be under the blocker, keeping the shoulders square to the line of scrimmage. He must not get any deeper than a yard penetration (no deeper than the heels of the offensive linemen). The lateral step and blow are one quick movement.

Be sure the defensive tackle delivers the blow; this initial movement is one of aggression! (See Diagram 5-2—A and B.)

Note: From initial movement the tackle should make contact with the offensive blocker that he is aligned over and deliver a hard blow; while he is moving he should eye the offensive guard (No. 1 man) and key him.

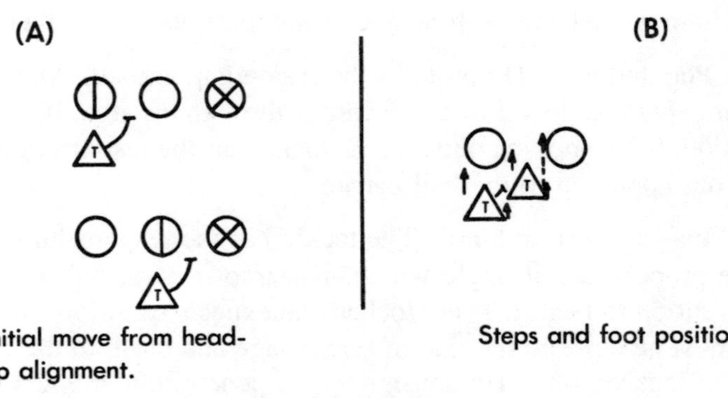

DIAGRAM 5-2

b. From gap alignment (regular gap and short-yardage gap): From this position the tackle's initial move is to spring for a yard's penetration, being sure to bring his feet with him. He attempts to create a new line of scrimmage—one yard deep in opponent's back-field, stay low and keep the head up but always grab legs. The gap technique on short yardage is similar to the above with these exceptions: There should be more of a bend in the elbow and the chin will almost be touching the ground. Buttocks will also be relatively high. Grab legs!

Note: On gap technique the tackle must not be stopped from penetrating straight. He must not be redirected.

5. Tackle Techniques, Keys and Ways He Will Be Blocked

Once the tackle has made his initial move he will be faced with keying and reading properly.

a. (No. 2 man) Offensive tackle's down block: This will probably be the most common block. If the tackle is blocking alone, which is most likely because of the defensive tackle technique, he should straighten the offensive tackle with his forearm blow and work laterally outside, and work through the blocker's head. Eye the football and go to it. The defensive tackle must not be driven down the line. At worst, he should just stay in the guard-tackle gap for a stalemate. If the block is made and the defensive tackle feels himself being pushed down the line, he should bend the outside leg and drop; if possible, he spins on buttocks and then moves to the ball. He must not get driven too far down the line. If the defensive tackle feels the blocker's head is behind him he may run around the tackle's block, but must stay close to buttocks of linemen (see Diagram 5-3—A and B).

Offensive tackle. Down block—fight outside

DIAGRAM 5-3 (A)

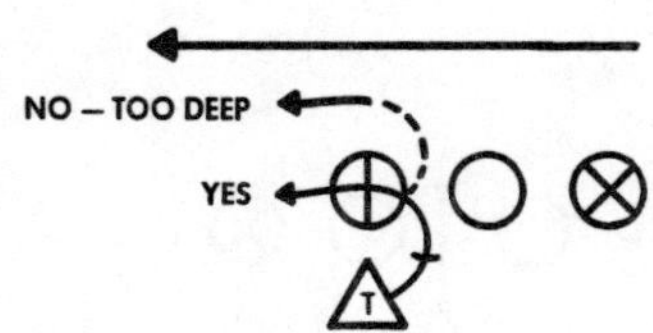

Blocker's head is behind our tackle; our tackle uses run-around technique, but must get close to buttocks of lineman and stay parallel.

DIAGRAM 5-3 (B)

Note: He only looks for the football when he is in a position under the blocker in all circumstances.

If the defensive tackle can see the ball and there is a chance that if penetration is made a big play can be made, then by all means he will move to the ball—but he must be right (see Diagram 5-4).

Note: You can see that by the tackle's initial movement he can give the offensive tackle a good down block, but he has protected the inside gap. He also becomes proficient at defeating the

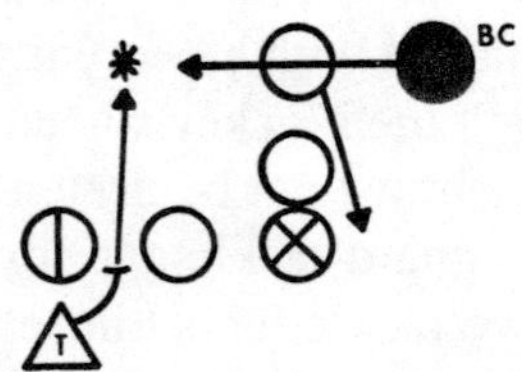

If the ball can be seen and there is a chance, he goes to it, but must be right.

DIAGRAM 5-4

tackle's down block. The tackle has protected his gap and now he can fight pressure and move to the ball.

From the gap position, the defensive tackle will have made penetration; grab his legs. He must fight to get into a pursuit pattern. However, he must be prepared since there might be a chance of the big play. He must not attempt to be redirected on contact (see Diagram 5-5).

Note: Remember—gap alignment puts the defender in his responsibility before the snap.

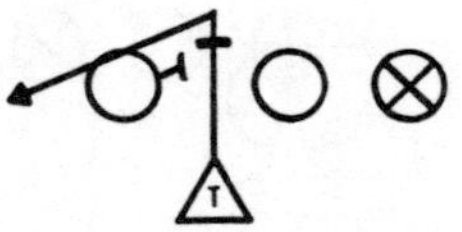

From gap alignment, defensive tackle faced with down block of offensive tackle—fights to outside and gets to pursuit angle.

DIAGRAM 5-5

When head up on the guard, the defensive tackle executes the same techniques.

b. (No. 2 man) The offensive tackle's turn-out (cut-off) block: If the defensive tackle is quick enough there will be no problem of turn-out block. On occasion, if the blocker gets position on the defensive tackle and blocks him outside, the defender should fight across the blocker's head and fight to the inside—fill the hole with the blocker.

Beating the turn-out (cut-off) block—fights through blocker's head and protects the inside gap with blocker's body. This block should really never occur.

DIAGRAM 5-6

This should not happen more than once or twice; if it does, the tackle is too slow. The defensive tackle must not be cut off by the offensive tackle (see Diagram 5-6).

c. (No. 1 man) Offensive guard's turn-out block: This is handled similarly to the turn-out by the tackle. Deliver the blow, drive the blocker down the line. Don't allow the guard to get position; shed him quickly (use previous techniques). Don't allow him into the body. From the gap alignment, the tackle just attempts to get his head in the hole. From the regular alignment, if the blocker's head is well behind our tackle, the tackle may use a go-around technique, but must stay close to buttocks of linemen and keep shoulders parallel (see Diagrams 5-7 and 5-8).

Offensive guard's out block—sheds and drives back into LOS.

DIAGRAM 5-7

Blocker's head is well behind our tackle—use run-around technique.

DIAGRAM 5-8

Note: This type of block is common with tackle trap and no fill block by a back.

d. Facing the trap block: Since the initial movement of the tackle has him protecting the inside gap, this also puts him in excellent position to defeat the trap block. If on the initial move the tackle feels no pressure from the offensive tackle and he sees the guard blocking someone else, then the defensive tackle is going to be trapped. The defensive tackle first looks inside; if no blocker is coming he looks to the backfield for a blocker or ball carrier. Basically, if the tackle reads trap early, he steps down, stays square with toes pointing to the goal line and shoulders parallel to the line of scrimmage. He meets the trapper with the inside forearm, braces the outside leg, gets into a good low breakdown position. He attempts to close the running lane that the offense is trying to create. Our tackle will attempt to expose only the tip of his shoulder pads (see Diagram 5-9).

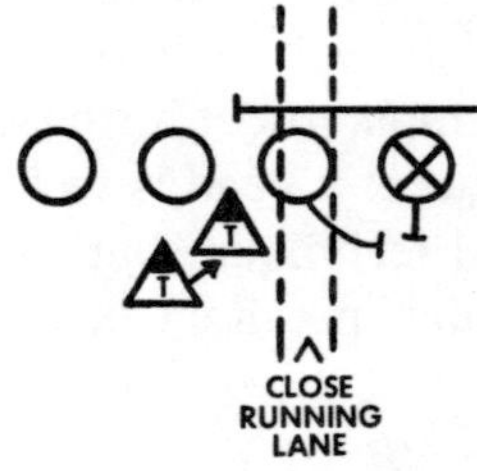

The defensive tackle reads trap early and is in position to close the running lane by using the inside forearm.

DIAGRAM 5-9

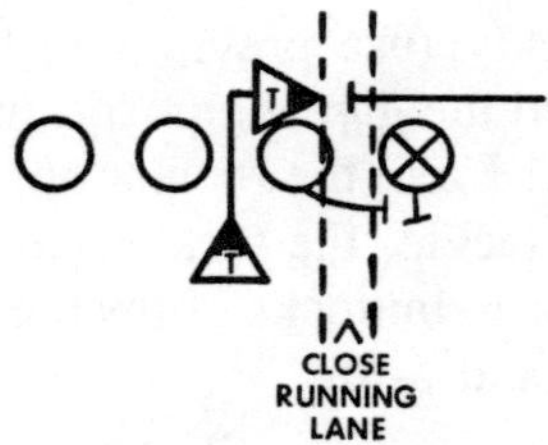

The tackle is in gap technique and must get his helmet back in the hole. He uses the "down the line" technique because he has penetrated and feels no one blocking him.

DIAGRAM 5-10

Another method we use is to meet trap "down the line." This is used when there is penetration by the defender—for example, in the gap alignment. The defender, having penetrated, realizes he is not being blocked, and therefore tries to get his helmet in the hole to his inside. The defensive tackle moves down the line and tries to find the trapper and meet him head on. Either method is acceptable as long as the running lane is closed for the ball carrier (see Diagram 5-10).

Note: He can't stop after meeting trap; he tries to make the tackle. Another coaching point to remember is that if he is not blocked by the time he is to the offensive blocker's toes he is going to be trapped.

e. The isolation block by the back: The defensive tackle should never be blocked by a back. The tackle feels no one blocking him, looks inside and sees no one coming, and immediately looks to the offensive backfield. If action is coming he penetrates and chops the lead blocker aggressively (see Diagram 5-11). You can see by the nature of our defense that the back isolation on the tackle is a distinct possibility since many teams try to isolate a linebacker in a standard 5-2 defense.

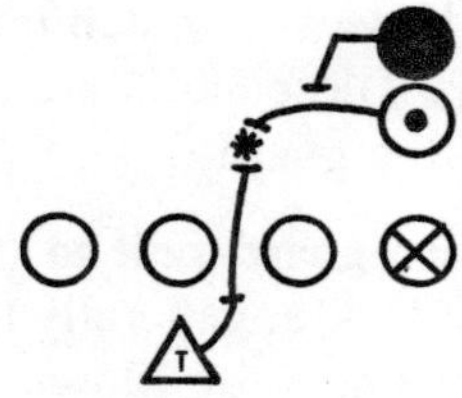

The isolation block requires penetration to beat it, but it is only made after the inside look by the defensive tackle is made to check trap.

DIAGRAM 5-11

f. Offensive linemen pull or trap away to the inside: Because of the initial move the defensive tackle is also in excellent position to get in the hip pocket of the puller or trapper. He moves down the line with the trapper; while moving, he grabs the trapper or knocks him off course and looks for the ball carrier. This trapping or pulling man will lead the defender directly to the play. The defensive tackle's initial move will make it easy for him to get on the hip of an offensive tackle. The initial move will also allow him to see the offensive guard. If he pulls away the defensive tackle may do one of two things: attempt to get in hip pocket if read early, or just take a good pursuit angle. Whether or not he gets on the hip or pursues depends on the defender's speed and quickness off the ball (see Diagram 5-12— A and B).

Note: He must stay on the hip closest to the line of scrimmage —this will prevent an effective fill block by a back.

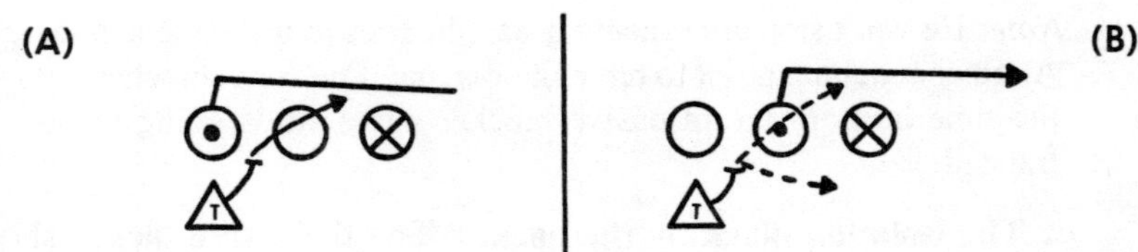

(A) Defensive tackle gets in hip pocket of offensive tackle. Initial move makes this very probable.

(B) Defensive tackle may get in hip pocket of offensive guard or take good pursuit angle.

DIAGRAM 5-12

If the opponent doesn't use a fill block by a back, the defensive tackle will generally be blocked by the guard blocking out; if he is not, he should have a field day. However, watch it if the tackle is too good as he may overrun the play. These skills are also followed when the defensive tackle is head on the guard.

g. (No. 1 man) Offensive guard pull to (to the outside): If the guard pulls to the side of the tackle, generally the defensive tackle will follow all techniques given under the down block of the offensive tackle. This is probably how the tackle will be blocked. He must be conscious of one thing if the guard pulls across his face—he should attempt to follow him. If this can't be done, he should cut him off and search for the ball. Otherwise, he follows techniques described earlier of beating down block. If the defensive tackle is in the gap, he is in

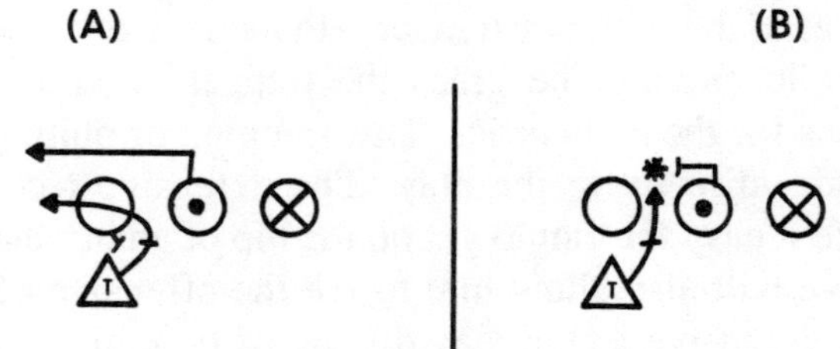

(A) Be conscious of following guard if he crosses tackle's face, he stays close to LOS.

(B) He must be conscious of penetration if guard crosses his face or cuts off *any* pulling linemen.

DIAGRAM 5-13

good position to cut off the pull of the guard and even make the play (see Diagram 5-13—A and B).

h. Our tackle head on the offensive guard (No. 1 man): Our defensive tackles will align a great deal of the time head on the opponent's offensive guards (our college 4-3 defense). We believe it is difficult to "sit" in one defense without superior talent. Therefore, it is necessary to have a change-up alignment or stunt and/or slant from the basic alignment. We prefer to adjust alignment so techniques remain the same and there is no loss of depth in our defense. We also feel that when playing a 5-2 defense there should be a companion defense that covers the opponent's guards since much of the opponent's game plan is based around their guards being uncovered. They will run many plays without a fill block when pulling guards or they will attempt to attack linebackers. The tackle techniques remain the same when aligned head on the guards. Beating the blocks is exactly the same as when aligned head on the offensive tackle, i.e., the tackle beating the center's turn-out block is exactly like beating the offensive guard's turn-out. The interesting point is that some opponents won't allow for the new alignment on a guard pull and allow our tackles to get on the hip (see Diagram 5-14).

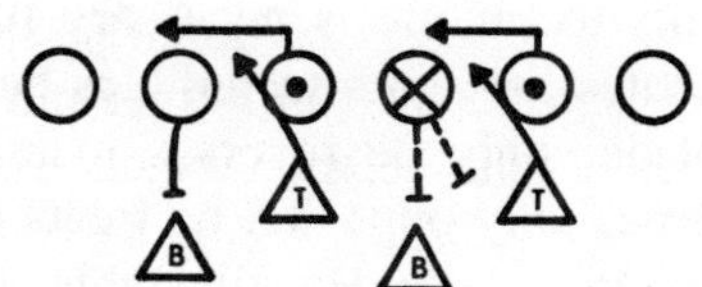

DIAGRAM 5-14

i. Vs. cup block and play-action pass block: The defensive tackle follows all techniques given under pass rush. He must attempt to get into the passer's line of vision (see pass-rush techniques).

j. What about the double team: No technique is given for defeating down block of tight end or double team (see methods of beating blocks). It should be difficult for the offensive end to execute an effective block on the defensive tackle due to the initial move of defensive tackle. If he does go for the tackle, our linebacker is absolutely free. (See Diagram 5-15.)

Initial move makes it difficult for end to make block. If he does, LB is free (to be discussed later).

DIAGRAM 5-15

k. Offensive tackle pulls outside (No. 2 man): Our tackle will find it difficult to get on the hip of a pulling offensive tackle that is moving outside. Asking the defensive tackle to get on the hip is impractical because of his initial movement so we ask him to penetrate and do the best he can. We make them aware that if the play is run it is almost always "flip."

6. Called Moves

These moves are predetermined and called in the huddle. They are executed on the snap.

a. Step-out: This technique is necessary for a change-up. The defensive tackle executes the same techniques he normally would on his regular move inside, only he reverses it and steps outside. All techniques are the same, only opposite; he treats the tight end's block as he would the offensive guard's. He still fights pressure. *The tackle is now responsible for the outside gap*. This is a most important move to success (see Diagram 5-16). It is mostly used when we find the tight end is just coming directly down on our linebacker. It is also used if the offensive tackle is anticipating the initial movement of our tackle.

The step-out move by the defensive tackle.

DIAGRAM 5-16

Finally, we like it when we expect the opponent to attack our corner, i.e., sprint pass, flip, etc. (See Diagram 5-17.) We use this call a great deal with our college 4-3. When we call this we have found our tackle, on occasion, completely unblocked.

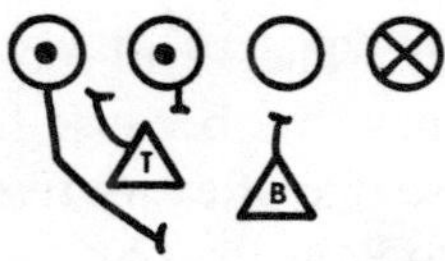

Good time to use step-out—defensive tackle is free vs. this blocking scheme.

DIAGRAM 5-17

b. Lock-up: This call is made to keep the offense honest. It is especially good if we can control the offensive blocker. It is a punishing move. The defender fires off the ball straight and locks face gear with the opponent while delivering a blow. It is all-out explosion into the opponent. After explosion, the defender attempts to control the opponent's shoulder pads and find the ball. He should control the gap to either side.

c. Pinch: This is penetrating move by the defensive tackle inside. The inside gap is still protected, but instead of just stepping laterally, keeping the shoulders square as he would on the regular, the tackle penetrates and pinches to the buttocks of the first inside offensive man (usually the guard). The defensive tackle uses a cross-over step and brings his outside arm across. When reaching the desired area, he will break down and find the ball. This is very effective when a trap is expected or the offense shows a tendency to run a particular play to the inside gap. It is also used on short-yardage situation.

d. Twist: When the defensive tackle hears *twist*, he will execute the following technique around our defensive end: He steps laterally outside and breaks off the buttocks of our defensive end who will be going hard. He dips the inside shoulder and breaks down. He must be ready to follow all technical skills from the new alignment. This is very effective against sweeps, to a split end side. Being perfectly honest, we have used this only twice in two years. It is one of those calls we know can be effective—but risky. We don't practice it as much as we should because to use this play we feel a team must have a strong tendency.

7. Common Faults

a. Too high: A defensive tackle is easy prey if he doesn't stay in a very low breakdown position at all times. He must think of staying under the opponent's shoulder pads.

b. Doesn't read keys: The "ball-looker" may make a big play once out of every ten times, but because he doesn't read his keys he generally costs the defense one of every five plays. It is easier to get to the football by reacting to keys than by looking for the ball too soon. The ball-looker usually lets opponents into his body. We have found this point must be sold to players: they must read on the move, *then* find the ball.

c. Doesn't step lateral but steps up: Another problem occurs when the tackle doesn't step laterally, but rather steps up and penetrates; now he is easily blocked down by the tackle and can't get into the play. Also, the guard now has a terrific angle on the linebacker. The tackle, by making a "pinch" move, leaves an enlarged off-tackle hole and can no longer squeeze it shut (see Diagrams 5-18 and 5-19).

d. Too much penetration: This can occur and when it does the tackle is easily trapped, and if he isn't trapped and the play is away he is usually slow in pursuit. Our tackles must play no more than one yard deep.

Another problem—when the tackle gets too much penetration, he is easy prey for a fill block by a back when he is trying to get on the hip of a pulling or trapping lineman (see Diagram 20—A and B).

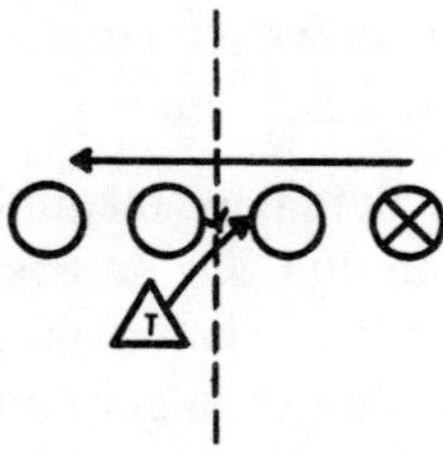

Our tackle slants and is easily blocked down by offensive tackle and can't recover.

DIAGRAM 5-18

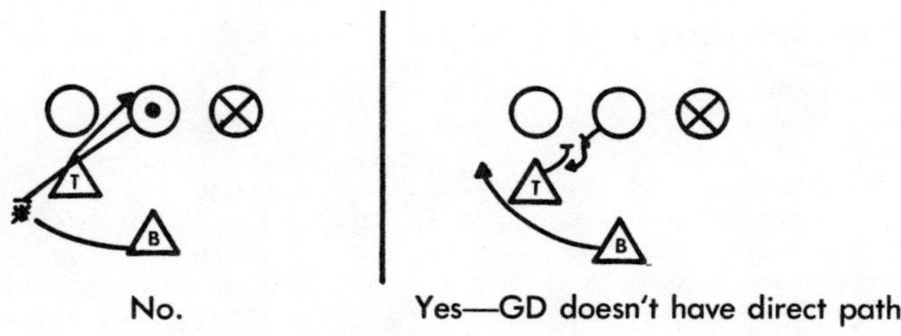

No. Yes—GD doesn't have direct path.

Also, guard has easy shot at LB since the guard doesn't have to go around our defensive tackle to get LB.

DIAGRAM 5-19

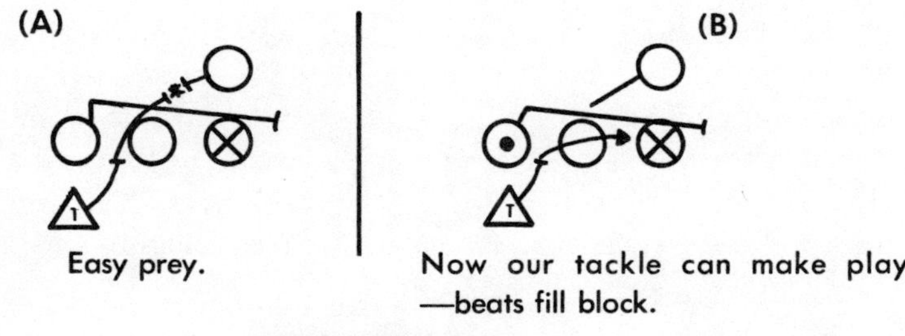

(A) Easy prey.

(B) Now our tackle can make play —beats fill block.

DIAGRAM 5-20

e. Shoulders turned: When a tackle gets his shoulders turned to the line of scrimmage he is worthless. He must attempt to keep his shoulders parallel to the line. He can now make a play even if driven back; no wall is created.

f. Not delivering blow on initial step.

g. Wipe-out: A wipe-out occurs when the offensive tackle drives our defensive tackle down the line and a large running lane is created. It is usually the result of too large a step by the tackle, similar to the pinch move.

6

Controlling Two Gaps with the Nutcracker

1. Stance

The nutcracker will assume a four-point stance (see tackle's gap stance).

2. Alignment

a. Head-on: Basically, he will align head on the offensive man who is in the middle of the offensive line. This is the regular alignment. The nutcracker alignment in regard to proximity to the ball will vary with the individual, the defense called, and the down and distance needed. However, for the most part, we would like him to get as close to the ball as is legally possible.

b. Gap: Another alignment is the gap alignment. These two alignments will each have their own technical skills. In a gap alignment, the nutcracker should get as close to the ball as possible. He aligns to the gap on either side of the center, depending on the call.

c. Up: This alignment puts the nutcracker in an "up" position off the ball (see No. 6, "Called Moves"). We may put a linebacker in place of the nutcracker, depending on the nutcracker's ability.

3. Basic Responsibilities

From the regular alignment, the nutcracker is responsible for the gaps to either side of the center. If he is in a gap alignment, he is responsible solely for that gap. He will always be head up or in a gap, but if he is aligned on someone other than on the middle man on the offensive line he is responsible for the gap to his immediate inside.

> *Note*: The nutcracker must have some freedom; he must move to the ball the best way he can. We only give him the technique that gets him to the ball. We limit his duties.

The most important part of the defense is the fact that the nutcracker must not be controlled by the center alone. If the nutcracker can *consistently* be controlled one-on-one by the center, we are in for a long game.

a. Play to: If the play is an internal play, the nutcracker must be able to control both gaps to each side in a regular. And after initial movement, he must be able to protect the playside gap. In a gap alignment, he controls the gap aligned in (see Diagram 6-1—A and B).

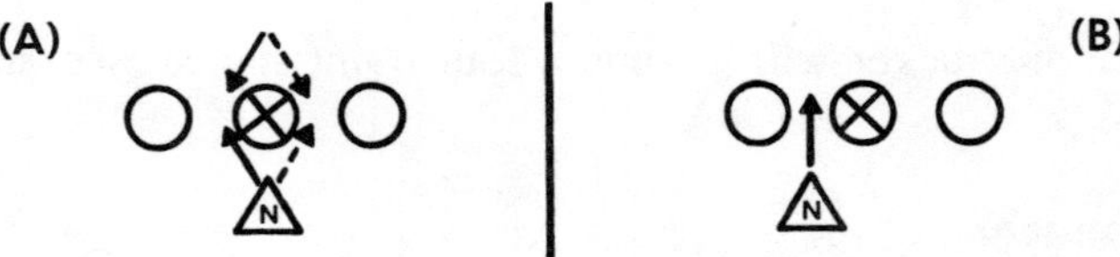

Controls gaps to both sides from regular (controls center) and moves to ball.

Controls that gap in a gap alignment.

DIAGRAM 6-1

b. Play away: The nutcracker must pursue to the ball from inside-out to either side. The angle will depend on the speed of the nutcracker. Also, he pursues along line or deeper on wide plays, while a forcing type of pursuit is more appropriate on tighter plays. However, the nutcracker can at any time move to an opening in the line if he feels he can get to the ball (see Diagrams 6-2 A and B and 6-3).

c. Play action pass: Rush and he takes first opening and gets in quarterback's eyes (see pass rush).

d. Drop back pass: After initial move on the center, the nutcracker takes a side; the center should seldom block the nutcracker one on one. The nutcracker just moves to the passer any way he can. (See pass rush.)

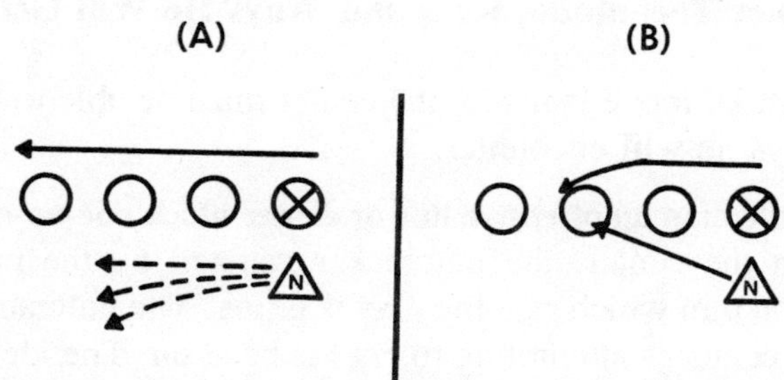

Play away wide—optional pursuit course.

Play away—off-tackle force pursuit pattern.

DIAGRAM 6-2

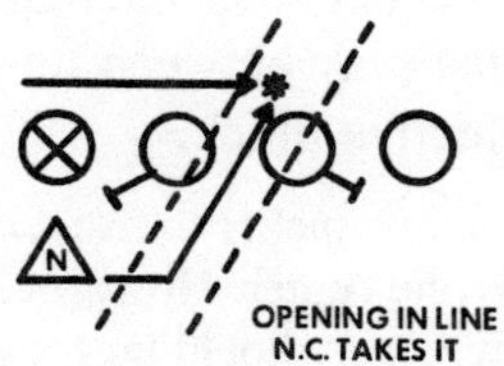

Nutcracker—can take an opening in the line if he feels he can make play.

DIAGRAM 6-3

4. Initial Movement and Technique

a. From basic alignment: This may vary, but basically, in a normal situation, he delivers a blow on the center. The arm will depend on the scouting report, and/or the individual defender. He should try to keep the arm to the side of the play free at all times. On long-yardage situations, the nutcracker may be asked to use a hand shiver. On initial blow he must be sure to bring the legs with him. He tries to keep the shoulders square to the line of scrimmage. On initial move, the nutcracker must control center and react to his head!

Note: Whatever arm the nutcracker delivers blow with leaves him vulnerable to double team on that side.

b. From gap alignment: (See tackle initial movement from gap alignment.)

5. Nutcracker Technique, Keys and Ways He Will Get Blocked

Once initial move is made, the center must be able to react to the blocking keys he will encounter.

a. Middle man on offensive line or center block one-on-one: After the blow on the center, the nutcracker can tell by the pressure the center puts on him which side the play is going. The nutcracker goes to the side the center is attempting to get his head on. The ideal situation is to control the center from under his pads, straighten the center up and find the ball. The nutcracker should try to keep his shoulders square to the line of scrimmage at all times and not take a side unless making a tackle or moving to the ball (see Diagram 6-4). All this sounds very nice, but in actual practice, the nutcracker may get cut off by the center. When this occurs, the nutcracker should try to get the shoulder that is opposite the play between himself and the center; this is only used versus an effective block.

> *Note*: We will allow the nutcracker to use a run-around technique if he is badly cut off by the center. However, this shouldn't occur too often since the nutcracker should be the first defender off the mark on the snap of the ball.

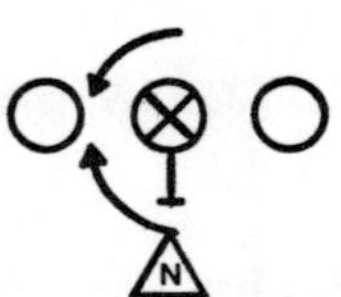

Fighting through center's head after initial move. He straightens center up and finds ball.

DIAGRAM 6-4

b. (No. 1 man) Offensive guards down block (double team): This should usually be a double team. The nutcracker should not allow the center to release unmolested. The guard is telling the nutcracker which side the play is going by his block. The nutcracker should fight back through the guard's head and try to get to his gap and find the ball. Follow applicable procedures for defeating double team (see methods of defeating double team). See Diagram 6-5.

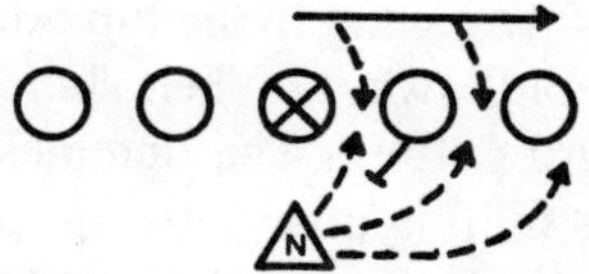

Nutcracker blocked by guard.

DIAGRAM 6-5

> Note: If the guard is constantly the man giving the nutcracker problems, the nutcracker is allowed to move off the ball in order to facilitate a read.

c. Other blocking schemes vs. the nutcracker: Basically, the nutcracker will be confronted by those two types of blocks. Seldom will he be trapped or isolated.

6. Called Moves (Predetermined on Snap)

a. Slant: The nutcracker will execute a pinch technique, but he must be squared up by the time he is to the offensive guard's buttocks to the side called (see pinch technique under tackle). It is called slant because it applies to the nutcracker. There are some points that the nut-

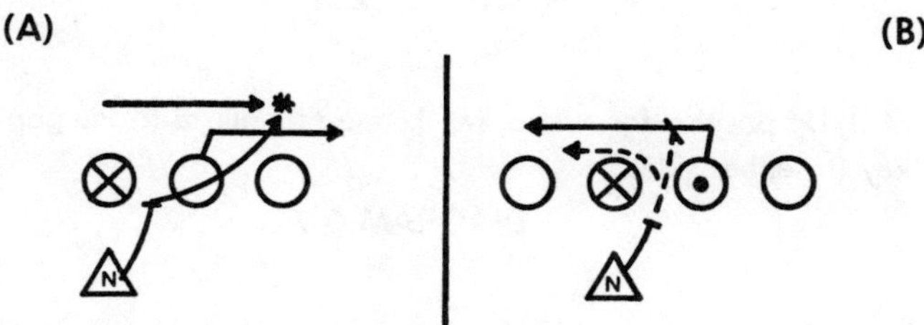

(A) Nutcracker slants and guard pulls away; he gets in hip pocket and looks immediately for ball.

(B) Nutcracker slants and guard crosses his face. Nutcracker executes a run-around technique, but nutcracker should first try to cut off guard; if he can't, then he stays close to center's buttocks.

DIAGRAM 6-6

cracker must know about getting in the hip pocket of a pulling lineman (see defensive tackle pull away). When slanting, the nutcracker can't help but notice a guard pulling. The nutcracker should get in the hip pocket if the guard is pulling away, disrupt pulling linemen and look for the ball immediately. If the guard crosses the nutcracker's face and the nutcracker can't cut him off, the nutcracker should turn and find the ball. He should execute a run-around technique. Remember, he stays close to the line of scrimmage and gets close to center buttocks (see Diagram 6-6—A and B).

b. "Up" position: This particular call may force us to put in a linebacker since this is a new technique for the nutcracker. However, if he can handle it we would like to leave him in the game. This call is usually made in passing situations or in a situation when we want our tackles on their offensive guards. The nutcracker takes a two-point stance over the center, off the ball. He must read the fullback and on his key fill the guard-tackle gap (to either side) on run. On pass drop read the quarterback. (See linebacker technique.) This is called in conjunction with our 4-3 defense (see Diagram 6-7).

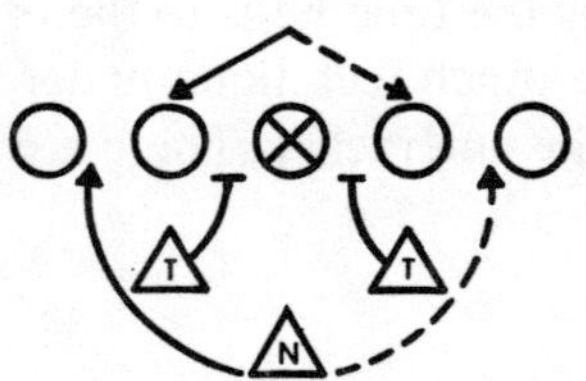

(4-3) Up position for nutcracker; he must fill guard-tackle gap on run key (to either side).

DIAGRAM 6-7

Note: If step-out is called from 4-3, the nutcracker must control center-guard gaps to either side on run. On pass we have him strictly read quarterback; he has no predetermined drop.

For scrape techniques, etc., see Linebackers.

7. Common Faults

a. Low block: The center will undoubtedly attempt to chop block the nutcracker at the ankles; he cannot let this occur. He must use previously described techniques of beating low block, and he must not be driven back as he will cut off linebackers.

b. Shoulders turned: If the nutcracker gets his shoulders turned perpendicular to the line of scrimmage, especially by the center, we are in deep trouble. Follow all techniques of defeating blocks. He may have to use run-around technique (see Diagram 6-8—A and B).

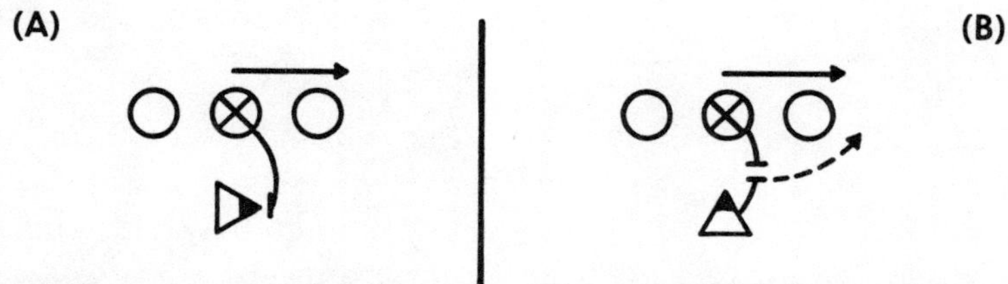

Nutcracker turned, we are in trouble. Okay, nutcracker beat center.

DIAGRAM 6-8

c. Wipe-out on guard-center double team: On the double team the nutcracker must not get wiped out! He must hold his ground and at least create a stalemate. (See methods of defeating double team and also see tackle faults.)

7

Developing the Pressure Fighter—the Defensive End

1. Stance

The end's stance is exactly like the breakdown position with these exceptions: The outside leg and foot are back further, at least past the heel of the inside leg. Also, the buttocks of the defensive end are facing slightly towards the ball. We feel this alignment will prevent an immediate hook by the tight end.

2. Alignment

a. Inside eye to outside eye of opponent: Basically, the end has one alignment that he will be in 80% of the time. He will align with his inside eye to the outside eye of the third man from the middle of the formation, provided his split rule allows it. If there is no one there, he aligns where an imaginary third opponent would be (see Diagram 7-1— A and B).

b. Outside shoulder alignment of opponent: In this situation, the defensive end aligns with his inside shoulder to the outside shoulder of the third man from the middle of the formation. This is common when the wing is the fourth man on the line and the wing is close enough to make an effective down block; also, it is common on a long-yardage situation.

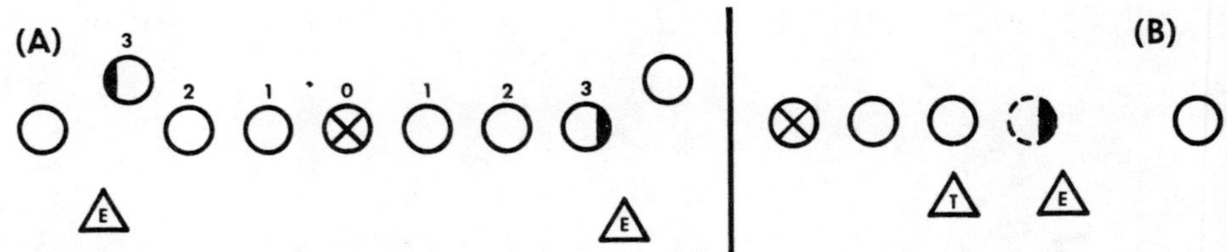

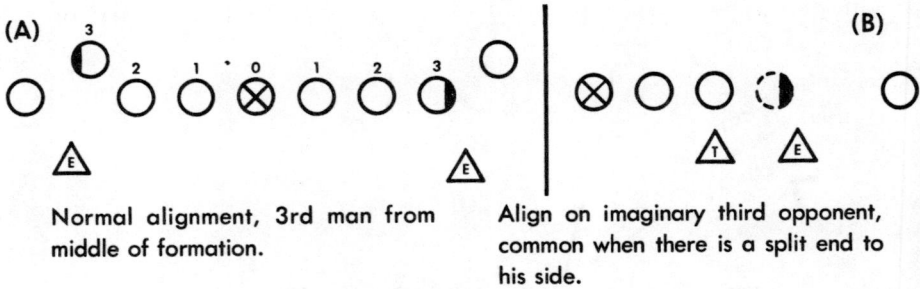

Normal alignment, 3rd man from middle of formation.

Align on imaginary third opponent, common when there is a split end to his side.

DIAGRAM 7-1

Note: All technical skills from this alignment are the same—also used if end is getting hooked by offensive end, but we like to think this will not occur frequently. If it does, we are in trouble.

c. Split rule: The defensive end is faced most frequently with a dilemma. If someone splits, when does the split man no longer count as the third man from the middle of the formation? If the end asks himself this question, he should have no problem: ''Can I carry out my responsibilities from the wider alignment?'' If the answer is ''yes,'' he stays there, if it is ''no'' then he moves back to a normal alignment. Generally at 2½ yards the end must move to a head-up alignment. At 4½ yards the end should move back to his normal alignment (see Diagram 7-2—A and B).

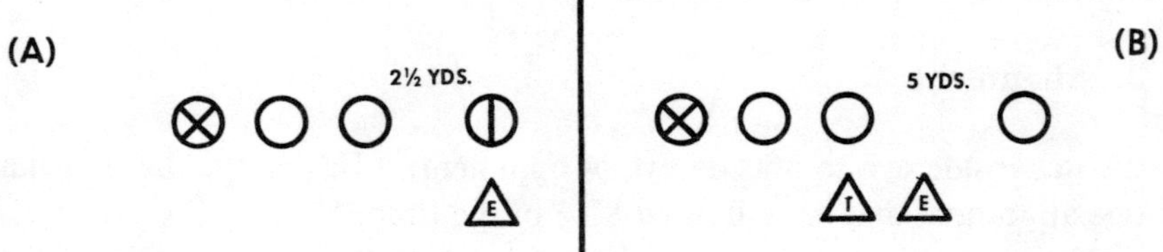

Ends move to head up on 2½- to 3-yard split.

Ends move back to normal alignment.

DIAGRAM 7-2

Note: The defensive end can split as far as he likes as long as he can carry out his basic duties.

d. Wide alignment: This is seldom used and must be called from the sidelines. It is used in conjunction with a ''switch'' or ''contain'' call. The defensive end aligns on the fourth man from the center, or counting from outside-in, aligns on first outside receiver. However, the split rule will still apply, only it applies on the 4th man from inside (see Diagram 7-3).

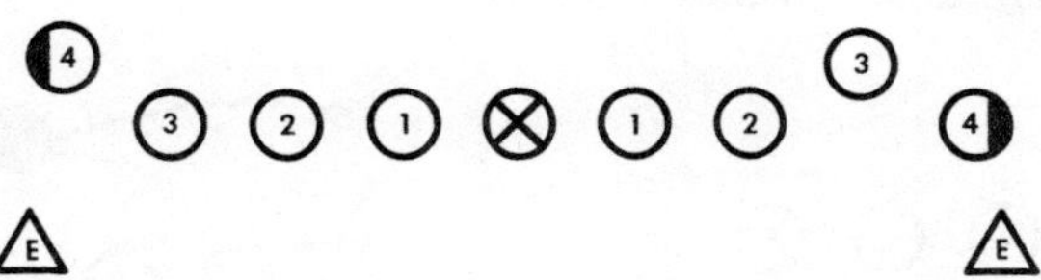

"Wide call"—end aligns on 4th man from middle of formation (wide alignment—this must be called from bench). Split rule may still apply.

DIAGRAM 7-3

Note: From this wide alignment the end becomes an aggressive contain man; no one can get outside. On option, he has pitch.

3. Basic Responsibilities (from Regular)

The end is the "pressure fighter." He is the apex of the defense; he has the duty of reading and playing accordingly. He must protect his outside leg and stay on his feet at all costs. He must not be hooked. He must read well; he moves to the ball. The end's duties and responsibilities remain the same from all alignments (except wide alignment and predetermined calls).

a. Play to: The end's play will be determined by the way he is blocked, but generally he must protect the gap to his inside first, move to ball, and finally, have containment. However, since he is the apex of the defense, his technique will allow him to properly protect each area one step at a time. There is one rule which he must always remember on a play to the defensive end: *Never allow a pulling lineman to cross his face; take him on*!

b. Play-away: The end's duty here is most important. He is responsible for all bootlegs and reverses. The defensive end is the only person we have left for bootleg and reverse. He takes one step inside, on play away, checks for "faces"—especially pulling guards. He doesn't chase! After checking bootleg and reverse, he pursues, taking deepest angle downfield. On plays to or away, generally the defensive end has no pass responsibility; however, he must never let a back cross his face, especially the quarterback on plays-away. He must knock them (backs) down or cover them to the best of his ability; they are potential receivers. This applies only to plays-away from the defensive end. (See Diagrams 7-4 and 7-5.)

Play away—check bootleg and reverse—step down line, one step, pursue.

DIAGRAM 7-4

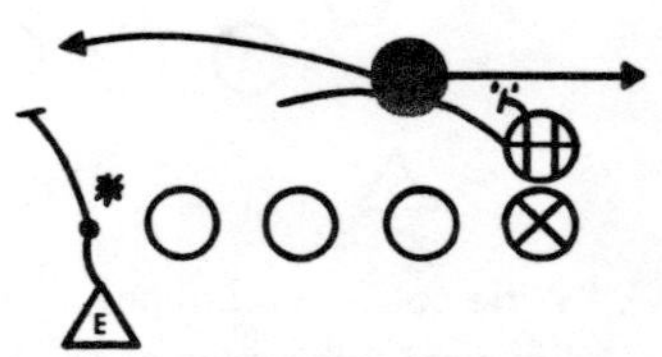

He never allows a back to cross his face, especially the QB, takes him or knocks him down (referring to plays away).

DIAGRAM 7-5

You can see that we have no chase man in the defense. We have found that for the most part he is wasted versus plays-away. On any bootlegs we have found that a chase man, pursuing as deep as the ball in the backfield, can be easy prey and knocked off his feet. Finally, on any inside reverse, i.e., the Delaware reverse, he is easily kicked out when he is a chase man. With our "sit home" technique we have prevented the big play. We have also been able to stop counters from breaking for long gains, and also the tailback "wind back" from the "I" formation breaking against the grain for long gain has been stopped. The coach must take care that the defensive end does not leave too soon on flow-away.

c. Play action and sprint-out pass: On all passes that threaten the corner, the defensive end is responsible for containment of the passer. The defensive end must not get knocked off his feet. The passer must not get outside.

d. Drop-back pass: Rush from outside-in hard. On occasion, if there is a chance, the end may take an inside path to get to the passer; however, generally the end will keep his inside shoulder to the outside shoulder of the passer.

4. Initial Movement and Technique

The end must always keep his toes pointed to the goal line (unless making a tackle) and always protect the outside leg. The initial movement will permit the execution of these things.

On movement, the defensive end will immediately give a hard hand shiver or deliver forearm blow to the offensive blocker he is aligned over. Control his head. Along with this, the end will shuffle step with both feet (never deeper than a yard), staying in the breakdown position with the outside leg back. Never square up to the backfield, keeping shoulders facing goal line.

Note: The end will be asked to deliver a blow on the blocker he is aligned over in many cases (see Diagram 7-6—A and B).

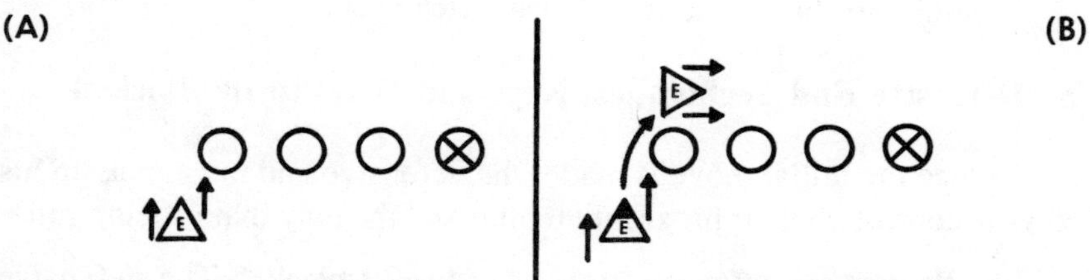

End's toes always pointed to goal line, outside leg back.

Never faces backfield; this is wrong.

DIAGRAM 7-6

The next move will depend on the offensive blocker's moves. The defensive end will step initially with the blocker over him. If the blocker moves inside, the defensive end will take one shuffle step inside, looking inside, staying close to the rear end of the blocker. If the blocker steps outside, the defensive end must shuffle step outside to protect his outside leg. If the blocker comes straight, the end must take him with the inside forearm and leg. If the defensive end reads the helmet of the offensive blocker, it should tell him everything he needs to know for initial movement (see Diagram 7-7—A and B). If the helmet moves outside and it is above the waist of our end, then the end need not continue moving outside since the end (offensively) is releasing. If the helmet is below the waist, the defensive end must fight outside because the tight end is "reach" blocking.

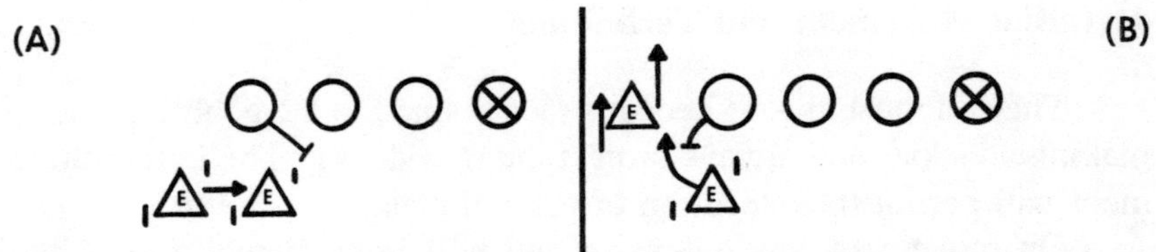

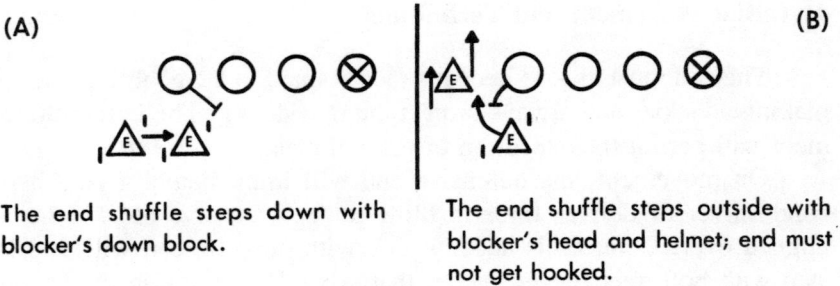

The end shuffle steps down with blocker's down block.

The end shuffle steps outside with blocker's head and helmet; end must not get hooked.

DIAGRAM 7-7

Note: If the tight end or slot blocks inside, expect the guard or fullback to kick-out block! Or, versus a 3-back offense (i.e., wishbone), find the near back and watch hook.

5. Defensive End Techniques, Keys and Ways to Be Blocked

Once the initial move is made, the defensive end must pick up his keys according to their proximity to him and the play that is being run.

a. Beating the offensive blocker's "hook" block: The defensive end cannot be hooked; he must protect his outside leg. Due to the defensive end's alignment, the offensive blocker's head must move across the body of the defensive end. The defensive end should keep the blocker away from his legs and the defensive end should step to the sideline and not too far upfield. If the hook block is made, the end fights through blocker's head to the outside (see methods of beating blocks). If the block is made, the end must try to get his opposite arm in the "V" of the blocker's neck and run with the blocker. He spins out as a last resort.

b. Turn-out block by the offensive blocker: Can be defeated by, once again, fighting through head, stepping with shuffle steps inside and back. *He doesn't try to go around the block* (see Diagram 7-8—A and B).

c. Down block by a wing: The wing has a very nice angle on the defensive end. However, the end knows exactly where the play is going—outside. The end's stance allows him to see the wing. He must protect the outside leg and arm. The end shouldn't be concerned about the wing until contact is almost made; then he should execute the

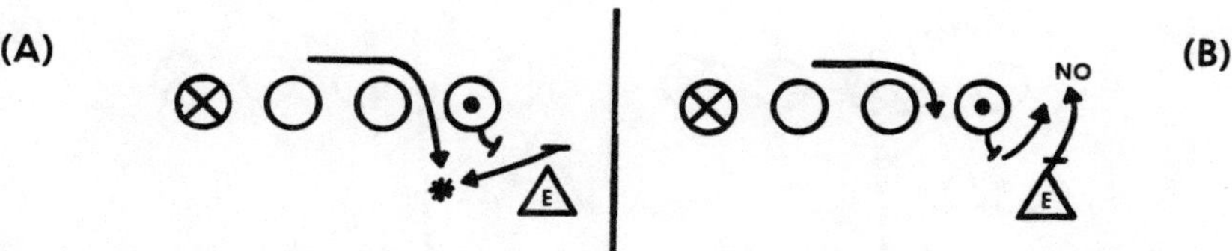

The defensive end facing the turn-out block should step back and inside.

Don't try to run around; this is wrong.

DIAGRAM 7-8

previously given techniques (the drop-step technique is especially effective. However, if the wing has help from offensive end (double team), the defensive end must not be driven back or down the line. The end drops to a knee and splits the seam (see methods of defeating blocks) as a last resort. All attention must be redirected to the wing down block.

d. Offensive lineman or back coming to block with inside-out approach: After initial move, the defensive end should be looking inside (if the offensive blocker on him has blocked down), reading the blocks. Assuming there is an offensive blocker coming flat down the line or a back coming with an inside-out approach, the defensive end should be sure to keep his toes pointing to the goal line and take the blockers on with the inside forearm and leg, staying under the blockers. He "squeezes" the off-tackle hole shut, and delivers a blow with inside forearm and leg—hard! He should not square up to blocker; he is an easy target and can't make the play if he squares up to blocker. A running lane is created if the defensive end exposes his chest to the blocker (see Diagram 7-9—A, B and C).

> *Note*: Remember, if the tight end/slot blocks inside, the defensive end's key that follows (his auxiliary key) will depend on the type of offense being faced, the type of plays, and the proximity of the next most dangerous blocker. For example, versus a wishbone his auxiliary key would be the near back. You see, the auxiliary key would depend on what you are facing offensively.

e. Offensive lineman pulling wide to block, crossing end's face: If an offensive lineman is trying to cross the defensive end's face, the defensive end must take him on aggressively. He must not allow a lineman to cross his face. He controls the puller's shoulder pads or head and moves to the ball. *The end must stay on his feet*. If a lineman

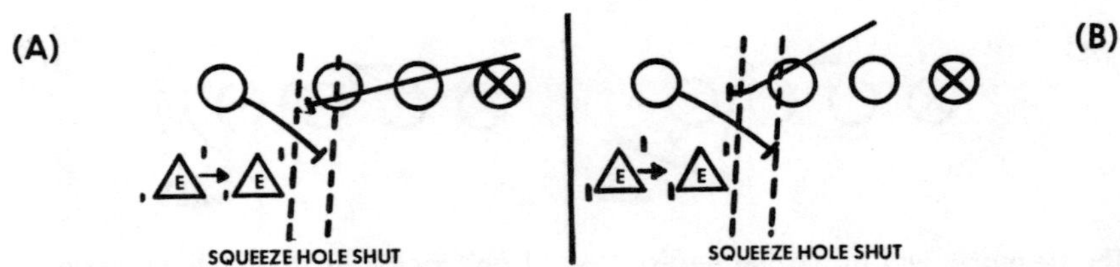

Lineman coming flat down line to kick out defensive end—squeeze hole shut.

Offensive back coming with inside-out approach to kick out—meet as mentioned.

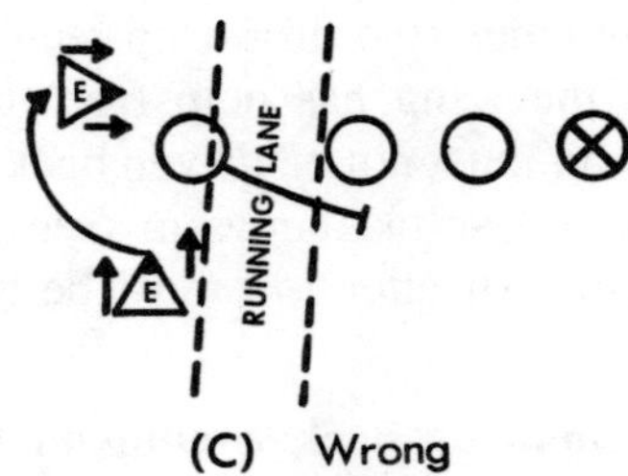

(C) Wrong

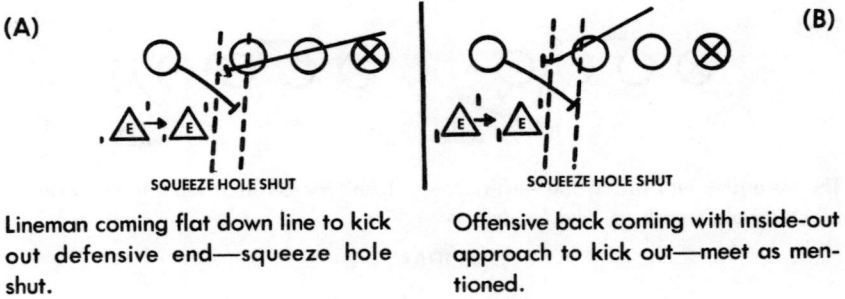

Don't square up to blocker; it makes an easy target, running lane is created and the defensive end doesn't have to be blocked (end can't make play).

DIAGRAM 7-9

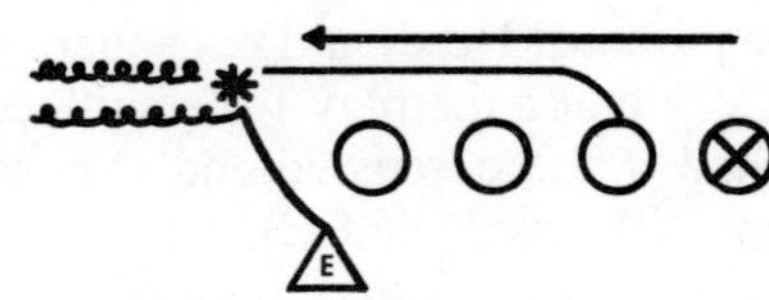

Defensive end must take on a lineman pulling wide aggressively. The blocker must not turn the corner, defensive end must stay on his feet.

DIAGRAM 7-10

can turn the corner on a defensive back, we will be in trouble (see Diagram 7-10).

f. Back coming to block outside-in or wide: If an offensive back comes directly at the defensive end with an outside-in approach, obviously to hook him, the defensive end must close on the blocker and meet him aggressively, always protecting his outside arm and leg. He meets him with the inside forearm and leg. If the back swings wide, it is up to the defensive end to use good judgment and get to the football (see Diagram 7-11—A and B). For the defensive end to move out with the offensive back, the back must be a blocking threat. The influence by the back will not pull the end out, we hope! Remember he must read the helmet (high no threat, low is a threat).

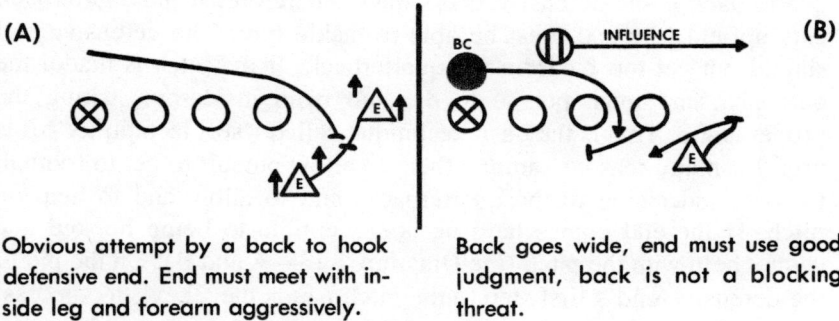

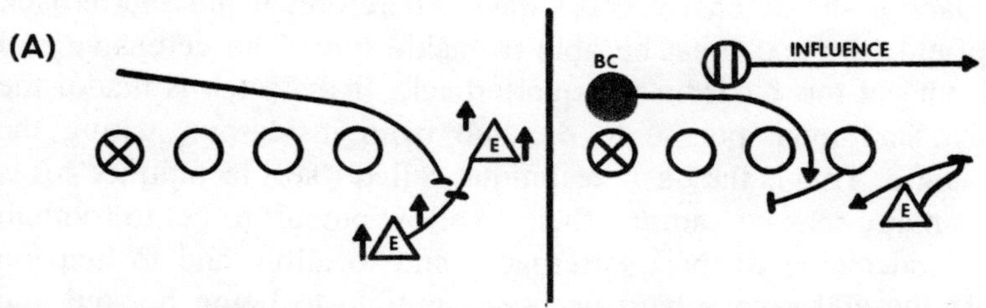

Obvious attempt by a back to hook defensive end. End must meet with inside leg and forearm aggressively.

Back goes wide, end must use good judgment, back is not a blocking threat.

DIAGRAM 7-11

g. Facing two blockers from backfield: This usually occurs on sprint-out pass or quarterback sweep. The defensive end must take on any blocker threatening his outside leg aggressively. If the blockers are shoulder to shoulder, he takes on the deepest one aggressively (see Diagram 7-12).

Note: He must remember to protect his outside leg at all costs.

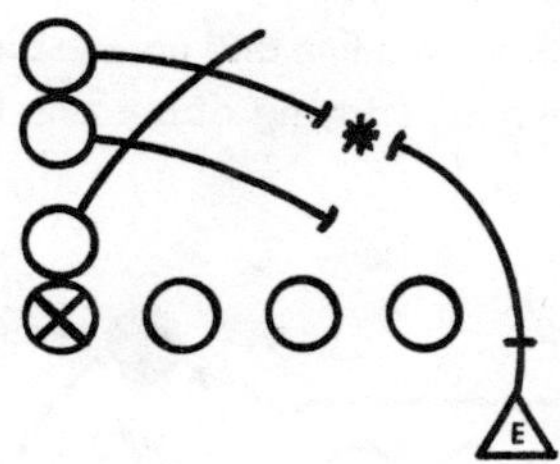

He takes on deepest back aggressively if they are shoulder to shoulder.

DIAGRAM 7-12

h. If no one blocks the defensive end and no one comes to block—option: The end may be confronted with not being blocked by anyone; then he will see the quarterback moving down the line at him. The defensive end must keep his toes pointed to the goal line. He must stay on the line, keeping the quarterback in front of him; he does nothing, he simply stays about one foot in front of the quarterback. The quarterback is the defensive end's man. Therefore, if the quarterback cuts upfield, the end must be able to tackle him. The defensive end should not get too far from the quarterback. If the pitch is made, the defensive end must pursue to the ball from inside-out, taking the proper angle. This is the basic technique called "soft technique." It is used for many reasons, among them to allow pursuit to get to football to force indecision to the quarterback, and to allow end to help on pitch. If the end comes hard he is susceptible to being hooked and cannot help with the pitch (see Diagram 7-13—A and B). On the pitch, the defensive end's first step to the pitchman is the "key" to success. He must step along the line of scrimmage and *not* toward the pitchman. If he steps toward the pitchman it will not bring the defensive end to a "collision point."

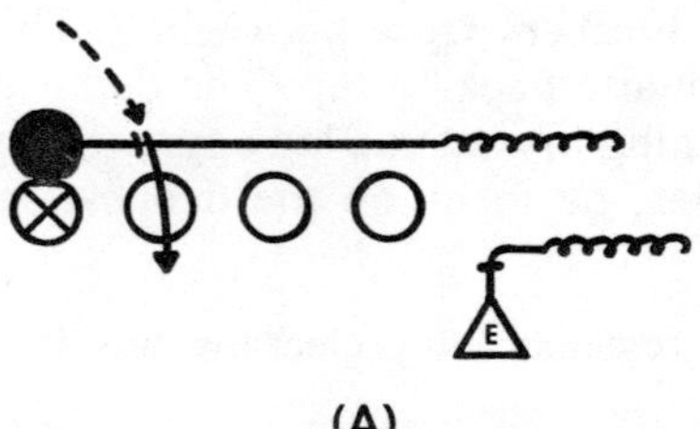

(A)

On option, the defensive end is responsible for the QB; he recognizes it by the QB coming down the line and no one blocking end. Defensive end plays "soft technique" (staying about one foot in front of QB).

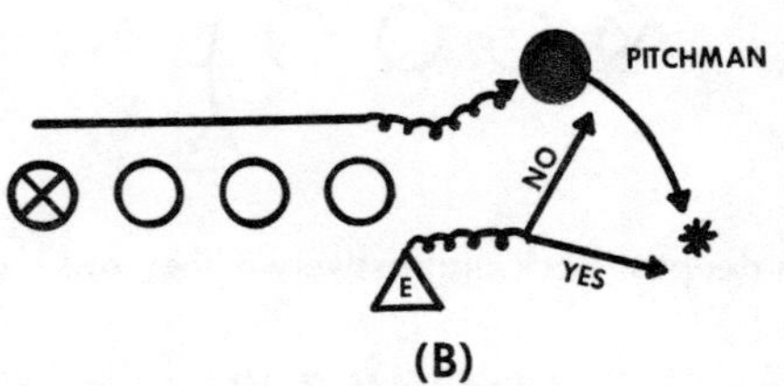

(B)

Defensive end pursues on pitch - he pursues down the line.

DIAGRAM 7-13

Note: The defensive end must be close enough to the quarterback to make the play if the quarterback keeps. Therefore, the distance away from the quarterback will depend on the defensive end's ability. The end will always keep the quarterback in reach of him.

i. Facing option on goal line: When we are in a goal line defense (opponent inside our 10-yard line), the defensive end must make something happen so he must attack the quarterback and destroy him, putting the face mask through his heart (called "tough technique"). The defensive end immediately plays option aggressively.

j. Beating bootlegs and reverses: The end must follow all technical skills given previously, remembering one important point—the quarterback on bootleg cannot ever be allowed outside. The defensive end must keep his feet. On reverue that is wide, the end keeps everything inside. Versus inside reverse, the defensive end must close cautiously on the ball. Besides keeping everything inside, the defensive end must not move upfield too soon. (See Diagram 7-14—A and B.)

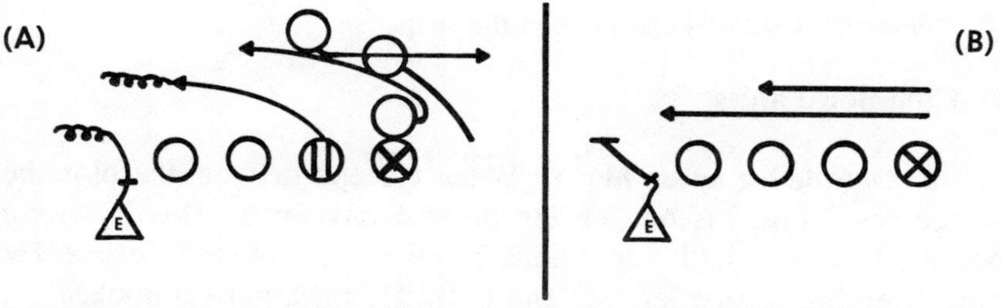

Defensive end vs. bootleg; don't let the play outside.

Wide reverse, keep inside.

DIAGRAM 7-14

6. Called Moves

These moves are called from sideline or predetermined for some reason before the game.

a. "Tough technique" on option: As mentioned earlier, the end may be told if option comes he should immediately destroy the quarterback. This is an excellent change-up, most effective against a timid or good-running quarterback. He hits the quarterback high and gets his arms between the ball and the pitchman. This is a must on the goal line.

b. Contain or switch call: From a wide alignment, the defensive end is now responsible for aggressive contain on flow his way. Nothing is allowed outside.

c. Fire: The defensive end will be told on occasion to fire from his position at a 45-degree angle into the offensive backfield; he moves to the quarterback or near back (see stunting techniques). This stunt may also be called with an "in" call, which means the end "fires" through the inside gap (see Diagram 7-15—A and B).

DIAGRAM 7-15

Note: This stunt is executed on the snap.

7. Common Faults

a. Outside leg up on blow: When the end delivers the blow he sometimes brings his outside leg up to apply force. This is wrong because he is susceptible to a hook block which can easily occur. He must keep his outside leg free and back. He must not get hooked.

b. Too much penetration: The defensive end can get too much penetration, especially when the tight end blocks down. He must step down with tight end's block *only one step across*, no deeper!

c. Square up to blocker: The only time the end should square up is to make a tackle, *not* to ward off a blocker.

d. Play away—getting hooked: Being hooked by a guard or tight end, especially when action is away (bootleg or reverse), is one of the worst things that can happen. Usually, it is the result of the defensive end not beating initial block or not watching for faces.

e. Playing the option wrong: The end overruns the quarterback and lets him cut up inside. The end must be sure the ball is pitched before he leaves the quarterback and moves to the man receiving the pitch—the pitchman. (See Diagram 7-16.) Another problem is when the end moves to the pitchman he moves too deep instead of moving to a collision point. (See Diagram 7-17.)

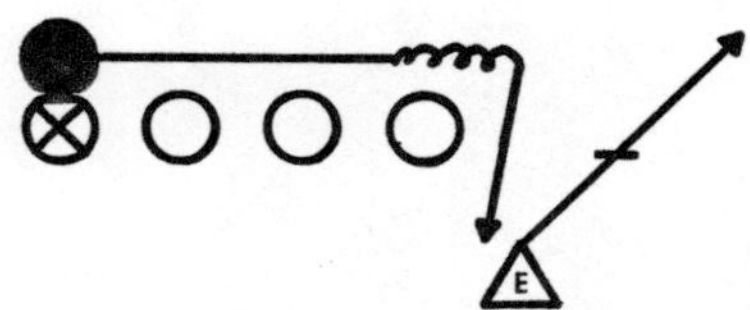

End leaves too soon, allowing QB to cut up.

DIAGRAM 7-16

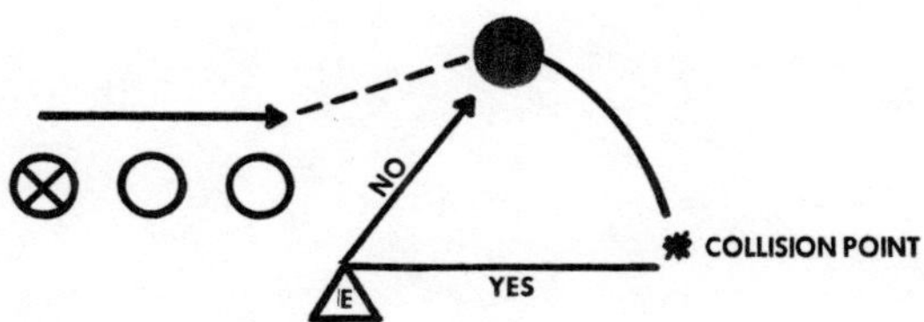

End must go to collision point on pitch.

DIAGRAM 7-17

f. No shiver or blow on tight end: When the end doesn't at least give a hand shiver to the tight end or tight slot he allows the tight end a free uninterrupted block inside. We don't ask for a great forearm blow all the time, but we do expect the defensive end to at least interrupt the tight end's release with a hand shiver.

DIAGRAM 18

DIAGRAM 19

8

How to Coach the Gap-Control Linebackers

1. Stance

The linebackers will use a breakdown position with the outside foot and leg slightly back. The linebacker must be sure he can see over front line to read his key. He stands just tall enough to read keys.

2. Alignments (see Diagrams 8-1—A, B, C, and D)

a. Inside eye of linebacker to outside eye of opponent: Usually on No. 1 man or No. 2 from center (usually the offensive guard is a regular). The toes are about six inches behind the heels of the defensive downman in depth. This alignment is also on the No. 2 man from the middle of the offensive line; usually it is the offensive tackle (this is our 4-3 defense and eagle). The alignment in depth may be deeper but usually not closer.

b. 40-contain alignment: Inside eye of tight end.

c. Stack alignment: Aligned behind a down lineman; these alignments do not change linebacker keys and, actually, do not drastically change their techniques. This stack alignment is seldom used.

d. Split rule: The linebacker will align normally up to 1½-yard split. Remember the rule—he aligns normally as long as the basic responsibilities can be carried out. Also, he is sure the keys can be seen.

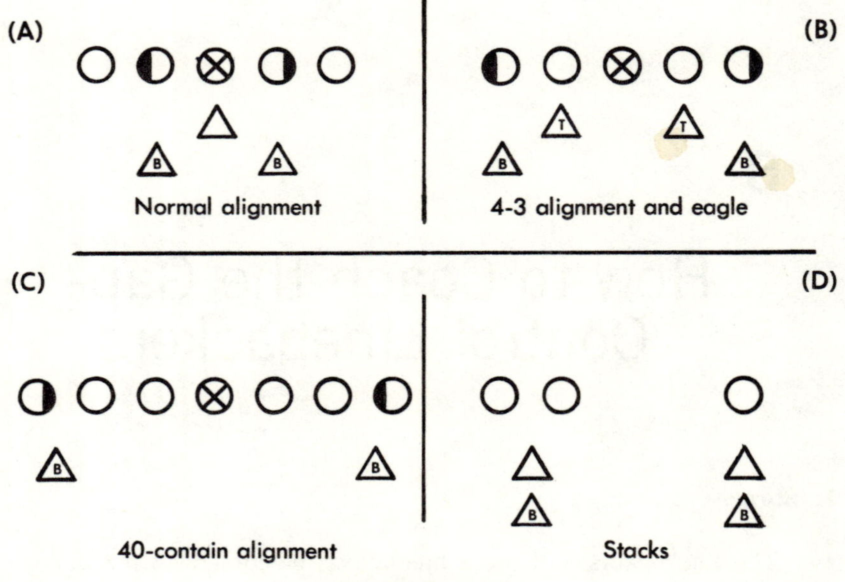

DIAGRAM 8-1

3. Basic Responsibilities

Generally, the responsibilities will be based on what the keys do. The keys are the offensive backs who are aligned in the backfield. If it is an "I" backfield, the backs that come to the side on which the linebacker is aligned are the key. If there is only one back, both linebackers key him. The linebackers key the backs that are nearest them in the backfield (see Diagram 8-2—A, B, C and D).

We key backs because we feel it is an easier key and one which can fit into the scheme of our defense, especially because of our tackles' initial movement. Sicce our linebackers are expected to scrape on a key if an offensive lineman is keyed, we believe it would slow our linebacker scrape to the playside. Finally, because of various alignments—but with techniques and responsibilities remaining the same—we find it difficult to key linemen.

Note: There are times when both linebackers will key just one back (even though there are 2 or 3).

a. Play to: A play to the linebacker is determined by his key. He is responsible first for the tackle-end gap, then outside for inside-out

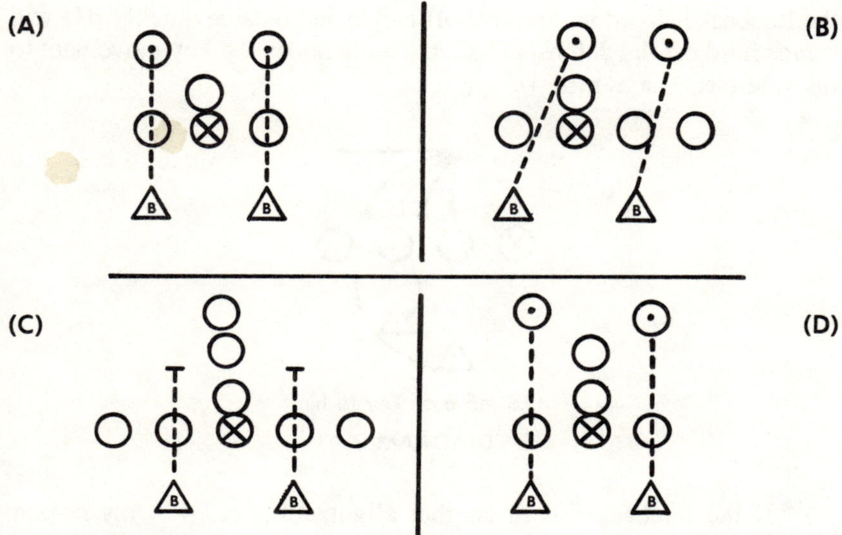

The key is first back in area, flow, or what the scouting report presents us with.

Key could be fullback (depending on scouting report).

DIAGRAM 8-2

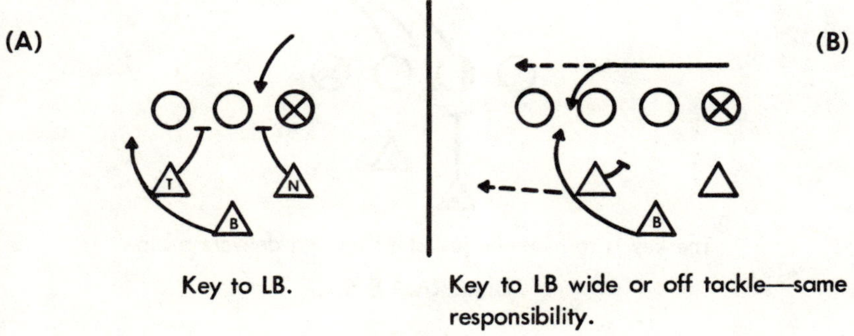

Key to LB.

Key to LB wide or off tackle—same responsibility.

DIAGRAM 8-3

pursuit on the ball (see Diagram 8-3—A and B). The linebacker is responsible for making tackles; he must get to the ball. There is no reason for him to be tied up with an internal fake inside our tackles. It is not his duty. His responsibility and technique on plays his way allow the linebacker freedom to move off tackle and outside quickly. He will scrape hard off the defensive tackle's buttocks on the key movement to his side (see Diagram 8-4).

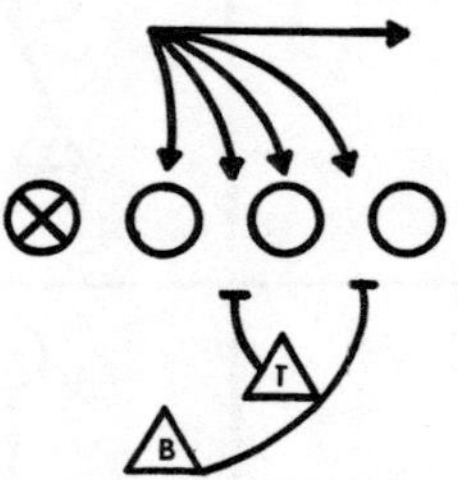

LB move on key to him.

DIAGRAM 8-4

If the linebacker is in another alignment, i.e., 4-3, his responsibilities remain the same. The difference lies in the fact that he does not have to scrape; all he must do is to step up and deliver the blow when his key is to him (see Diagram 8-5).

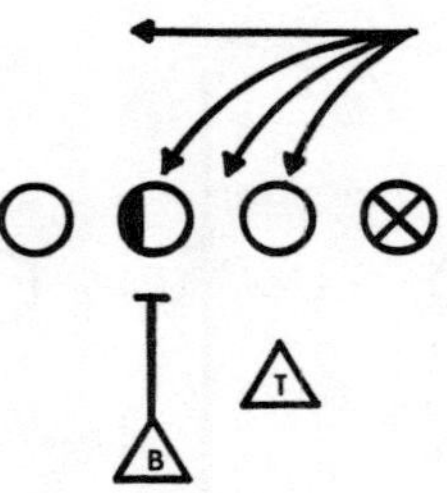

The key is to him—he just steps up and delivers a blow.

DIAGRAM 8-5

b. Play away: If the linebacker key goes away, the linebacker must immediately pick up the other back. This is to assure that the linebackers will not collide if the backs cross (to be shown later). The away linebacker is responsible for the center-guard gap on the opposite side of the nutcracker. The linebacker must be careful to take a so-called "slow" read—keeping lag on the ball (see Diagram 8-6). If the ball goes to the away center-guard gap, the backside linebacker must fill there very hard. If the ball continues outside, the linebacker must move outside (see Diagram 8-7).

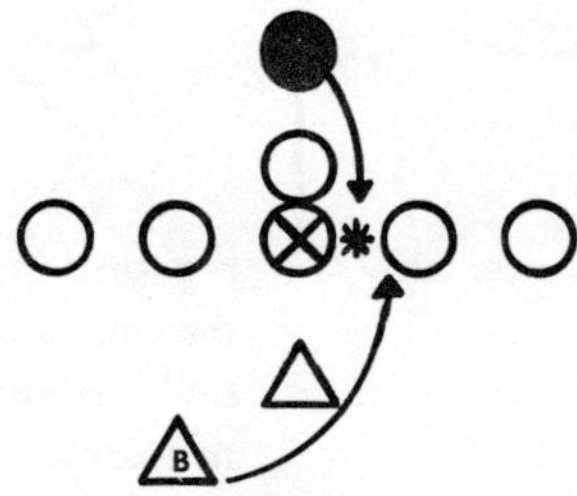

Key away—LB responsible for center-guard gap opposite side.

DIAGRAM 8-6

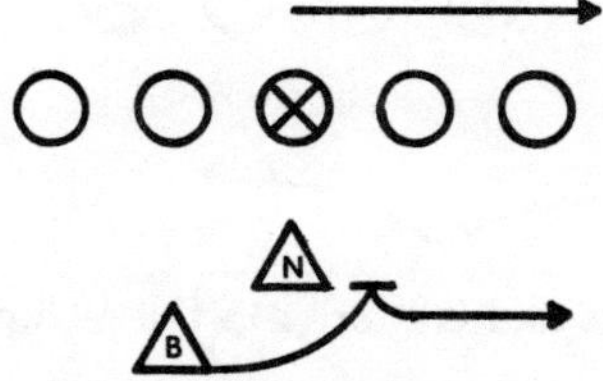

He checks away center-guard gap; if ball goes past, the LB goes past.

DIAGRAM 8-7

Note: Backside linebacker must always keep a lag on the ball. Also remember that responsibility remains the same from all alignments unless there is a special call.

c. Pass responsibility: The linebackers have backs (their keys) man for man. If they release, the linebackers take them; if they block, the linebacker immediately looks to the quarterback and moves to the side the quarterback is looking. Then the linebacker finds the receiver the quarterback is looking to and immediately looks back to the quarterback for the ball. If it is a flow pass and the linebackers key goes away he will get depth and look for pass in the middle or any back sneaking through the line. (See Diagram 8-8—A, B and C.)

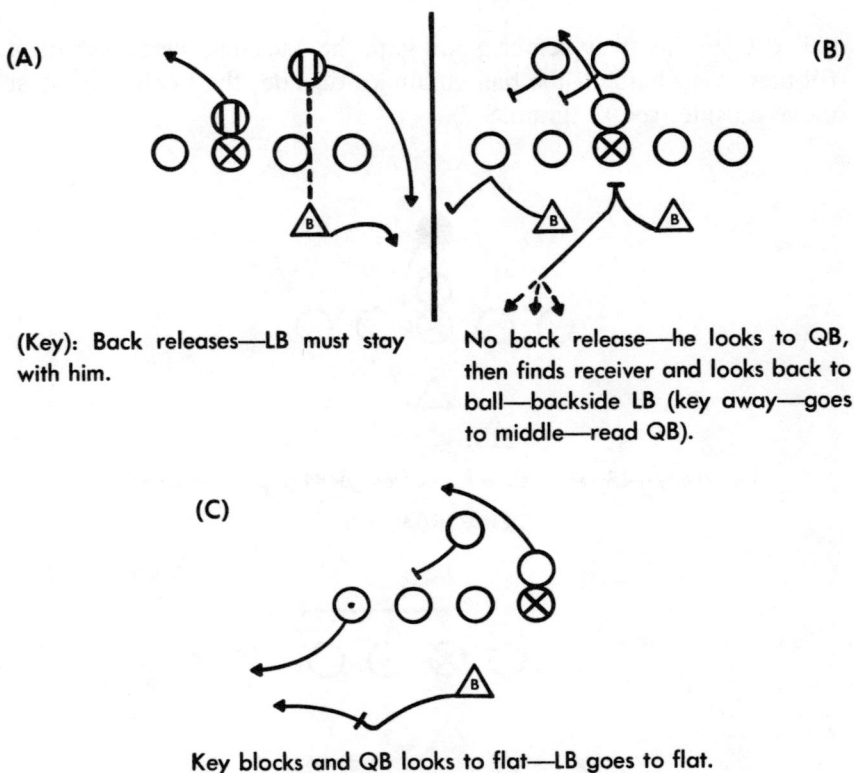

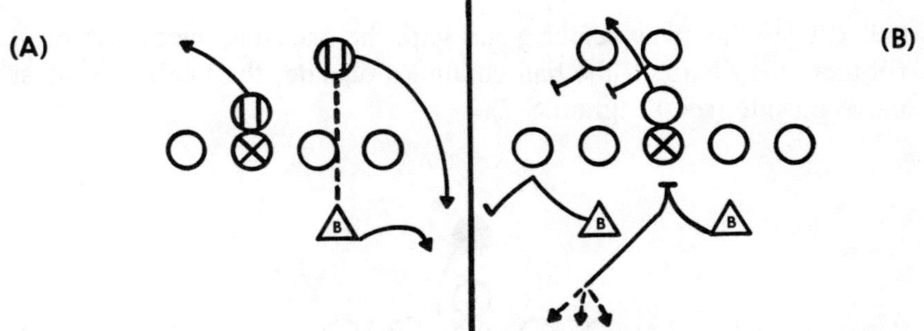

(Key): Back releases—LB must stay with him.

No back release—he looks to QB, then finds receiver and looks back to ball—backside LB (key away—goes to middle—read QB).

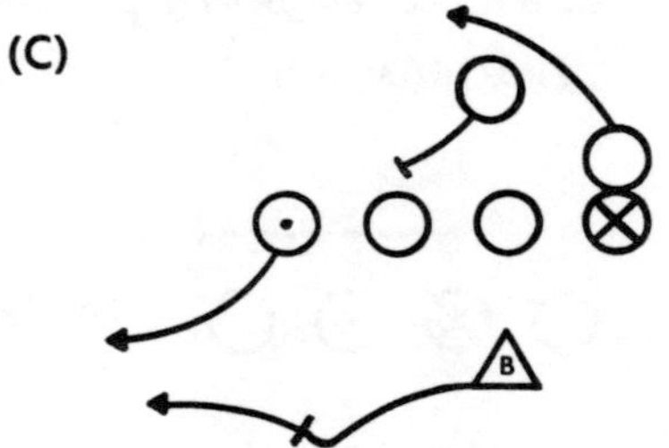

Key blocks and QB looks to flat—LB goes to flat.

DIAGRAM 8-8

You have noticed that our linebackers don't necessarily drop to the hook zones, but rather read the quarterback if they're key blocks. The reason they play backs man for man is simple. We have found that in high school football, when a back is sent out of the backfield, he is the prime receiver about 75% of the time. When we are in zone coverage, we ask our linebackers to drop to hook areas; however, if a back releases and the quarterback is read looking to the back, we ask our linebackers to get on the back. Whenever our linebackers are in doubt they cover the backs. However, we would like the linebackers always to run through the hook area even when covering a back out of the backfield in the flat.

It should be noted that if there is a play fake, the playside linebacker can't help but go for it, but as soon as the linebacker recognizes pass he must immediately get depth and, depending on his location, get width. He fights to recover! If the linebacker crosses the line of scrimmage on play action fake, he keeps going. (Responsibility is the same from all alignments.)

4. Initial Movement and Technique

a. From regular: The linebacker, on reading his key as coming to him, will step up and laterally with the outside foot, take a crossover step close to the defensive tackle's buttocks, and by the third step should have his toes and shoulders pointing to the goal line, square in his area. He must be at least to the line of scrimmage; he must scrape up but not penetrate too deep. As soon as he starts his scrape he must pick up the tight end to see if he (the tight end) is going to block him (see Diagram 8-9).

Note: The first step of the linebacker should replace the far foot of our defensive tackle.

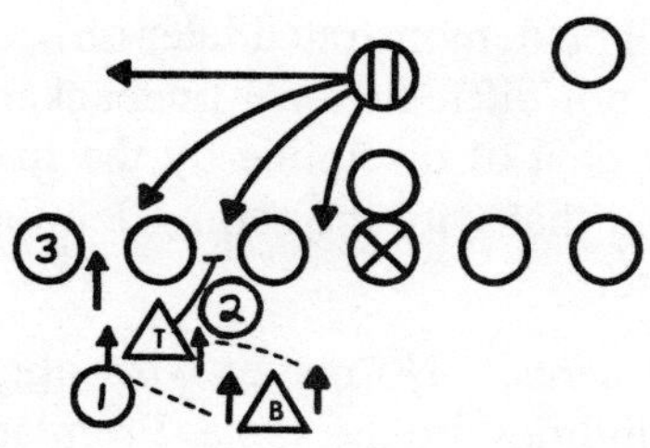

LB reads initial key as to him; therefore, the LB makes his initial move to protect tackle-end gap.

DIAGRAM 8-9

The backside linebacker who has read his key going away will step laterally with the inside leg, keeping his shoulders facing the goal line. The backside linebacker will eye the center guard gap on the other side of the nutcracker. The backside linebacker will scrape to the playside leg of the offensive center (that is located on the far side of the ball). Remember, he tries to keep a lag on the ball carrier. If the ball goes to that area, he fills it (see Diagram 8-10).

You have probably said to yourself, "How can you tell a

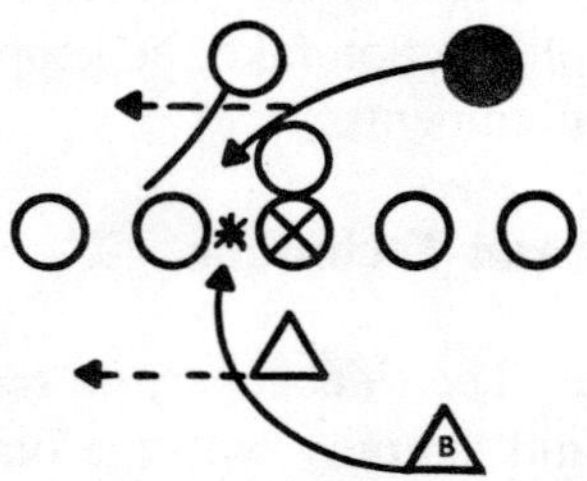

Backside LB reads flow-away, checks center guard gap opposite the nutcracker.

DIAGRAM 8-10

linebacker to run away from a back who is running at him?" We convince him that he will make more plays that way than any other way. We feel a minimum of 50% or more of every offensive play starts with an internal fake and goes somewhere else and therefore he is not tied down by internal fakes. We also feel we have three people moving to the internal move—the playside tackle, nutcracker, and backside linebacker (this will be demonstrated later on). Contrary to what might be thought, it was not difficult for a linebacker to do. We thought it would take a great deal of discipline by the linebackers but we were surprised to find out that with the selling job they felt it was the only way to play defense.

b. Other alignments: No matter what alignment the linebackers are in, the responsibilities are the same. From an eagle, the linebacker to flow just needs to step up. The linebacker away from flow must make his initial move from a long distance away. The playside

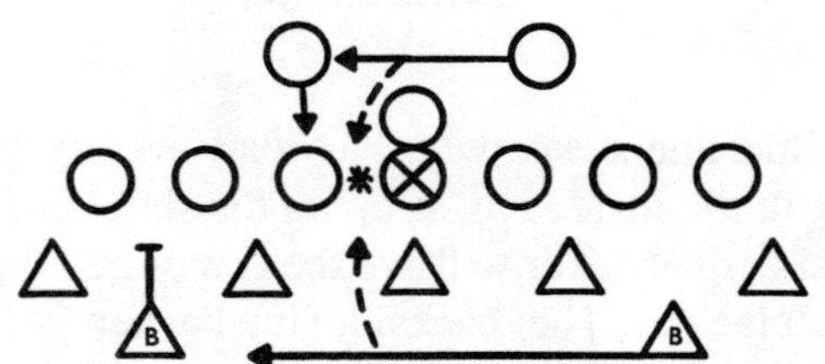

Playside LB must deliver a blow (can't take a side).

DIAGRAM 8-11

linebacker on step-up must deliver a hard blow on blocker—usually the tackle. (See Diagram 8-11.)

> *Important Coaching Point*: The linebacker's keys, the backs, are just a preliminary start to the ball. The linebacker should step as cautiously as does his key. This means that if a back steps one false step in the opposite direction of the play, the linebacker does not run himself out of the play in an all-out scrape. This is common sense to most boys, but we take nothing for granted. We will use a step-out call a great deal (see step-out at end of chapter) if false steps are primary to a team attack—something which we have never faced. Also, there should be no problem if the backside linebacker keeps his proper lag.

5. Linebacker Technique, Keys and Ways to Be Blocked

a. Guard block on linebacker to side of flow: There is no excuse for the guard making this block if the linebacker reads his keys properly and executes well. However, if for some reason the guard makes his block, the linebacker should attempt to free his outside arm, work across the blocker's head, shed him and move to the ball (see methods of beating blocks and see Diagram 8-12—A and B).

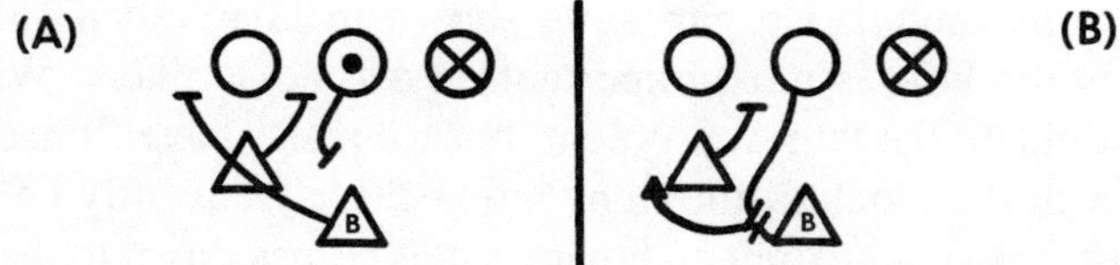

Offensive guard should not be able to get to playside LB.

If he does get to playside LB, free the outside arm and work outside.

DIAGRAM 8-12

b. Offensive guard on backside linebacker: This could occur if the blocker gets position on the backside linebacker. The linebacker must attempt to work through blocker's head, using the hands or, if necessary, bringing the opposite arm across and using it as a rake to redirect the blocker. Find and move to the football. It is a good idea to keep the forearm between the blocker and the linebacker's body. Using the opposite arm as a rake is a maneuver used when the block is made.

Coaching point: Versus all blocks, a linebacker must attempt to stay low and never allow the blocker to get under his shoulder pads and into the body.

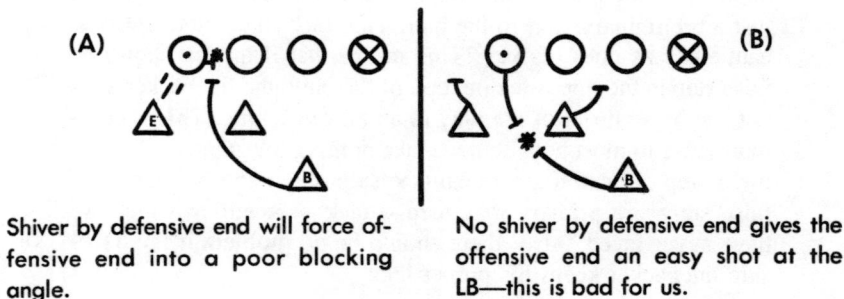

Shiver by defensive end will force offensive end into a poor blocking angle.

No shiver by defensive end gives the offensive end an easy shot at the LB—this is bad for us.

DIAGRAM 8-13

c. Down block by offensive end: This could be the largest problem the linebacker is faced with in his technique. This is the only blocker with a chance to get to the linebacker. However, if the defensive end gives the offensive end a shiver, the offensive end will not have a clear shot at the linebacker (see Diagram 8-13—A and B).

If the linebacker must take on the tight end we would like the collision to take place in the end/tackle gap (see Diagram 8-13 A), not away from the end/tackle gap as is shown in Diagram 8-13B. This collision in the hole is most important on off-tackle plays. We stated that this could be the largest problem, but we really haven't had a great problem with the block of the tight end because frequently he is not a proficient blocker. The tight end many times comes down to the tackle, then tries to get the linebacker and it is too late, and finally, the defensive end, who is also squeezing the off-tackle hole shut, needs only to give a good hand shiver to throw the tight end off course.

The technique involved for the linebacker may vary in what he feels the play may be; that is, if it is a wide play he will take the blocker (tight end, usually) on with his far shoulder (inside forearm), keeping the outside arm free, and attempt to disconnect from the blocker, redirecting the blocker's head. If the linebacker feels it is an off-tackle play (it usually is when the tight end or slot is blocking our linebacker), he must get in the end/tackle gap. The linebacker will usually take the blocker on with the outside arm on the line of scrimmage. There is nowhere for the ball carrier to run with the defensive end also squeezing the off-tackle hole shut.

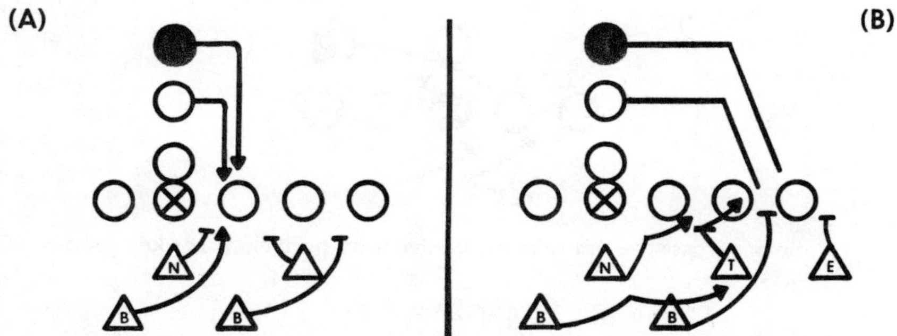

Isolation over guard will look like this. Isolation over tackle will look like this.

DIAGRAM 8-14

d. Block by a back—isolation guard or tackle: This presents no problem. The linebacker should always take a back on aggressively with inside shoulder (see techniques of meeting and defeating blocks and see Diagram 8-14—A and B).

e. Beating the guard-tackle step-around (fold block): This block is taken on by the linebacker aggressively. He should try to beat the guard to the hole. Keep clearly in mind that the linebacker should also be able to move outside on wide plays. He stays low and under the offensive blocker. The key for the linebacker is to meet the guard in the hole. This fold block presents no real problem.

f. Offensive line down blocks on counters (crossing keys): Since linebackers are not directly responsible for counter, their recovery and reaction to counter are most important. The linebacker must redirect himself and take a proper path to the ball carrier as soon as he recognizes counter or as soon as he feels pressure by the offensive lineman, whichever occurs first. (Also, see method of beating blocks.)

Coaching Point: The linebacker on play away must check for faces. If he reads counter, he must redirect and take first daylight to the ball carrier.

The only counter that should present a problem is a counter to the wing or slot since the linebackers are keying the men in the backfield. If the men in the backfield cross, there should be no problem. It is important for the linebacker to be careful when his key goes away so that there is no collision with the other linebacker. This should not occur as long as both linebackers realize the problem. When key goes

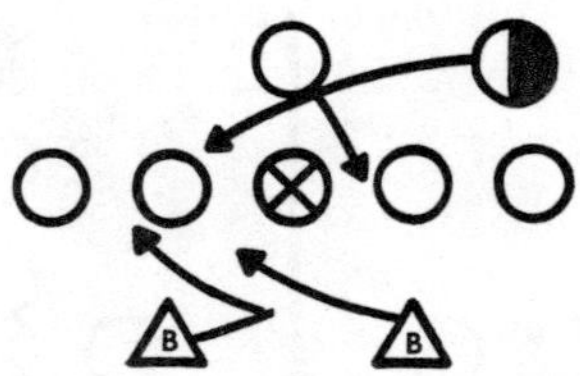

Back's crossing—this type of counter is no problem if LBs key properly.

DIAGRAM 8-15

away the linebacker immediately looks to opposite back. The linebackers have never collided in our defense. Also notice our tackles are squeezing the counter hole shut and giving the linebackers time to recover (see Diagram 8-15).

g. Defeating the option: The linebacker's technique should especially free him for option. If the fake is made in the off-tackle area, he may get caught for a while but, if he is not, he is then free to go to the pitchman. It is especially important for the linebacker to keep his

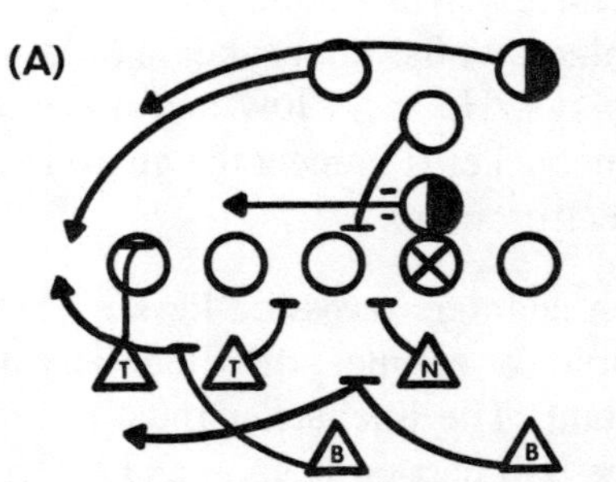

Regular option—no problem for LB.

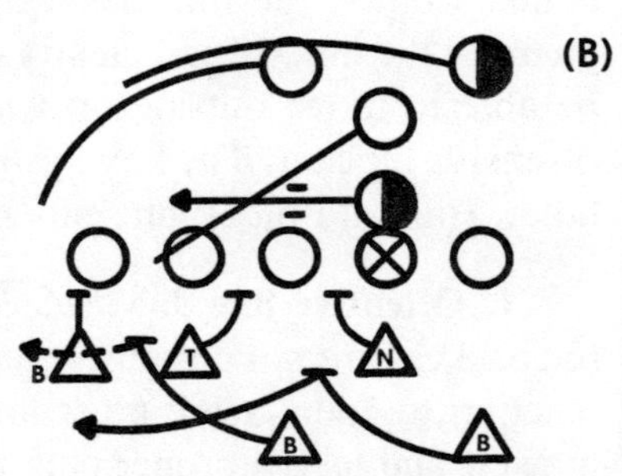

Wide fake option—LB must recover.

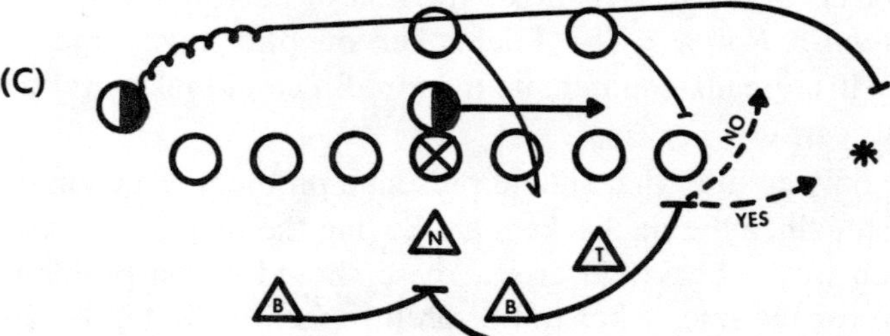

LB must move along LOS, not upfield unless the LB is sure of a tackle.

DIAGRAM 8-16

outside arm free versus option. He has no quarterback responsibility on option, but must keep a lag on the ball. The linebacker must keep a lag on the pitchman, stay along the line of scrimmage and not move upfield unless he is sure of a tackle (see Diagram 8-16—A, B and C). We have been very fortunate with our defense versus standard options. The option has been very unsuccessful against us for the most part.

h. Covering backs on pass: The linebackers can lock on immediately or may keep a cushion. This depends on their speed, speed of the back, position of the linebacker, etc. He must be sure to get in the quarterback's throwing lane. The linebacker will usually have help if the back goes very deep. Covering a swinging back is always done by going through the hook and curl area first, then to the back (see Diagram 8-17).

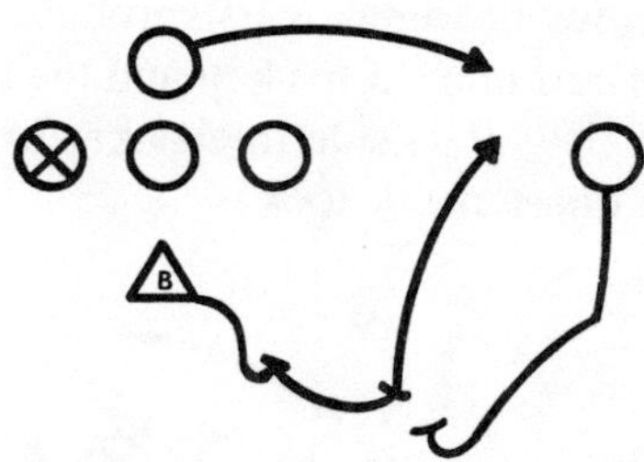

Covering swing back—LB must go through hook and curl area first, then to the back.

DIAGRAM 8-17

i. Defeating reach block by offensive tackle: If the offensive tackle tries to block the linebacker, the linebacker must read the tackle's head, following all methods of beating blocks. The linebacker should beat the block being sure not to allow the tackle to cut him off. It may mean taking on the tackle with the inside forearm and working into the "V" of his neck. We seldom see this block and spend very little time against it (see Diagram 8-18).

j. Offensive tackle block in 4-3/or eagle: When our linebacker is over the offensive tackle and key comes his way, he must step up and deliver a blow on the offensive tackle. The blow is delivered by the linebacker with his inside forearm to the outside shoulder of the offensive tackle. Now the linebacker is in his responsibility, the off-tackle area. The most important point for him to remember is that he must *not*

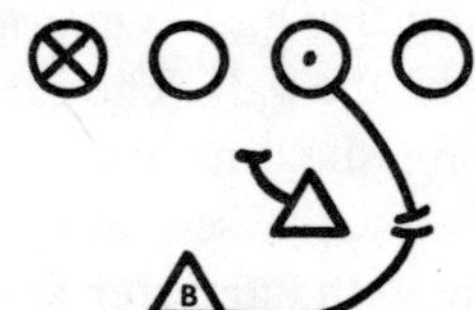

Offensive tackle reach block on LB.

DIAGRAM 8-18

get his shoulders turned perpendicular to the line of scrimmage. They must remain parallel. It is better for him to get driven back with his shoulders parallel than it is to get his shoulders turned.

k. Linebacker covering play-action curl: On a good play-action fake the frontside linebacker may go for the fake and be slow in dropping back. It now becomes very probable that the backside linebacker gets to the curl man, if his key and the quarterback take him there (see Diagram 8-19). Backside linebacker in a 5-2 can get to the offside curl area (on quarterback look).

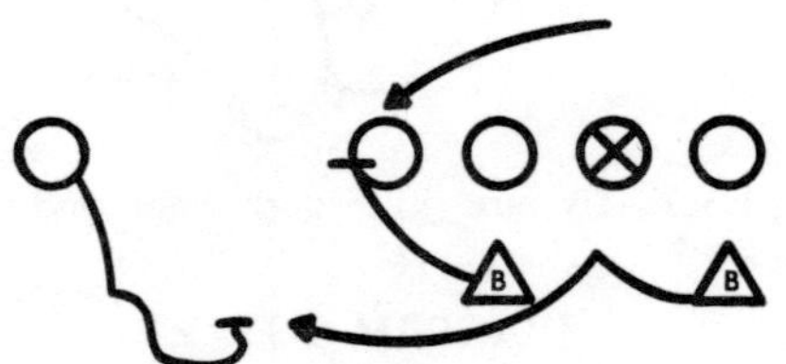

Play-action fake backside LB to curl on key.

DIAGRAM 8-19

6. Called Moves and Called Techniques

a. Blitz: This is simply a penetrating maneuver by the linebacker on the snap of the ball to an open gap. The gap will depend on the team and situation. We seldom blitz.

b. Nutcracker stunt: This is a stunt executed on the snap of the ball. The stunting linebacker fills the opposite center-guard gap, while the nutcracker fills the gap to the call side (see stunting technique). See Diagram 8-20.

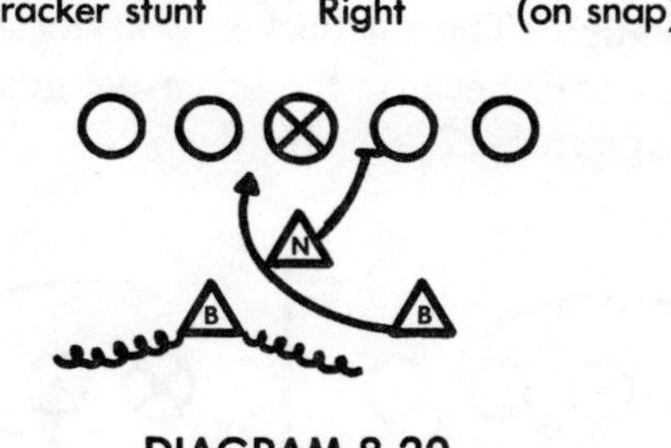

DIAGRAM 8-20

c. Step-out: This is on the snap for the linebacker. He will step up and fill the guard-tackle gap since the defensive tackle is stepping out (see Diagram 8-21). We use this call more than any other. It is most effective if teams are "false-stepping" or if teams are attempting to use blocking schemes to take advantage of our regular defense. This call is a *must* change-up.

Note: On the step-up the linebacker must deliver a blow with the inside forearm.

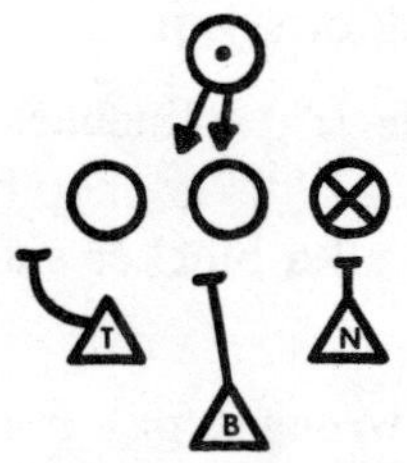

Step out techniques—LB keys normally unless key goes to him.

DIAGRAM 8-21

d. Lock-up: This call means that our tackles will lock face gear with the man they are aligned over. The linebackers will play regular technique since this is basically a call for our tackles to change up.

7. Common Faults

a. Backside linebacker—no lag: The backside linebacker not keeping a lag on the ball in a regular is bad, but a backside linebacker in a 4-3 or eagle not keeping a lag is disastrous! The backside linebacker *must* keep a lag on the ball.

b. No scrape-up: The linebacker who does not scrape up to the hole is making an error because the offensive guard can block him by the hole (see Diagram 8-22—A and B).

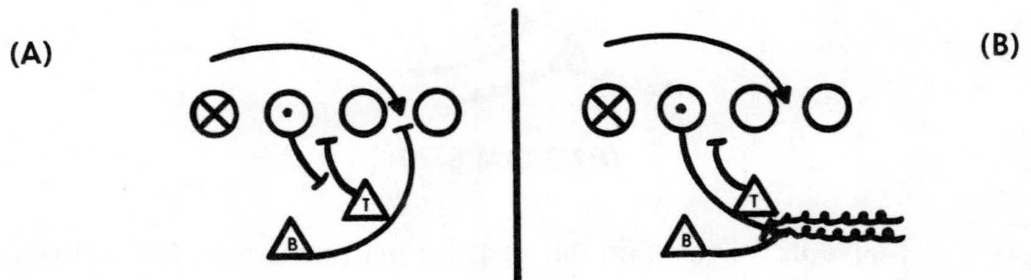

Right; guard can't block him past the hole.

Wrong; LB didn't scrape up, now guard can push him by the hole.

DIAGRAM 8-22

c. No step-up in eagle or 4-3 alignment: On key to him the linebacker must step up from his alignment in 4-3 or eagle and deliver a blow, being sure never to get his shoulders turned. His shoulders must stay parallel to the line of scrimmage.

d. Letting blocker into legs: A linebacker cannot allow himself to be blocked, either by letting a blocker chop him or by letting a blocker into his body. But most of all a blocker can't be allowed to knock a linebacker off his feet.

e. On key-away taking wrong step: For some apparent reason we have a problem with the linebacker taking one step in the wrong direction (off-tackle area) on play-away. We make an effort to make linebackers conscious of the problem.

f. Slow scrape: Slow scrape by a linebacker can allow the tight end a chance to block our linebacker before he reaches his assigned area.

9

Coaching the Defensive Halfback in the Gap-Control Rover Defense

1. Stance

The stance must permit free movement in any direction without loss of time. Therefore, everyone will vary slightly. The guidelines to be followed are: feet staggered, knees flexed, hips lowered, shoulders over the hips, arms hang but are bent at the elbows and forward for balance. Shoulders and hips are parallel and square to the line of scrimmage. The outside foot is generally back with the weight on the balls of the feet. We like the heels on the ground. The stance must be low enough to prevent dipping by the defensive halfback on his initial movement.

2. Alignments

There is one alignment we never want our pass defenders in, and that is head-up alignment. This alignment does not fit into our defensive schemes.

a. Basic alignment: This is usually outside of the first eligible receiver on or off the line. This outside position will vary in width according to field position, pattern tendency and specific technique. In a normal situation, with the receiver in tight, the alignment is about two to three yards outside the outside shoulder of the receiver. If the wide side of the field is to the defensive halfback, he may take more of an outside alignment. If the receiver is split wide to the wide side or from the middle of the field, the defender will close his outside shoulder alignment to one yard (provided his inside alignment doesn't take preference (see Diagram 9-1).

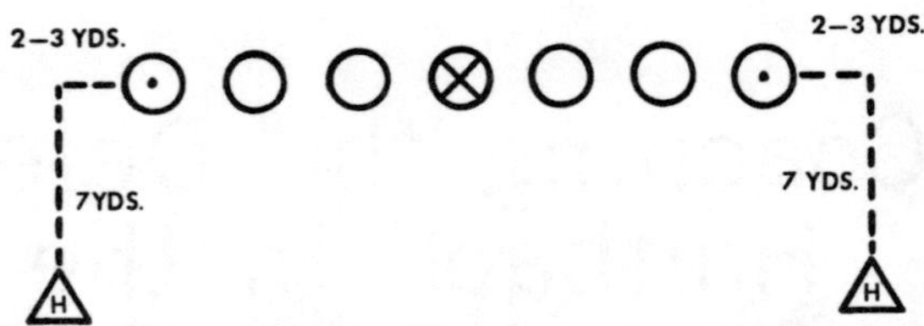

Normal alignment is outside receiver.

DIAGRAM 9-1

The defender's alignment on a tight receiver is about seven yards deep. This will vary according to the speed of receiver, defender's speed, situation and tendency. As the receiver splits wide, the deeper in depth the defensive back will align, but no deeper than 12 yards (unless the situation is unusual). The defensive back must ask himself one question and adjust his alignment in depth accordingly; the question is: "Could I cover this receiver if he streaked straight downfield?"

Note: We have discovered that most defenders underestimate their own speed.

b. Inside alignment (see Diagram 9-2): This is a sideline adjust-

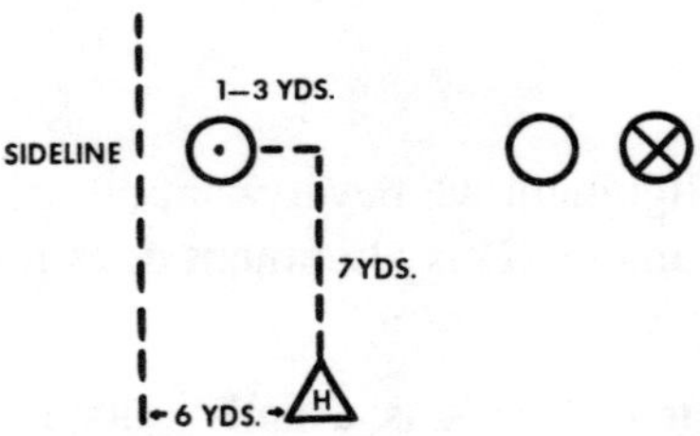

Inside shoulder alignment: he uses the sideline as an extra defender.

DIAGRAM 9-2

ment rule to split receiver. If the receiver is split to the short side of the field or the opponent has a tendency, the defensive back may be asked to align inside the receiver; he follows all rules of alignment from the inside shoulder alignment. The defensive back will never align closer than six yards to the sideline. Also, the defensive back must be sure his stance doesn't face too far towards the receiver. The defender's hips are facing the line of scrimmage. The sideline acts as an extra defender for us. Remember, this may be used anywhere in certain circumstances. This alignment is also taken when no post help is available.

3. Basic Responsibilities

If in a man-to-man pass defense, the halfback will cover the man he is assigned—the first outside eligible receiver on or off the line of scrimmage. The defensive halfback will cover him all over the field on pass. If in a zone he will align the same way, but will protect an assigned area either on snap or on the reading of a key. On run he has contain duty of some type, which will be discussed.

a. Run to: The defensive halfback is responsible for bringing the ball carrier back to the inside. Nothing must ever get outside him. The defensive back will have two types of contain—aggressive contain or auxiliary contain.

b. Run away: The defensive halfback will keep everything in front of him; he never lets a receiver behind him. There should be 21 players in front of him. He is responsible for cutback, after ball carrier crosses the line of scrimmage and he is the last line of pursuit on break-away. He is the deepest defender on ball-away. Naturally there will be some variations in a man-to-man secondary; the defender must move according to the action of the receiver who is his responsibility.

c. Pass action: Whether it is drop back, sprint out, or play action, much will depend on the call that is made—especially if it is a zone. When a man-for-man is called things are relatively simple in regard to responsibility: the defensive back will just cover his man.

4. Initial Movement

The first three steps are most important for positioning. We never want to allow the receiver to get a head-up alignment. The purpose of the initial movement is to prevent this from occurring. Positioning is

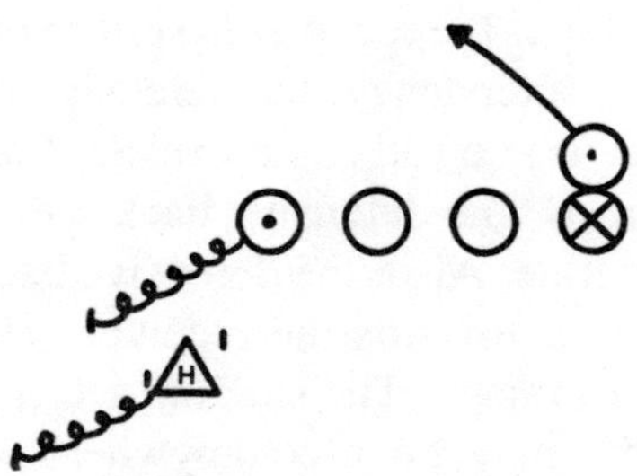

Maintaining outside position—being able to see the receiver and the ball.

DIAGRAM 9-3

most important to the success of a defensive back. Initial movement will also allow the defensive back to maintain balance and complete body control. Again the first three steps of a back pedal or shuffle are most important (see Diagram 9-3).

a. Basic alignment: The initial move from this alignment, as the receiver comes downfield, is a shuffle step back and out with the outside foot, then bringing the inside foot back approximately to the original position of the outside foot. This procedure is followed again until the key the defensive back must read can be read. Remember, it is most important to maintain outside position. The defensive back may, if he so desires, use a back-pedal technique to move backwards and maintain position. This movement will allow the defender to see through the receiver to the quarterback while reading his key yet maintaining his cushion. The legs must not cross in preliminary movement. The shoulders must face the line and be square to the line, and the hips must also face the line. The shoulders should be over the knees as the defensive halfback moves backward. Remember, we want the defensive back to keep outside leverage when we are in a normal alignment.

b. Inside alignment: From this alignment the defensive halfback should maintain his inside position following all the above techniques, only executing them from the inside alignment—never losing the inside position.

Note: The defensive back must remember to give the receiver only one way to go. Don't get head up to the receiver.

5. Defensive Halfback Techniques and Keys

a. Key release in man-to-man (hawk): Once the initial move has been made and it is apparent that the receiver is going on a pass-route, the defensive halfback must maintain his position horizontal (outside) and his cushion (depth) from the receiver. The defender will back-pedal, maintaining a three-yard cushion. The deeper the receiver goes, the larger the cushion may be, up to four yards. Naturally, the farther the ball must travel, the more time the defender has to react to the ball. The defender will keep his arms pumping and his feet moving rapidly just over the ground in his back pedal, keeping his shoulders over his knees and his hips facing the line of scrimmage without crossing his legs as he moves backwards. Most receivers will have their final cut made at 12 yards; all receivers seem to show at 15 yards what move they are making.

We spoke of the outside leverage in all of our coverages. Most coaches have realized already that if we are in a man-to-man there is usually a free safety, and therefore there is post help. We will discuss this more later in the chapter (see Diagram 9-4). You can see that our defensive back will be a step behind the post route of the receiver (this is by design).

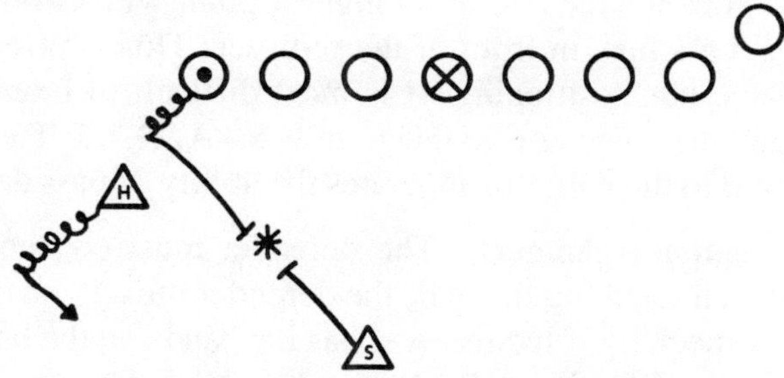

Safety gives post help—reason for outside angle on positioning.

DIAGRAM 9-4

b. Covering the break or change of direction by receiver: If the receiver moves downfield straight or if the receiver gets any closer than one yard from the defender, the defender must turn and run with the receiver. If the receiver makes his final move, the defensive halfback should turn (plant the leg, whip the arm) and sprint for a few steps to the receiver to regain lost ground and lost positioning. Recovery! That is the secret to pass defense. The defender must close the cushion, cut down the interception distance and move to the ball. After a few steps of recovery, the defensive back must look for the football.

The ideal situation is where the defender can see the ball released and also see the receiver. We will cover all outside patterns very aggressively. On the inside patterns we may be a step behind the receiver, but the pass will have to be perfectly thrown and will have to avoid linebackers and our safety. We feel teams can't live with that type of pass against us.

> *Note*: On the pivot the defensive back drops the weight over the ball of the pivot foot and gains ground with the lead foot, and he will also drive off the lead foot. On recovery by defensive back he must sprint to the far shoulder of receiver.

c. Ball in the air: Now is the time when the defensive back must explode! He can't be timid in this situation. The pass defender must use good judgment as to whether to go for the interception or play through the receiver. This decision is based on the distance he is from the ball and where the ball is thrown. If going for the interception, naturally, he goes for the ball at its highest point with two hands. He attempts to get his hips in front of the receiver. This is possible since we should have our positioning. It is most difficult to intercept from directly behind the receiver (see Diagram 9-5—A, B, C). The defender must drive hard to the ball; this separates the ability of pass defenders.

d. Interception technique: The defender must concentrate hard on the ball; when touching the ball, the defender must twist away from the receiver, especially if the receiver has his hands on the ball. On the interception, the defender yells "Score"—depending on the situation—but generally moves to the sideline. There should be a wall forming. He must be sure to go for the ball at its highest point and with his hips to the receiver. He must look the ball in and not look upfield.

> *Note*: Everyone yells "Pass" when pass is recognized and all yell "Ball" when ball is in the air, especially those players on the bench. But since I have been coaching I have only heard one of our players yell "Score" on an interception and he dropped the ball.

e. Strip the receiver: If there is no chance for an interception, the

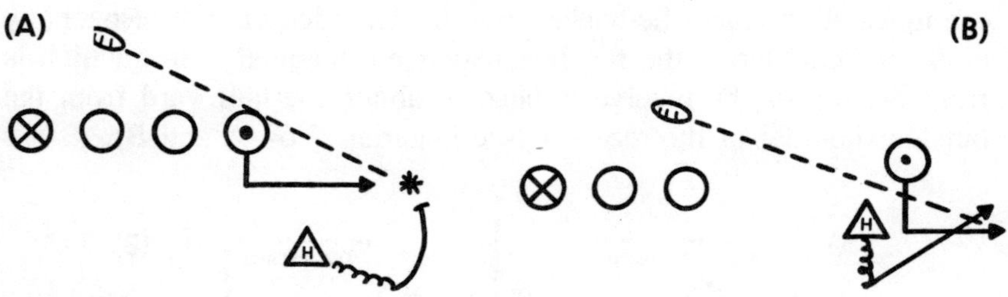

Going to ball from outside—position, good.

Going to ball from underneath—good *if* interception can be made.

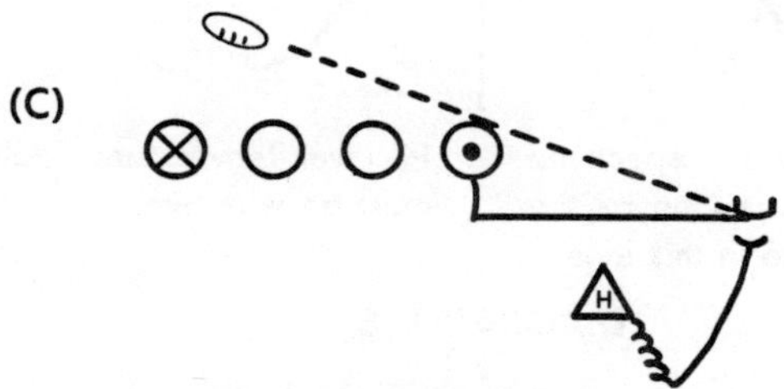

It is most difficult to intercept from directly behind receiver.

DIAGRAM 9-5

defender should destroy the receiver. Put his helmet on the receiver and pull at the receiver's arms. If only one arm is used to knock down the ball, the other should be used to control the receiver. However, we always attempt to go for the ball with two hands. Whatever occurs, we don't want to miss the tackle! We attempt to play through the receiver and work on his arms.

f. Keying just the receiver in a man-to-man on his release: There may be times when the defensive back, in order to maintain position or from initial alignment (inside), may be forced to see only the man he is covering. When this occurs, the defender will be able to tell how deep the receiver is going by the receiver's body lean. If the receiver's shoulders are forward and the cushion is being closed quickly, he is going deep. If the shoulders of the receiver are back, he is making a break. Body lean determines the depth of the pattern. The "roll" of the shoulders determines receiver depth.

If the defender just maintains his position he should have no problem with fakes and moves. To maintain horizontal positioning, the defender may use "shoulder-lane" technique. This means the receiver can make all the fakes he wishes, but the defender will not respect any until the shoulder of the receiver leaves an imaginary alley which is from the top of the receiver's head to about one-half yard from the outside shoulder of the receiver (see Diagram 9-6—A and B).

Shoulder lane—defender respects no fakes by the receiver as long as the receiver's shoulders are in this lane.

Receiver leaves lane, defensive back must go with him.

DIAGRAM 9-6

Finally, the defensive halfback can also get horizontal position by looking at the belt buckle of the receiver and moving with the receiver only when the belt buckle moves. However, we have found this type of concentration seems to allow the receiver a chance to get on top of the defender and beat him deep.

g. Some basic zone principles: The defender goes to an assigned area when in a zone either on the snap or on a "key." In a zone the defender will play the ball and the quarterback and not the man. However, at some point in every zone the defender must play man-to-man, following all the man-to-man principles. The defender must play as deep as the deepest receiver in his area. Adjust the zone in width according to the formation being faced and the field position (wide side/short side). The defender will "shade" his zone on the look of the quarterback; the defender goes to the boundary of the zone.

h. Covering deep outside: This zone coverage is apparent in our invert, with the rover to the halfback's side. The halfback will take his initial read steps. On recognition of pass, the defensive halfback will move to the deep outside area of the zone (this will vary). When to the sideline, we never go more than a yard and a half past the hash mark to the sideline if the ball is not thrown.

When moving to the deep outside zone, the defensive back must, after the initial read, use a cross-over step, crossing the inside leg over the outside leg. While moving backwards the defensive back's head should be facing the passer; he should "eye the ball" and play the ball fronting the zone. The defender should be able to see any receiver in the area of his peripheral vision. The coverage area starts at about 15 yards in depth and extends from the sideline to the original position of a second receiver, provided the receiver is in a normal alignment. If not it goes to the offensive tackle. The angle of the drop will depend on field position and on formation, i.e., wide side-drop wider angle (see Diagram 9-7—A and B).

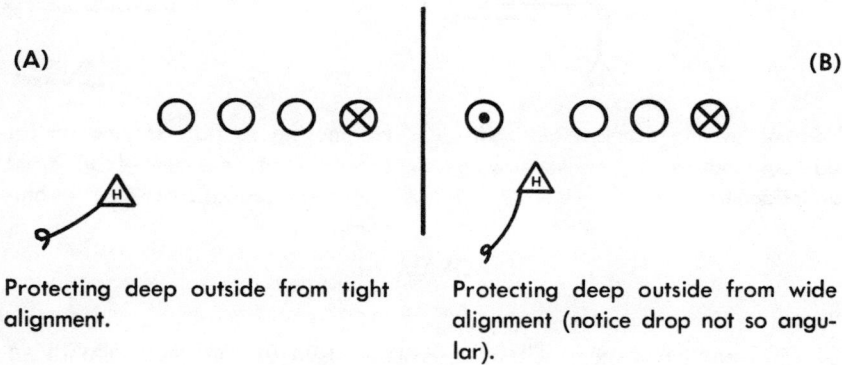

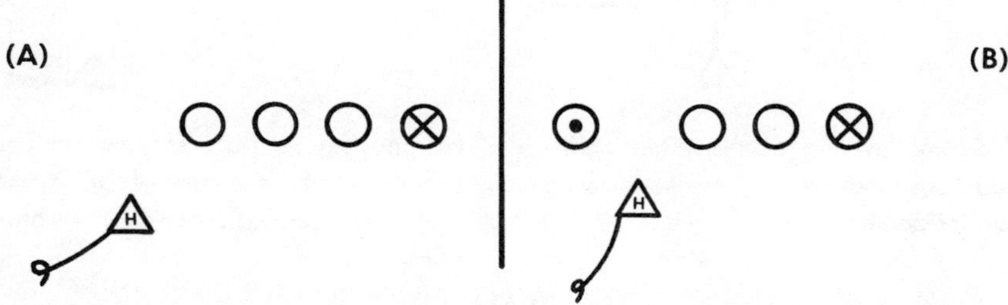

(A) Protecting deep outside from tight alignment.

(B) Protecting deep outside from wide alignment (notice drop not so angular).

DIAGRAM 9-7

Note: A zone is just a head start in a man-to-man coverage.

i. Covering the flat and short flag: This may be executed from a deep alignment or tight alignment. If executed from a deep alignment, the defensive back will rotate up, executing a "level" technique. He will move up under control, never getting closer than five yards to the line, yet being able to cover as deep as 15 yards. The depth will be determined by the route of the receiver and the action of the passer. When leveling off, the defender must be either inside or outside the receiver, staying to the receiver's shoulder and making sure he gets enough width and depth. Usually, if the receiver is split wide, the defensive back will come inside the receiver. When leveling, the defensive back will set his feet under him, sliding according to play action and receiver routes. When moving, he keys the ball and picks up the receiver from peripheral vision.

If covering from a tight alignment and being forced backwards, he executes the same technique as used when covering deep outside, except the depth is only 15 yards deep. The area of responsibility is from the sideline to the original position of the second eligible receiver or where a tight end or slot would normally be aligned. The depth of responsibility is 15 yards (see Diagram 9-8—A and B).

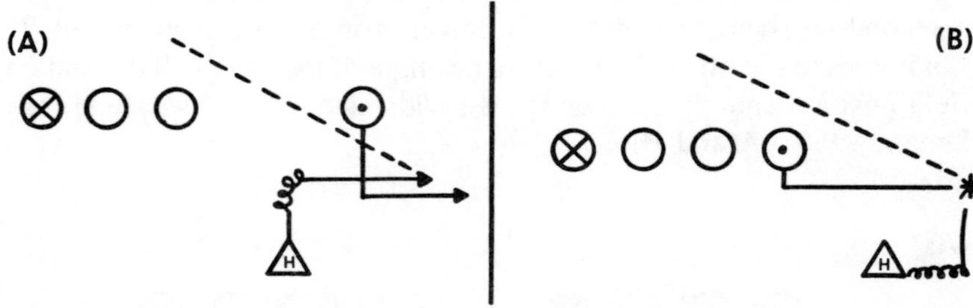

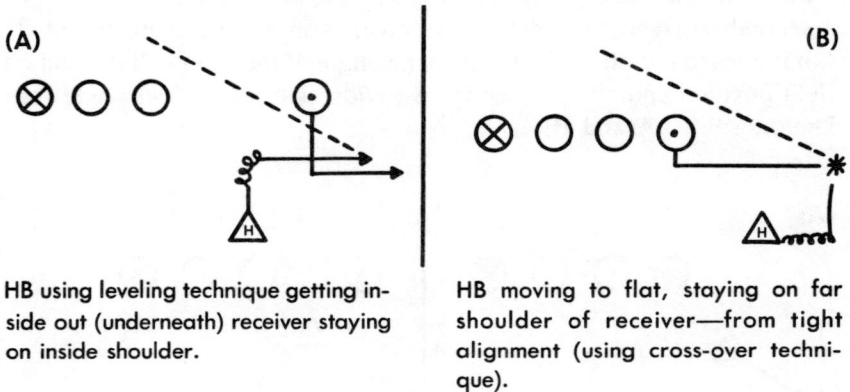

HB using leveling technique getting inside out (underneath) receiver staying on inside shoulder.

HB moving to flat, staying on far shoulder of receiver—from tight alignment (using cross-over technique).

DIAGRAM 9-8

j. Lane coverage: This is coverage used in conjunction with an "invert" call. It is used by the defensive halfback away from the rover's side. It is a zone coverage. The defensive back will cover all outside patterns and hooks whether the patterns are short or deep. He does not cover any patterns that go inside; for instance, posts, square-ins, slants, etc. The defensive back plays man-to-man on all patterns in his lane, but not on patterns over the middle. When a pattern is run over the middle, the defensive back will stay in his lane, just getting depth looking for receivers out of the backfield and crossing receivers (see Diagram 9-9).

k. Goal line technique (also called bump and run): In a goal line situation, the pass defender will attempt to get as close as legally possible to the receiver, attempting never to align with his heels past the goal line. On a tight receiver man-to-man techniques are followed. Against a wide receiver, the defensive halfback will take an inside

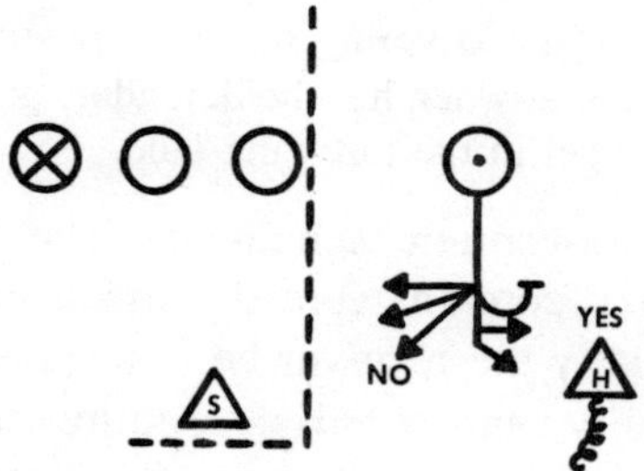

Lane coverage (with invert call): he plays m/m on outs, hooks, etc., but leaves patterns alone that are to the inside.

DIAGRAM 9-9

alignment as close as possible to the receiver. The halfback will not allow the receiver an inside release. He will have his inside foot advanced and his hips at a 45-degree angle to the line of scrimmage. He will keep the weight from the waist up forward, *never stepping toward* the receiver to hit him. He does not move with receiver until receiver's hips are even with defender's nose. The receiver must be shivered if he attempts to move inside. If the receiver moves on an outside pattern, the defensive halfback will get his hips in front of the receiver, getting as close as possible to him. The defensive back must go for the arms of the receiver if he, the defender, can't intercept the ball. By going for the arms he may force the receiver to drop the ball. A hard tackle after a touchdown does us no good; this is why we play through the arms on the goal line (see Diagram 9-10—A and B).

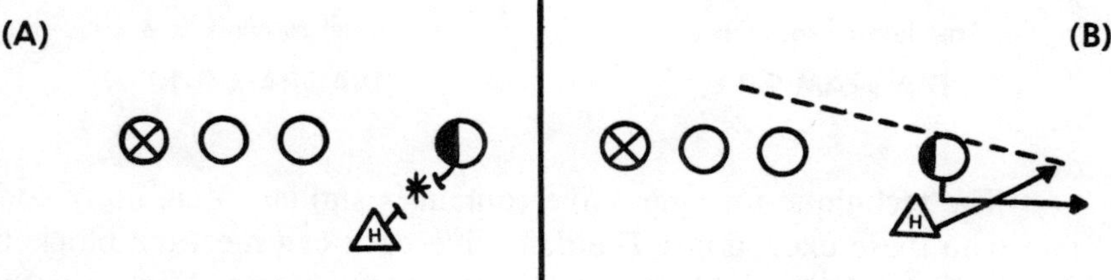

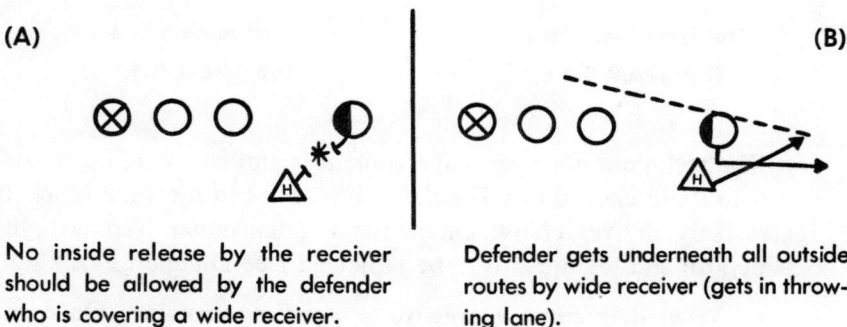

(A) No inside release by the receiver should be allowed by the defender who is covering a wide receiver.

(B) Defender gets underneath all outside routes by wide receiver (gets in throwing lane).

DIAGRAM 9-10

Point to note: When covering the wide receiver the defensive back will be sure that when he, the defender, gets underneath the receiver he must get in the throwing lane.

l. Key shows run-contain technique: The theory of aggressive contain and auxiliary contain were discussed earlier. Assuming the defender's key (usually the receiver he is responsible for covering, if zone the key is usually snap or ball depending on type of zone) shows over, the defender will proceed to his run responsibility, which is to contain the ball carrier, bringing him back inside and not allowing him to get outside. The technique for auxiliary containment for the defense halfback is to come up to the line of scrimmage with not more than one yard of penetration, and get in a good breakdown position with his toes pointing to the goal line. He should take on blockers with a hand shiver and give ground grudgingly. He must not get knocked down. In this situation the defensive halfback is the last contain man; he can't allow anything outside of him. He always protects the outside leg and arm (see Diagram 9-11).

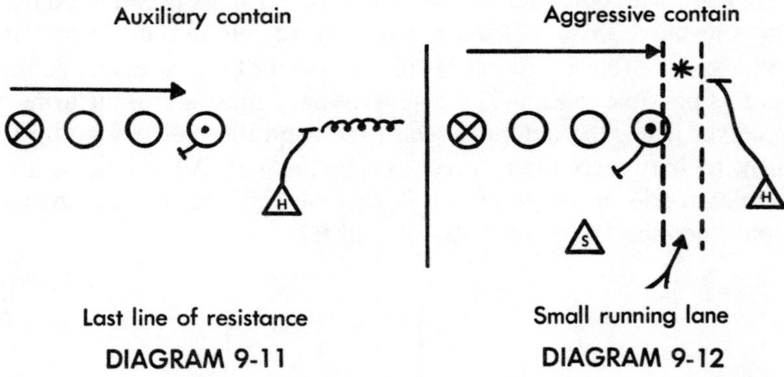

DIAGRAM 9-11

DIAGRAM 9-12

The technique for aggressive contain is similar to auxiliary contain with these exceptions: The defensive back can meet the blockers aggressively, deliver a blow, cut the running lane down. Naturally, the outside arm and leg are still to be protected (see Diagram 9-12).

m. What determines aggressive or auxiliary contain: Once run keys are established in man-to-man defense, a run to the rover gives aggressive contain to the rover. Auxiliary contain is left to the defensive back to the side of the rover who must be absolutely sure that the offensive back will not throw the ball. Once this threat is gone, the halfback can help contain. The defensive halfback away from the rover is responsible for aggressive contain and must react to run recklessly. His most difficult task is aggressive contain when he is covering a split end man-to-man and the split end releases and run action comes his way; however, if he can read the action, he will be able to react quickly enough to contain aggressively. To the split end side (and away from rover), the halfback must react up as soon as the ball is handed off or as soon as option is determined.

The safety who is away from the rover checks the halfback's pass and has auxiliary contain. The safety must be especially conscious of a split end if there is one. This will relieve the defensive halfback of some pass responsibility on run action his way. (See Diagram 9-13—A, B and C.)

There are situations when the aggressive contain to the rover's

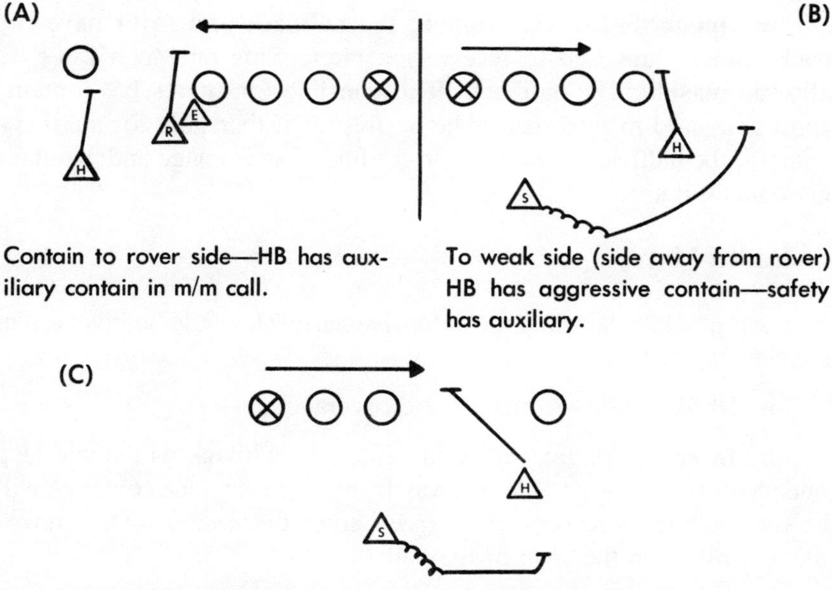

(A) Contain to rover side—HB has auxiliary contain in m/m call.

(B) To weak side (side away from rover) HB has aggressive contain—safety has auxiliary.

(C) S.E. side to defensive HB—he must take sharp angle and read well for aggressive contain.

DIAGRAM 9-13

side will be switched. If we call a ''keying'' secondary, this is one situation that will allow an automatic switch of contain responsibilities. Rover has auxiliary contain, while the halfback has aggressive contain; this is especially effective vs. tight wing formation (see Diagram 9-14).

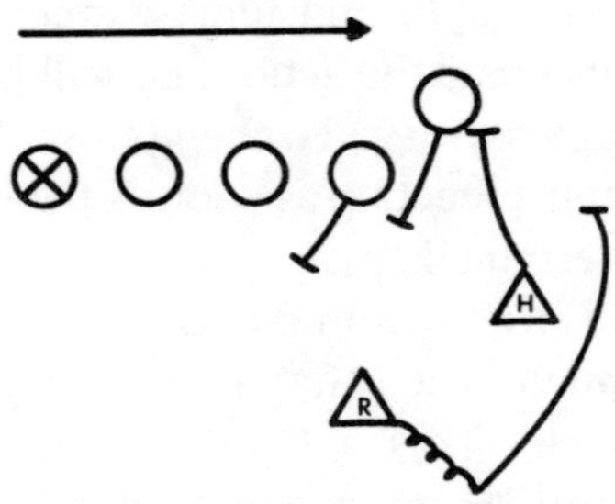

Assignments on run support switch on "keying"—secondary call.

DIAGRAM 9-14

n. Option duties: On option, the halfback and rover have the back who is supposed to receive the pitch. This pitchman can't be allowed outside. The halfback, if responsible for aggressive contain, can come hard to pitchman if he desires. If responsible for auxiliary contain, the halfback must hang on the line of scrimmage and maintain his contain duties.

6. Called Moves

All possible calls that the defensive halfback would be involved in are below.

a. Hawk: Man-to-man. Basic coverage.

b. Invert: Zone coverage in which the halfback will cover deep outside if to the rover's side. If away from the rover, lane coverage will be the halfback's responsibility (see earlier discussion). This movement is made on the snap of the ball.

c. Keying: This call is a zone call in which the halfback will rotate to the flat on drop-back pass or action his way. The ''keying'' refers to the movement of the ball. This gives the halfback aggressive contain duties on run. If flow is away, he will have deep outside responsibilities.

d. Bump and run: This is used on the goal line but may be called anywhere. If called before the secondary call, the halfback will align tight and bump and run. If called after the secondary call, the halfback will execute a bump technique after the snap while moving to the receiver.

e. Weak rotate or level: This is a predetermined rotation to the weak side. On snap, the halfback away from the rover levels to the flat and may or may not make contact with the receiver, depending on the situation. Safety protects the halfback deep (see Diagram 9-15).

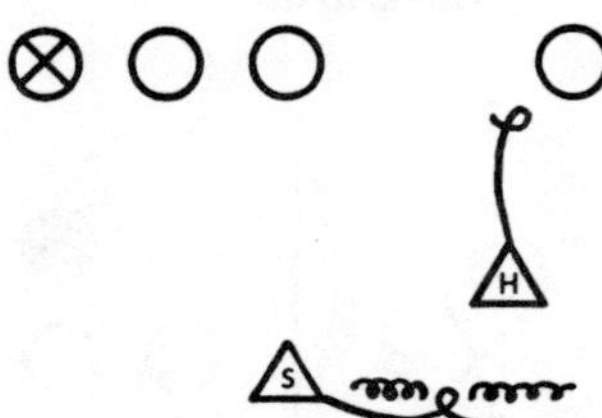

Weak level (also called weak rotate)—HB moves on snap.

Note: Deep call is simply a zone call used on long-yardage situations late in game or late in half. The Hbs drop to the deep outside quarters of the field to their side. This is used in place of prevent coverage (prevent will be covered under specific defenses).

DIAGRAM 9-15

7. Common Faults

a. Creating a running lane for ball carrier: On run, the defensive halfback, whether responsible for auxiliary contain or aggressive contain, cannot run away from the ball carrier and get too wide on containment. This leaves a large running lane (see Diagram 9-16—A and B).

b. Too deep on containment: Another fault we find with young defensive backs (I say ''young defenders'' because it isn't supposed to happen to our seniors, but it does) is that they over-penetrate in containment and they get deeper than the ball and allow the ball carrier a chance to get outside again (see Diagram 9-17—A and B).

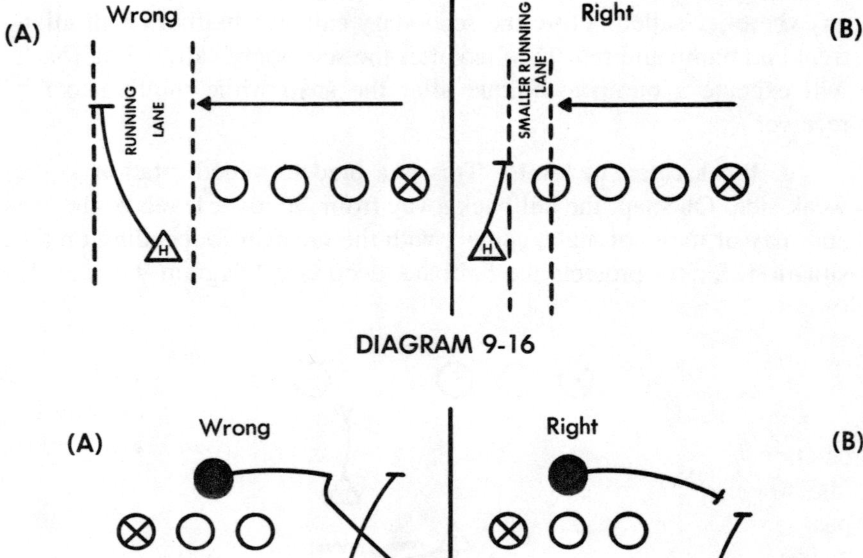

DIAGRAM 9-16

Def. H.B. too deep. B.C. allowed back outside.

Def. H.B. not as deep as ball. B.C. kept in front of Def.

DIAGRAM 9-17

c. Losing cushion and/or positioning: There are many reasons for losing cushion, such as the defensive halfback concentrates too intently in the backfield, ignoring the receiver; the defensive halfback does not take his initial steps, therefore losing proper positioning and allowing the defender to get on ''top'' of him. Another reason for losing cushion is that the defender stands flat-footed and doesn't move his feet. Finally, the defensive halfback, instead of going backwards from his stance, will dip before moving backwards in his stance, thus losing valuable time. He is too high in his stance.

d. Halfback coming inside on run: Never should the halfback come inside to the ball carrier (unless the ball carrier has obviously broken through the line). The halfback must never lose his contain

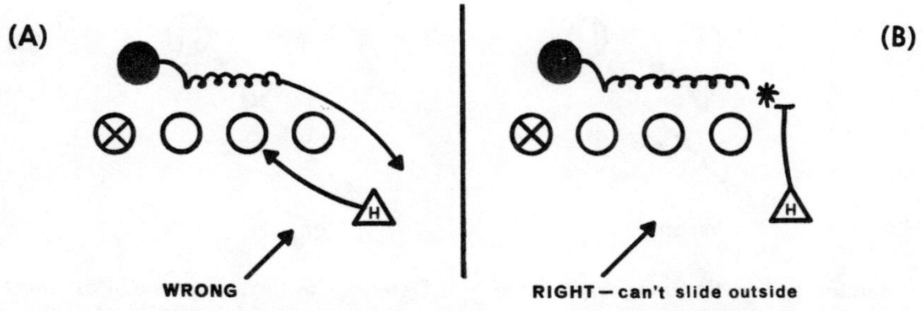

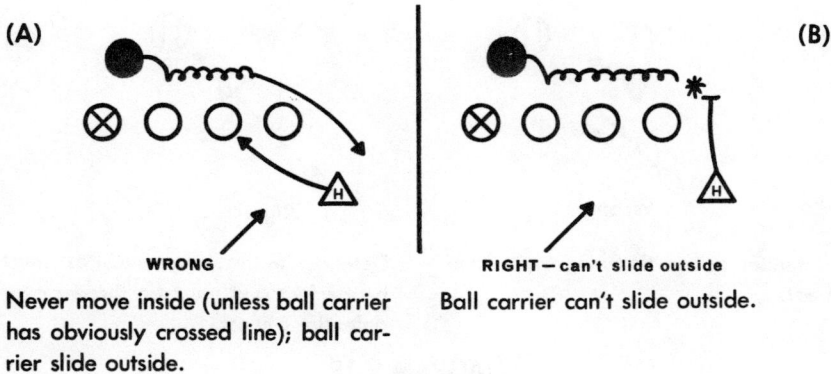

Never move inside (unless ball carrier has obviously crossed line); ball carrier slide outside.

Ball carrier can't slide outside.

DIAGRAM 9-18

position. It is easy for the ball carrier to slide outside or for an internal fake to occur and the play to come outside. This occurred twice in the past season—once for a touchdown. There is no excuse for a defensive back respecting an internal fake (see Diagram 9-18—A and B).

e. The chop block: The defensive halfback must never allow a blocker to get to his legs. He must never be knocked down, slip or be tripped (see methods of beating block).

f. False stepping: The pass defender, seeing the ball in the air, must not take an extra step back before planting and moving to the ball. He should plant immediately and move to the ball.

g. Not moving to ball in air: This is one of the worst errors a defensive back can make. He must close the cushion to the ball from any position on the field.

h. When beat, get in throwing lane: It will occur when the defensive back is beat deep. He must learn to get into the throwing lane to force the passer to throw over the defender's head. This forces the passer to throw a perfect pass. (See Diagram 9-19—A and B.)

i. Look back and ball seen: For some reason there is a tendency for a pass defender to slow down when he turns his head and sees the ball in the air. We try to make our defenders aware of this problem. We show them that if they slow down just because the ball is sighted they have a good chance of being beat deep!

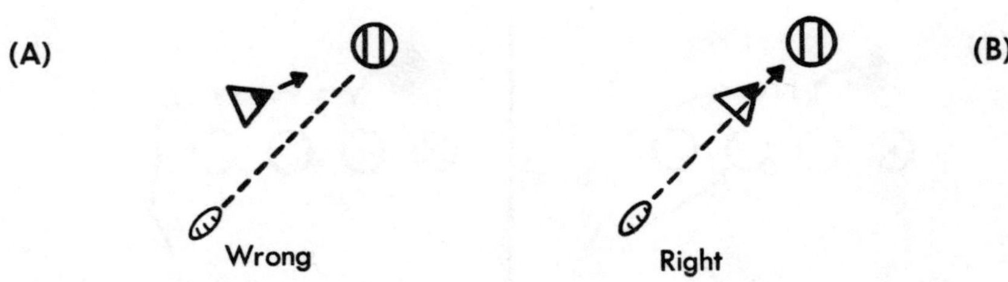

Defender not in throwing lane when beat.

Defender in throwing lane. Pass must be perfect and must be thrown over defender's head.

DIAGRAM 9-19

j. Turn and run too late: One mental error a defender can make is that he may turn and run too late, allowing the receiver to beat him. The defender must make a conscious effort to maintain his cushion. We would rather see him turn and run too early than too late. At about 15 yards the defender will realize his cushion is closing. We will take our chances with a 20-yard square-out.

10

Developing the Rover

The rover will be asked to do more things than any other defender. He is half linebacker and half defensive back. On some occasions his job is the most demanding. Don't think that he must be a super athlete, as he really doesn't have to be. Naturally, the better any defender is the better the defense will be. We have found that the boy playing this position can be whatever a coach desires. He can be a linebacker if a coach is geared that way, giving an 8-man front— or he can be a defensive back type of player geared to stop pass. Our type of player is similar to a strong safety in a pro defensive secondary.

1. Stance

See Defensive Halfback.

2. Alignments

a. Basic: The rover's alignment may vary from week to week with the scouting report and other variables. Basically, the rover will align one yard outside the outside shoulder of the second eligible ''quick'' receiver on or off the line of scrimmage. The depth of alignment will depend on whether or not the receiver is getting hit or what the scouting report tells us. Generally, the alignment in depth will be about four to seven yards. (See Diagram 10-1.)

Note: The man he is aligned on is generally his key in a man-to-man.

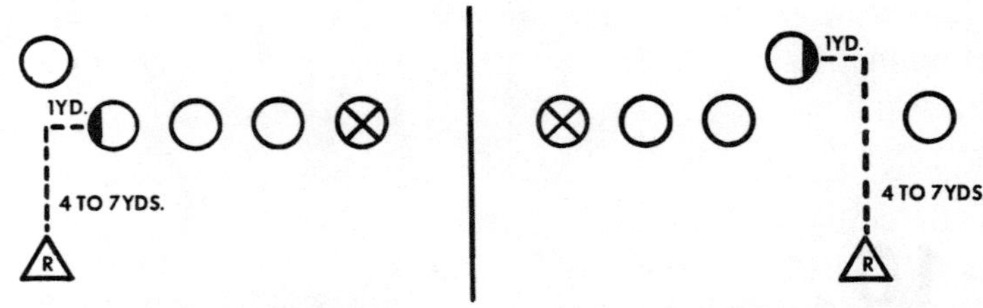

Rover alignment—2d eligible "quick" receiver.

Rover alignment.

DIAGRAM 10-1

b. Inside alignment—split rule: This alignment is seldom used and will not be discussed at length. In the alignment all duties remain the same. The rover will move to inside shoulder if the second receiver is seven or more yards wide.

c. Rover-free alignment: With a signal from the sideline or with a predesignated alignment that has been established before the game, the rover can align anywhere. Here is the beauty of the rover or "monster" defenses. One man can be put anywhere and there are no technical skill changes for anyone else. The front seven remain the same, while the defensive secondary can play man-to-man with the safety taking the rover's man, or an adjusted zone can be used. The possibilities are endless. We have put him on a great receiver, especially a wide-out, and have had double coverage. We have put him opposite the strength of the formation if a team has a tendency to run away from the strength. Versus teams that like to run internally, we have made him an extra linebacker. One common maneuver is to put him wide side. Of course, unless a coach uses short side and wide side personnel or is prepared to handle the short side attack with other adjustments, keeping the rover wide side as a regular diet is something that may not fit into the scheme of our defense, especially in regard to pass defense. You can see that the possibilities are many.

The rover must know his duties when he is put in a rover-free. Naturally, the coach can do this during the game; for example, let us assume a team is constantly hurting us off-tackle with the same play. Because of the gap control theory, the coach can place the rover in the off-tackle area (calling rover-free) and tell his rover to stop the play that is hurting us. We believe that there are times in a game when a coach cannot figure out *why* something is working against his team. He must act immediately, then try to figure out *why*!

d. On the line invert: The rover will align on the line of scrimmage on the outside shoulder of a designated receiver (usually the first quick receiver). He will generally be an "invert" coverage, which will be discussed later (see Diagram 10-2).

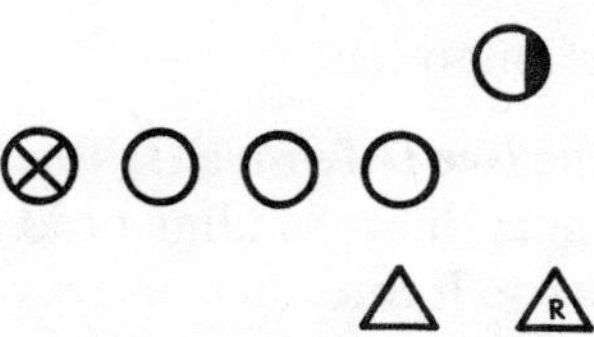

On-the-line alignment for rover (invert usual call).

DIAGRAM 10-2

3. Basic Responsibilities

a. Run to: Aggressive contain or auxiliary contain, depending on call.

b. Run away: Pursues to ball; much will depend on rover's speed as to the angle he will take (see pursuit).

c. Pass to: Responsibility depends on call.

d. Pass away: Ball in air—he sprints to it.

e. Drop back: Responsibility depends on call.

4. Initial Movement

See Defensive Halfback—exactly the same.

5. Rover Techniques, Keys and Ways to Be Blocked

a. Key releases in man-to-man (hawk): See Defensive Halfback.

b. Basic coverage technique: For all the previous coverage techniques, see the section on Defensive Halfback Techniques and Keys.

c. Covering deep outside: The rover will be asked to cover deep outside in a keying secondary. In this situation the rover will align a little deeper and follow all coverage techniques given in the defensive halfback section. If we were facing sophisticated passing teams that read our coverage constantly we could not make alignment changes with our rover for fear of check off and automatics.

d. Covering the flat and short flag: See Defensive Halfback section. One point should be mentioned: If the rover is covering from his ''on the line'' alignment, the rover must work to get depth along with width, but width is most important.

e. Goal line technique (see Defensive Halfback): The rover versus a tight alignment on the goal line may align head up to read his key, but only if absolutely necessary. Remember, the rover still must be able to keep the ball inside from this alignment (see Diagram 10-3). The reason for this allowance on the goal line is that we want the rover in a position to guarantee that the tight end look-in will be stopped!

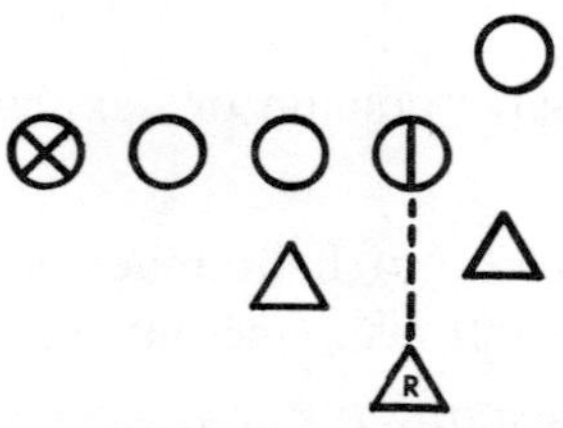

Goal line situation—rover may align head-up on his man.

DIAGRAM 10-3

f. Keys show run-contain technique (see Defensive Halfback): The rover follows basic principles given previously. Generally, the rover is responsible for aggressive contain except on a keying secondary call. The rover is then the auxiliary contain man.

g. Option duties: On option, the rover has the back who is going to receive the pitch (along with the defensive halfback). See Defensive Halfback.

h. Beating the tight wing block: If we are not in a keying secondary and there is a tight wing, there is a problem for the rover on run his way. He has aggressive contain. Naturally, all methods of beating blocks could be used, especially drop-step technique. Beating the down block of the wing could be a problem, but this frees the defensive end and, on contact by the wing, the defensive halfback will also be there for contain. If the wing is very tight, the rover may align a little wider and come off the buttocks of the wing (if the wing blocks the defensive end). See Diagram 10-4—A and B. The rover must realize that with this wider alignment he is giving the "look in" pass to the offense. He must react to this pass (see Diagram 10-5).

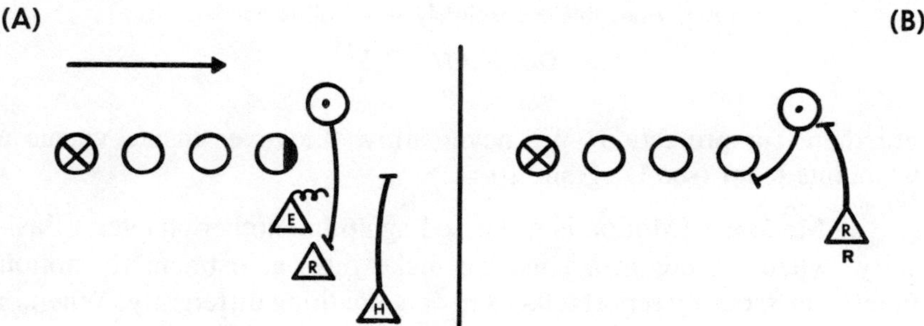

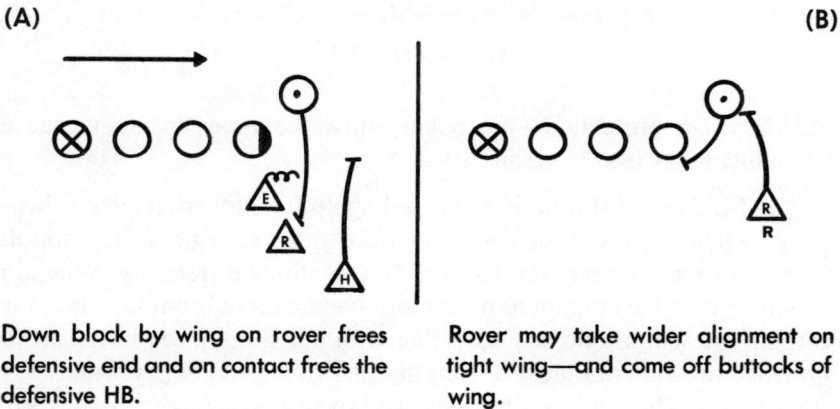

(A) Down block by wing on rover frees defensive end and on contact frees the defensive HB.

(B) Rover may take wider alignment on tight wing—and come off buttocks of wing.

DIAGRAM 10-4

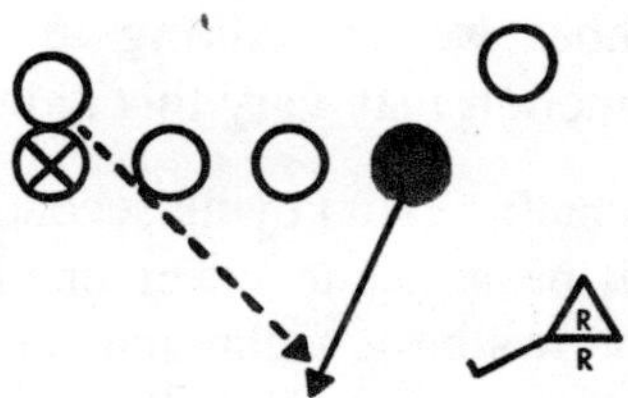

Wider alignment by rover leaves defense susceptible to quick pass. Rover must react to it if playing man-to-man.

DIAGRAM 10-5

i. Ball handed inside: The rover may move inside to a ball he definitely sees handed off inside. But he must be sure and we must be in a man-to-man. We are taking a chance since we feel our halfbacks

Ball handed inside.

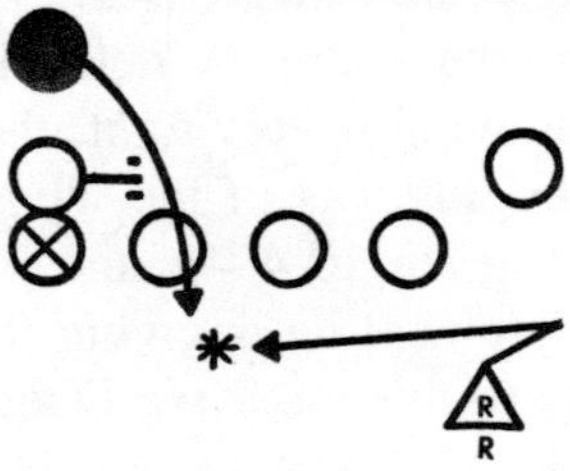

He only does this if absolutely sure ball is handed off.

DIAGRAM 10-6

are there for protection. We never allow the rover inside versus a wishbone team (see Diagram 10-6).

j. Motion: (Motion is discussed again in another chapter.) Basically, when we are in a zone we make little adjustment to motion unless our scouting report tells us to do something differently. When in a man-to-man we attempt to have rover handle all motion. One thing is certain, we will not do any adjusting with our front seven in regard to pre-snap movement unless a team has an obvious tendency when they use motion. The tendency must be well over a 90% tendency for us to make any adjustment with a member of our front seven. When we say the rover handles all motion in a man-to-man, we mean that, if possible, we would like the rover to go with the motion and play him man-to-man. Remember we are talking in generalities. Various reasons and types of motion may vary this philosophy.

k. Covering deep half: In a keying secondary, if drop back pass occurs, the rover will be asked to cover one-half of the field. The technique involved follows basic techniques in covering deep outside with less of an angle; he must get depth. The rover must take longer in his initial movement and we ask him to drift to the hash and be sure to drop deep. (Also see safety.)

6. Called Moves and Techniques

a. Hawk: Basic man-to-man.

b. Invert: Zone coverage; rover is responsible for the flat and short flag.

c. Keying: Rover keys ball and will have responsibility of deep outside on play to him; on play away the rover will have deep middle. On drop back, deep half is the rover's responsibility. On run to him, he is responsible for auxiliary contain.

d. Rover free: This call frees the rover of responsibility or it puts the rover on a designated alignment and gives him a specific duty to perform. This changes from week to week.

e. Bump and run: (See Defensive Halfback.)

f. Rover fire: This is a blitz by the rover. He will be sent in to a specific area according to the scouting report. We have seldom used this call.

g. Switch call: The rover may be asked to switch assignments with the defensive end. The rover will be responsible for the off-tackle gap while the defensive end is responsible for aggressive contain. The rover's pass responsibility will remain the same, but this call changes his run responsibilities (see Diagram 10-7).

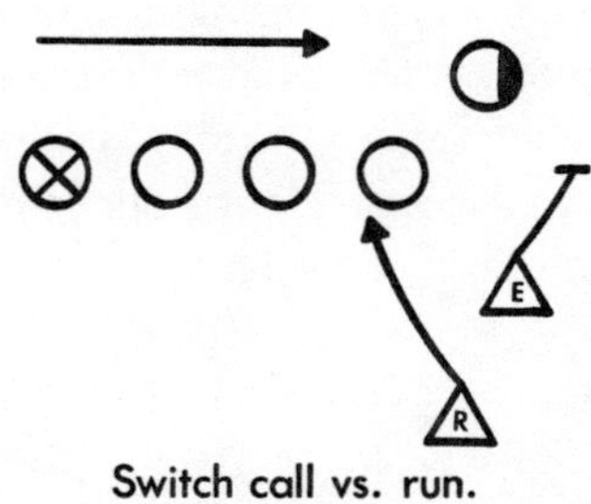

Switch call vs. run.

DIAGRAM 10-7

7. Common Faults

See Defensive Halfback for rover's faults. One fault that is common to the rover is that he can easily lose his cushion on a receiver especially versus a play-action fake in the backfield because of his, the rover's, proximity to the line of scrimmage.

11

How to Coach the Gap-Control Rover Defense Free Safety

The free safety is a must in our man-to-man pass defense. He allows the rest of our defenders the freedom to play outside routes aggressively. You will notice that our free safety is seldom (actually, never) asked to have aggressive contain. One obvious reason is that his basic alignment would prevent aggressive contain; another reason is that the free safety spends very little practice time on aggressive corner support.

1. Stance

(See Defensive Halfback.) The safety must stand tall enough to see his keys (usually the quarterback is his key).

2. Alignment

a. Basic: Basically, the safety will align opposite the rover in the area of the weakside offensive guard. He will never be closer than eight yards to the line. Generally, he will be ten yards deep (see Diagram 11-1).

b. Double rover: This alignment puts the safety on the second eligible receiver opposite the rover. In depth he aligns like the rover, about four to seven yards deep. If he is in a ''hawk'' call he takes on

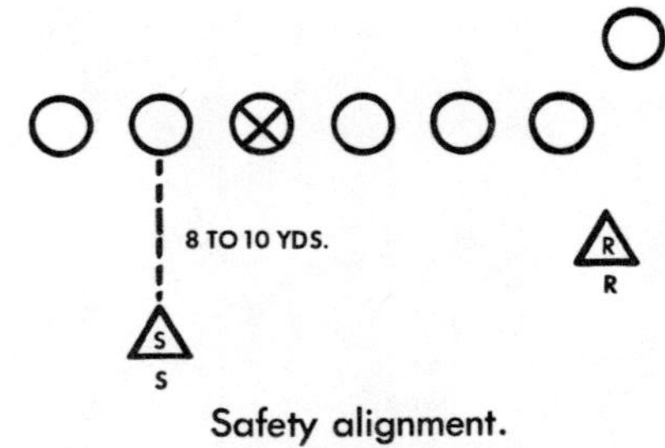

Safety alignment.

DIAGRAM 11-1

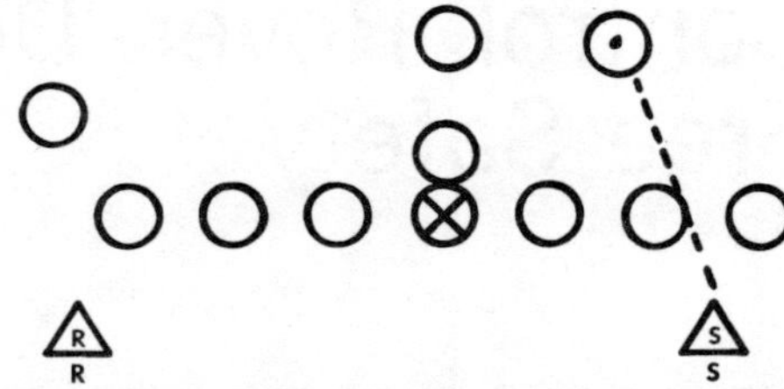

Safety in double rover takes second eligible receiver opposite the rover.

DIAGRAM 11-2

same duties as the rover. If he is in a keying secondary he will execute all safety duties from this alignment. The task in a keying secondary call from this alignment is especially difficult and seldom used. In reality, this double rover call is seldom used (see Diagram 11-2).

c. Rover free: When "rover free" is called, the safety must cheat slightly toward the rover's man because the safety will be covering the rover's man (see Diagram 11-3).

3. Basic Responsibilities

The free safety is free and is expected to protect the deep area between the hash marks. He must help on all internal routes, posts, etc. He is expected to be all over the field and lead the team in interceptions. He is expected to be in on every pass thrown over 15 yards. In most cases, he is responsible between the hash on every secondary call.

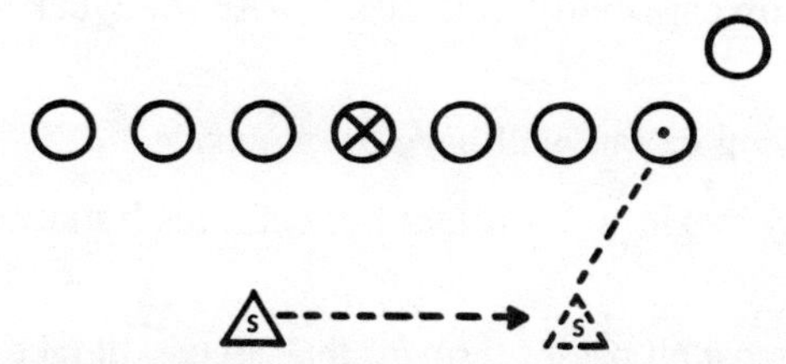
Rover free—safety must cheat over to rover's man.

DIAGRAM 11-3

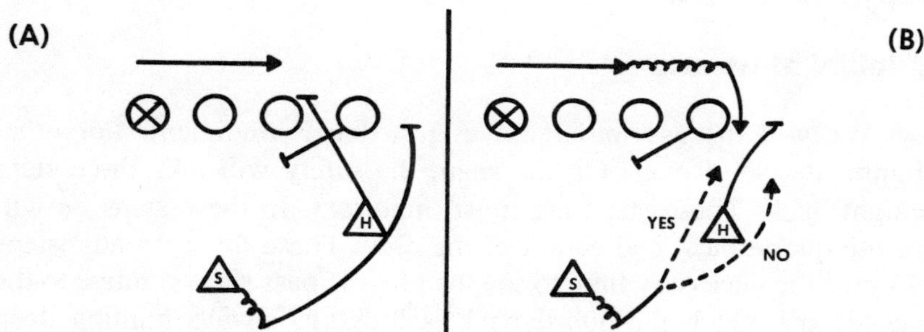

Safety has auxiliary contain on run to him if he is absolutely sure it is run.

Safety must use good judgment if the ball carrier is obviously cutting back.

DIAGRAM 11-4

a. Run to: Once the safety is absolutely sure run is apparent (ball should almost pass the line of scrimmage before moving to the line), he is responsible for auxiliary contain. However, he must use good judgment if it is obvious that the ball carrier is back inside; he must not overrun the play (see Diagram 11-4—A and B).

Note: Safety is responsible for halfback pass and all trick pass plays to both sides.

b. Run away: On runs away, the safety will keep lag on ball carrier, yet will keep an eye on halfback pass. He will jump on any deep receiver. He will stay deep.

c. Pass to: On pass action to his side, the safety will protect the post area, first reading the quarterback. This is especially true if there is a split end to his side. If it is a play-action fake to the weak side, the free safety must be especially concerned with the weak side halfback's man.

Note: In keying call he will have deep outside.

d. Pass away: He will protect between hash marks, keying quarterback.

Note: On almost all passes thrown, the safety will take an inside-out approach to the ball.

e. Drop back: He will drop and key quarterback, looking for deep quick receiver.

4. Initial Movement

We will discuss initial move from basic alignment. For other alignments, see Rover. On the snap, the safety will take three steps straight back. These steps are most important. In these steps he will eye the quarterback and action of the play. These three "read" steps will give the necessary time to see the play. If pass shows, move to the side toward which the quarterback is looking, always hunting deep receivers. No matter what action the safety sees, the three drop steps should be taken—the angle of drop can be adjusted to a roll pass (see Diagram 11-5).

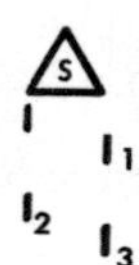

Three-step drop, look where QB looks.

DIAGRAM 11-5

Note: The importance of the safety's initial movement can't be overemphasized.

5. Safety Techniques and Keys

For coverage techniques in man-to-man moving to ball and interception technique, see Defensive Halfback section.

a. Keying the quarterback: Usually in high school the quarterback will look to where he is throwing by the time three initial steps are taken by the safety. The safety will move inside-out to the direction the quarterback is looking (see Diagram 11-6). He will find the receiver the quarterback is looking towards, get in proper relation with the receiver (inside-out), then look back for the ball and get the interception! If the safety is having trouble keying the look of the quarterback, then he will key the quarterback's shoulders. The quarterback must point them in the direction in which he plans to throw the ball.

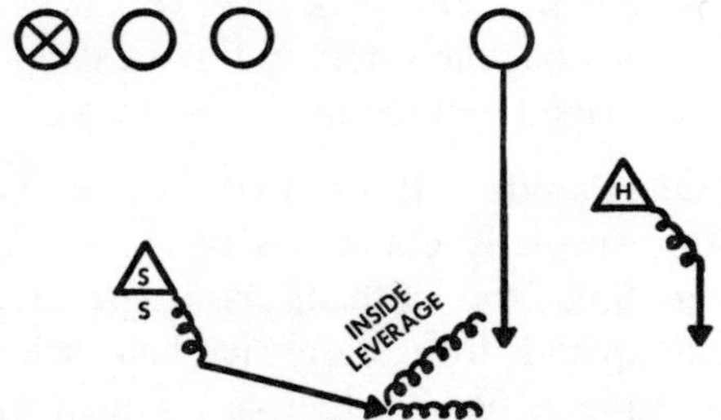

Notice that the free safety will always attempt to keep inside leverage on the receiver and on his movement to the ball (excluding a "keying" call when the safety is responsible for deep outside).

DIAGRAM 11-6

Note: The safety must "hang" in the post area. We call this the "hole." Because of his three initial steps the safety is in great position to cover bootleg pass.

b. Keying receivers: If all else fails, he simply keys the fastest and deepest receiver. The safety must attempt to stay on the receiver's far shoulder. The safety must get in stride with receiver as soon as the cushion closes to about two yards.

c. Moving with flow: After the initial movement of the safety, all flow should have been established. The safety must realize that as the

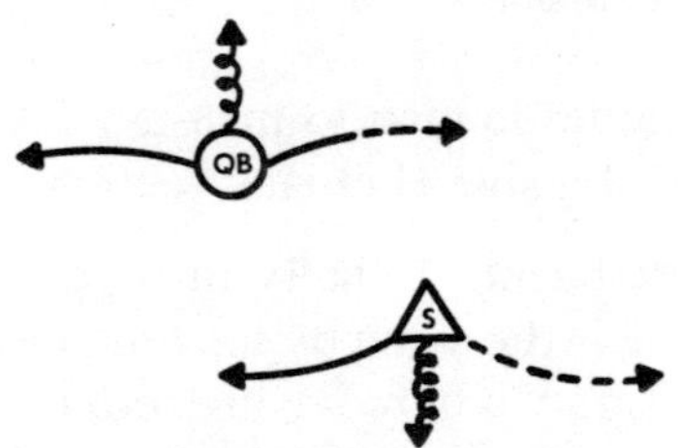

Safety's area of responsibility—moves with QB.

DIAGRAM 11-7

quarterback moves so does his, the safety's, area of responsibility (see Diagram 11-7).

d. Covering deep half: On weak level (rotate) and keying secondary with drop-back action, the safety will have deep-half responsibility. All previous described techniques are followed.

e. Run key, safety's side: If a run key shows to the safety's side, the safety must be especially conscious of the weak side, defensive halfback's receiver. Since the halfback has aggressive contain he will be anxious to come up and, if the defensive halfback reads wrong, the safety must protect the defensive halfback's man or deep area (see Diagram 11-8).

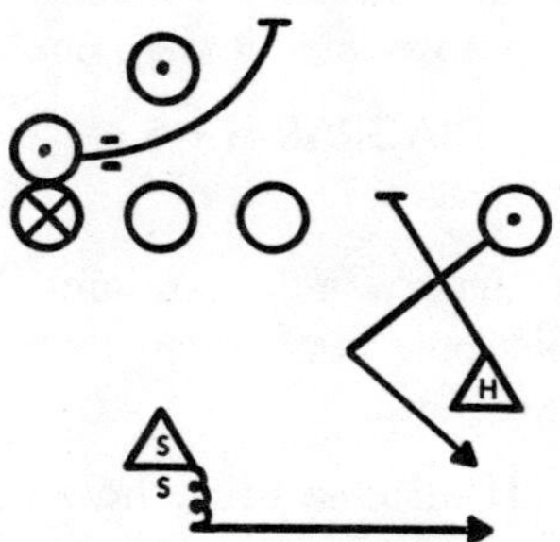

HB moves to contain play and pass shows; safety must cover up for defensive HB's error.

DIAGRAM 11-8

f. Covering deep outside: See Defensive Halfback section.

g. Breakthrough by runner: If the ball carrier has a breakthrough in the line, the safety must realize he is the last line of resistance. He *must* make the tackle (use previous tackling techniques). He must not be too close to the line of scrimmage unless sure of a tackle; he must be under control. The worst thing that can occur is to let the ball carrier break away clean (see Diagram 11-9). He must maintain depth on internal running plays.

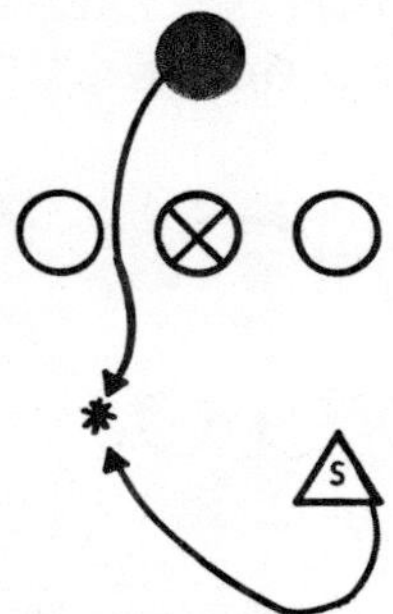

Breakthrough line, safety is last resort.

DIAGRAM 11-9

h. Option duties: The safety will have the back receiving the pitch as his responsibility, but only after all threat of pass is gone. That means the ball carrier must have almost crossed the line of scrimmage.

6. Called Moves

The safety will play from hash to hash. The following are just some calls that may change his responsibilities slightly:

a. Hawk (man-to-man): Free.

b. Weak level (rotate): On snap, the safety protects the deep half to his side.

c. Keying: This affects the safety if action is to him or drop back; he has deep outside. Versus drop back he has deep half.

d. Double rover: The safety, as mentioned previously, aligns in the rover position and plays as the rover would unless a keying secondary is called; then the safety plays normal from the rover alignment.

e. Rover free: The safety cheats to the rover's man and covers him man-to-man on this call.

7. Common Faults

a. Poor timing on post receiver: One error that is made by a safety is that he has poor timing to a receiver running a post route. He may overrun the post receiver instead of getting in stride with the receiver if the ball isn't thrown (see Diagram 11-10). Anticipation is fine as long as the defender is right.

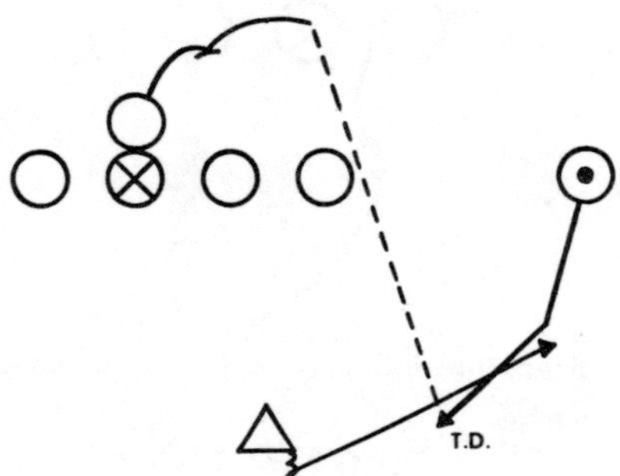
T.D.

Safety overruns receiver—very costly.

DIAGRAM 11-10

b. Getting in stride with receivers: Another problem we have trouble with is that the safety fails to get in stride with a deep receiver. The safety comes underneath only to find that the ball is thrown over

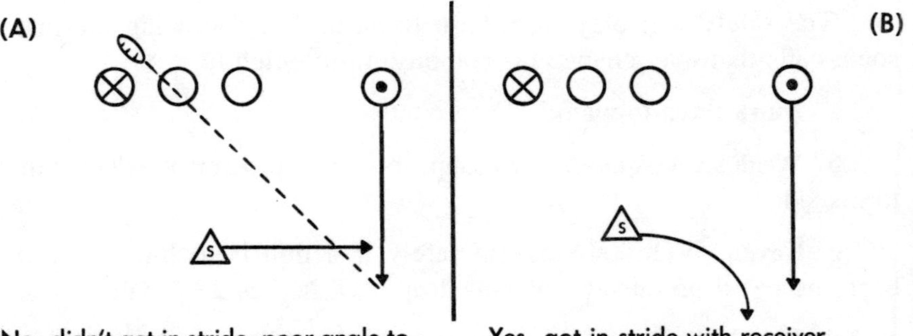
(A)
(B)
S
S
No, didn't get in stride; poor angle to receiver.
Yes, got in stride with receiver.

DIAGRAM 11-11

him (see Diagram 11-11—A and B). Generally, it is the result of taking a poor angle to the receiver.

c. Caught standing flat-footed: The safety, on occasion, can get caught standing flat-footed and wait too long to turn and run with receiver.

d. Coming up too soon on run: The safety must stay back. If he comes up too fast on run up the middle he can only cover limited ground. Of course, he should come up if he is sure of a tackle, but if he hangs back he can cover more area on a break-away (see Diagram 11-12—A and B).

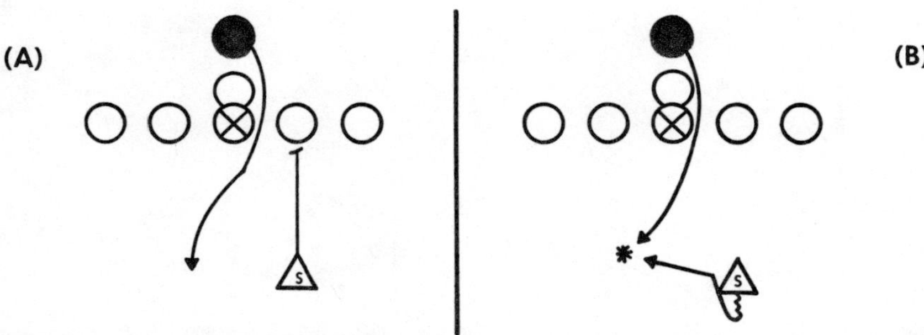

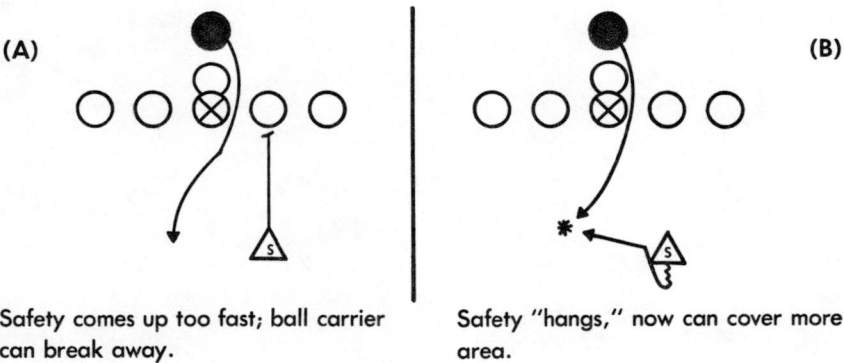

Safety comes up too fast; ball carrier can break away.

Safety "hangs," now can cover more area.

DIAGRAM 11-12

e. Sight of ball slows safety down: For some reason, when a deep defender sees the ball in the air there is a tendency to automatically slow down to play for the interception. The safety must be sure and accurate on his interception. Seeing the ball in flight should not make slowing down automatic.

12

Defensive Considerations

1. Defensing the Option

We have definite assignments on the option which seldom change. Unless a team runs the option constantly against us, we see no reason to change responsibilities to destroy the read of the quarterback. We have found it gives us more trouble to change duties than it does our opponents. We have been most successful against all types of option teams, mainly because our playside linebacker is free of the internal fake responsibility (unless it is a wide fake).

Regardless of alignment, the duties on the option generally stay the same. All techniques for playing the option have been discussed for each position. The defensive end (who is usually unblocked) will play his soft technique. He is responsible for the quarterback, but once the pitch is made he can move to the pitchman. His soft technique allows this to occur.

The playside linebacker is free to play football but is usually going to the pitchman. The backside linebacker is free to play football, but is usually held up with an internal fake if there is one. If he sees the ball removed he is free to move to it, but the backside linebacker must keep a lag on the quarterback, especially if the quarterback decides to keep the ball on the option.

The nutcracker and tackle will also have to respect the internal fake (if there is one).

The entire secondary know they are responsible for pitch. You can see that every option is covered by at least two defenders and sometimes three (excluding the quarterback). We feel the end should be able to handle the quarterback himself (see Diagrams 12-1 and 12-2).

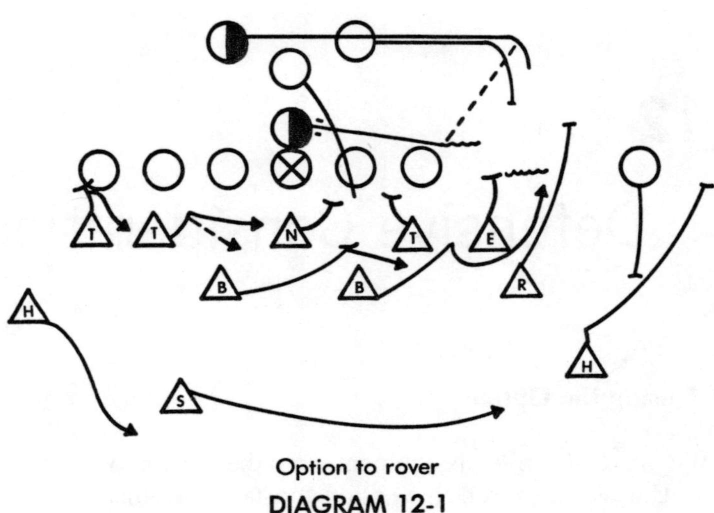

Option to rover

DIAGRAM 12-1

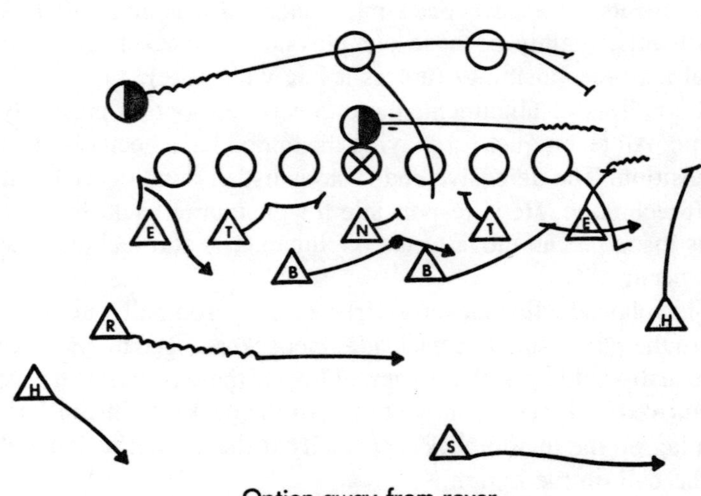

Option away from rover

DIAGRAM 12-2

2. Defensing Motion

With motion, the defensive backs just ask themselves the question: "What was the formation when the ball was snapped?" This will allow the defensive backs a chance to discover the rules in reference to first or second outside quick receiver. We want our rover to handle all motion when possible. If a wing (or slot) goes in motion, the rover will go with the motion man (see Diagram 12-3). If motion is from the backfield to the rover, we will go automatically to "invert." If it goes away from the rover it forces a man-to-man situation (see Diagram 12-4). If there is short "quick" motion, no adjustment is made. When in a keying (zone) secondary, no adjustment is made at all to motion.

Note: The defensive halfback naturally in all defenses cannot allow an offensive back to get too far outside without adjusting to the offensive back.

The front seven make no adjustment to motion, only the secondary adjusts. We have done things on the snap of the ball when motion is used by a team. We have found that many teams that use motion limit their offense to a degree and have definite tendencies when they use motion. We are by no means downing the use of motion (we use it a lot ourselves), but we are saying self-scouting becomes a must for teams using motion.

We have many automatic maneuvers to motion, and this isn't always a good idea since the opponent can attack accordingly. How-

Rover goes across formation with extended motion—everyone else goes "hawk" (man-to-man) unless in a "keying" secondary call.

DIAGRAM 12-3

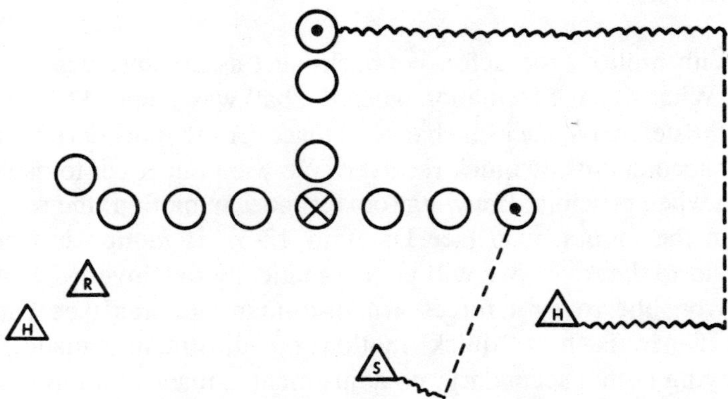

Motion from backfield—away from rover—"hawk" call (unless "keying" call).

Note: If back gets outside offensive end, the defensive HB must take him since the offensive back is the first outside receiver on the snap.

DIAGRAM 12-4

ever, we refuse to make elaborate adjustments or spend more time than necessary because of motion. That is what the opponent would like to see happen to our practice time.

3. Defensing the Unbalanced Line

We do not align on the ball. We align on the middle man in the offensive line. The front seven men align on numbered men—for instance, the linebacker lines over No. 1 from the middle of the line, tackle lines on No. 2 from center of the line, etc. The secondary adjusts, as usual, to backfield strength or any other called alignment (see Diagram 12-5).

Note: Generally, the nutcracker just moves to the next man alongside the center; he is usually the new zero man on whom the nutcracker must align.

4. Defensing the Screen Pass

It will be difficult for teams to screen against us since our linebackers are keying backs. The defensive ends are not directly respon-

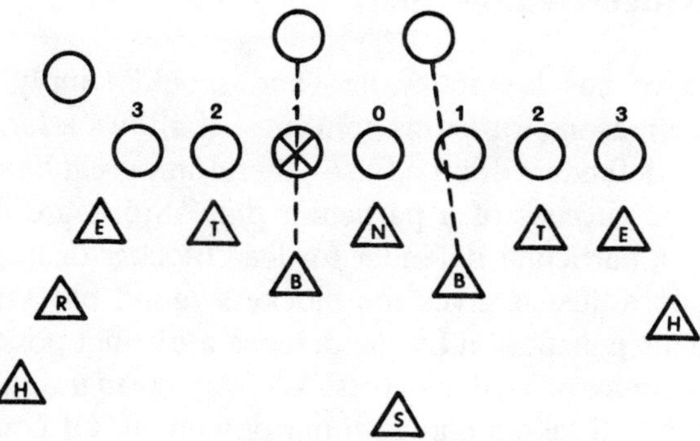

Adjustment to unbalanced line, keys remain the same.

DIAGRAM 12-5

sible for screen; however, if a back crosses a defensive end's face, the end should hang with him if that back crosses his face on a straight line. If the back waits until the end goes by and the defensive end recognizes screen, the defensive end should put on the "brakes" and go to the screen man. First man to screen should approach from outside-in. We don't want to allow the screen outside! (See diagram 12-6.) Screen is detected by sliding offensive linemen and by an unusually deep drop by the quarterback.

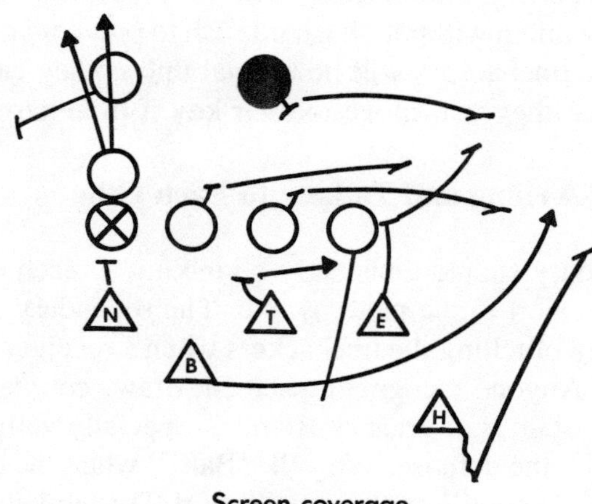

Screen coverage.

DIAGRAM 12-6

5. Defensing Offensive Line Splits

Every player has his split rule—and should simply follow it. There are many reasons for teams splitting—it allows a larger hole to be created if the defenders don't adjust—therefore, great blocks are not necessary for the success of a particular play. Splits are used many times to isolate a particular defender for lead blocker or trap block. If the defenders do adjust it gives the blockers good blocking angles. Large split makes penetration by the defense a distinct possibility and we can destroy many offensive drives. We stay normal until the splits hurt us, then we will take a gap with our downmen. Of course, much will depend on the type of offense run and the tendency of the offense, as to what defense we will call. The important point to remember is that we will stay in a normal alignment as long as we can carry out all of our responsibilities from that alignment. Large offensive line splits can hurt any defense, but they can also cost the offense some consistency because of stunting of linebackers and penetration by down linemen.

6. Weird Formation Philosophy

There is nothing worse than watching a defensive team run all over the field trying to adjust to a weird formation. We would rather be unsound with our front seven but ready to play football. With anything unusual our secondary immediately will go to a zone (keying or 4 across). The downmen will put on a hard rush to prevent anything from developing. The linebackers will be normal unless they can find their proper key. Then they will move to their key if time permits.

7. (Score Call) Yelling and Talking to Each Other

The secondary should constantly be talking to each other, being sure everyone is alert to the patterns, etc. The secondary people have the responsibility of telling the linebackers when a receiver runs a hook or curl pattern. Anyone recognizing screen, draw, counter or reverse must yell it. This talk is of great assistance, especially yelling "Pass!" when it is seen by the defense. We yell "Ball!" when the ball is in the air. We also yell "Score!" on the interception. This will alert everyone to form a wall on the hash marks. It also alerts the defender nearest to the defender who is yelling "score" to block the nearest receiver. The man making the interception heads for hash marks, to the forming wall.

Note: Our players on the bench are responsible for yelling "pass" and "ball"; they help out a great deal, especially when a screen pass shows.

8. Two-Minute Defense

The two-minute defense is the defensive strategy used in that time span before the end of the first half and the end of the game. There are two situations that will prevail during this time period.

The first such situation is when we are ahead and must prevent our opponent from scoring. In this situation we will utilize the best defense for the occasion. Time is important—we will keep the clock running whenever possible. We must attempt to keep the ball in bounds and never take a time out. We do not take chances when covering a receiver; when in doubt, we make sure of the tackle—let him catch the ball if the interception is not positive. We must be alert for "trick"plays and quick plays without the use of a huddle.

The second situation that could prevail is that we are behind and need possession of the ball. We will play an aggressive type of defense. We must get the ball and preserve time. We attempt to get the ball by grabbing at it, tackling the ball, forcing fumbles and going for the interception. We throw all caution to the wind and do everything within our power to give our offense a chance for victory. We force the ball carrier out of bounds when tackling him; don't let him in bounds. If the clock is running and if we are going to call time out, we call it immediately—we don't wait. These things are common sense to the coach, but a player must be more than just aware of them. He must be drilled for them—because common-sense situations in the heat of battle are the situations that cost football games.

9. Calling the Defense and Offensive Recognition

Many defenses are called from the sideline by hand signals from the head coach. The first signal is for the front seven, the second signal is for the secondary. The defensive signal caller will give the defense as received from the coach. Following this, the signal caller will give the situation (down/distance, yardline, etc.) and then caution as to which play to watch out for under these conditions. Any stunts will be given after the preliminary call of the front seven.

Once the offense comes out of the huddle, the defense will call the strongside. This is determined by the side a back aligns on, away from the normal backfield alignment. If this is not possible, then the side the tight end is located on is strong side. If this is not possible, it is a balanced offense. This call is made for the front seven. Following this call, the defensive backfield alignment is called. These calls are most important, especially if we have a formation tendency on our opponent.

Any coach can devise a system for the defense to declare the offensive formation as long as it is consistent, simple, and understandable to everyone. We like to be descriptive in our calling offensive formation, i.e., slot right, Delaware left (see Diagram 12-7). Less verbiage would be needed if the color method of defining offensive formation were used. It is used more and probably easier for the coach.

> *Note*: We call defensive signals from the sideline to make it easier for them to play football without having to think about proper alignments. The only time we are automatic on the field is when the opponent has an obvious formation tendency.

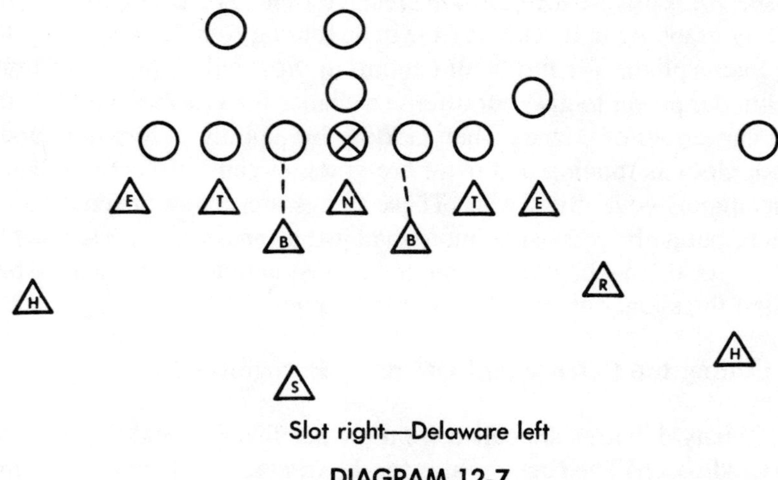

Slot right—Delaware left

DIAGRAM 12-7

13

Problems Facing the Gap-Control Rover Defense

It would certainly be a lie to say nothing ever hurts our defense. No defense can stop everything all of the time. For everything a defense does there is a counter move by the offense and vice versa.

The following problems have never cost us a football game. Some of these problems are unique to the defense in a theoretical way. Every defense ever created has problems within its structure, but most coaches, including myself, hate to admit it. Every problem can be corrected with the proper call.

We are proud that we play the best competition from four states. Our defense has been tested by the best talent and by some of the best coaching minds around.

Some of the following problems are common to every defense:

Tight End Flex

The defensive end who is faced with a tight end flex (sometimes called the "nasty split") can be a problem. Every defensive player asks himself this question: "Can I carry out my responsibilities from this alignment?" One defensive end may feel he can stay in a normal alignment versus a three-yard tight end split (flex), while another feels he cannot, so he may move inside. How do we handle the problem of a flexed end? Well, we really don't! We try to find out why the end is being flexed. There are many reasons for the flex, but one reason is that the opponent is trying to throw the ball and would like the tight end to get a free release.

Another reason for a tight end flex is that the play is being run inside or off-tackle (with a tight end release). Obviously, the flex will create a running lane inside. Occasionally, the flex is used by the tight end to force the defensive end back inside so an effective crack-back block can be used to aid a running play that is going outside. However, this does not occur too often since the corner may be stretched too far to get outside quickly. Finally, the tight end flex may be used in conjunction with some type of option so there is an easier read for the quarterback. You can see that regardless of the reason for the flex, the defensive end is forced to do something. Therefore, it is important to learn from the scouting report why a team would do this and, naturally, what is the basic offensive philosophy. In this way the coach can assist the defensive end in the choice of alignment. Be assured that the problem is still not resolved. Our defense is in a better situation versus the flex because of the hard and tight scrape of the playside linebacker into the running alley.

Don't Get Hooked

Another problem the defensive end must face is that he is asked to squeeze the off-tackle hole and still protect the outside leg (don't get hooked). We call him, as mentioned earlier, the pressure fighter. Let us assume we are faced with this situation. The first back comes to the defensive end's outside leg aggressively but doesn't block him, yet the defensive end is told to protect his outside leg so he must move outside with the potential blocker. Then another blocker (it can be a lineman or a back) is now able to execute an easy kick-out and, because of the influence block, a large off-tackle running alley may develop (see Diagram 13-1). What is the answer? There is no easy answer but we have had some success with just sending the defensive end on a "fire" call and having him attack the first back to squeeze the hole and not allow the influence to develop. Also, remember in our base defense the playside linebacker will be scraping hard to the off-tackle hole.

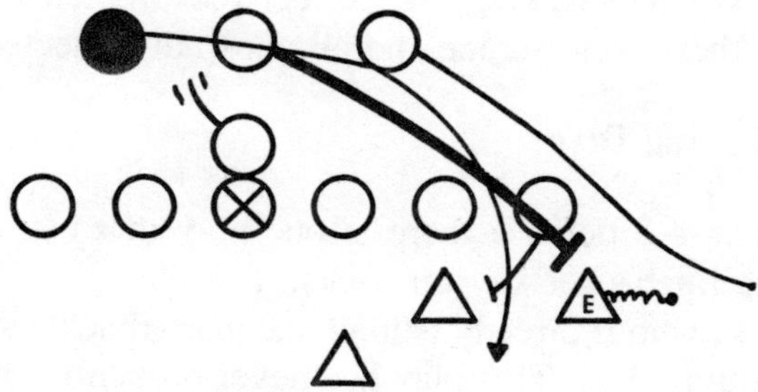

The dilemma of the end—don't get hooked but squeeze the off-tackle hole shut.

DIAGRAM 13-1

The Apex of the Scrape

The tackle and playside linebacker scrape has been severely tested by all offenses. The Houston Veer offense with the quick dive play has hurt us more than any other play—not insofar as big gains go but for five-yard consistent gains. The reason for that is the dive back hits at the apex of the scrape. This in itself is not a problem, but if the linebacker doesn't scrape as he should—tight to the tackle—a gain is the result (see Diagram 13-2). The reason for an improper wide scrape is that the linebacker becomes too conscious of the pitch man on the option. Also, the offensive back is at an excellent angle to read the play

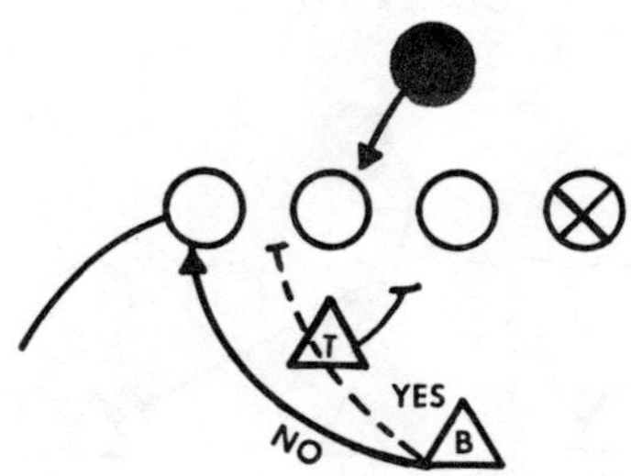

LB may scrape too wide and allow the back to hit the apex of the scrape.

DIAGRAM 13-2

of the linebacker and tackle. We correct the problem by calling a step-out; now there is no scrape and all gaps are protected.

4-3 Defense Facing Dive

Versus our 4-3 defense there is one play that can disrupt keys because of the linebacker key on backs. The play is a dive with the remaining back, who is directly behind the quarterback, flowing opposite (see Diagram 13-3). This play has never broken for a large gain, nor has it been exploited. Then you ask, "Why discuss it?" The reason is to be sure the coach knows the possible problems he will face (see Diagram 13-3). You can see the guard/tackle gap is unprotected. Even with that the linebacker could still make the play. Also notice that all keys must be exactly right for this offensive play to succeed. We correct the problem with a step-out call, so our defensive tackles are now in the guard tackle gap prepared to stop the dive.

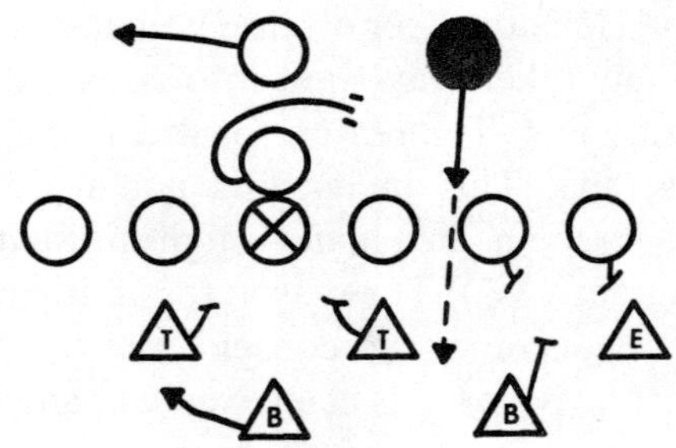

DIAGRAM 13-3

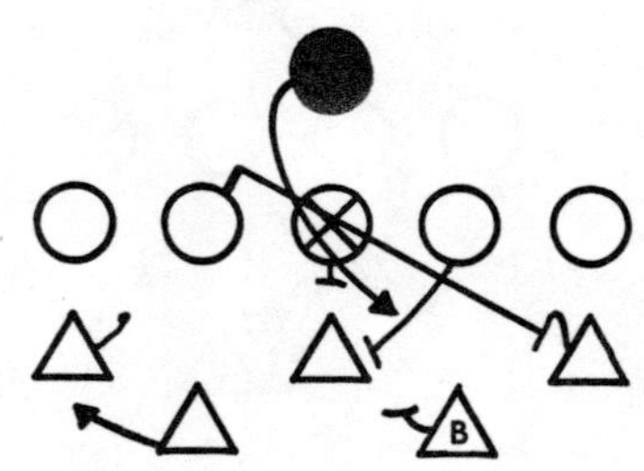

Buck wind back, backside LB hang.

DIAGRAM 13-4

Step Out vs. Trap?

One call we do not like to make on a slot counter-oriented team is the step-out call from the base defense. This leaves a large running alley because both tackles are moving outside and our linebackers are moving with flow of the backs and/or their keys. There is no chance for the tackles to get on the hip pocket of the trapper, or to close the trap alley.

Buck Wind Back

We ask our linebackers to pursue quickly, yet we ask our backside linebacker to keep a lag on the ball but still fill the center-guard gap to the opposite side of the nutcracker. This is a dilemma for the linebacker; that is, he must scrape to the gap yet keep a lag on the ball. This is most important to the success of our defense. Every defense has a dilemma, but it isn't as severe as one might think since there is only one situation with which we have been faced that has hurt us when in our base defense. That play is what we call buck wind back (see Diagram 13-4). This is done with guard trap. The reason it hurts us in our base defense is that the backside linebacker over pursues. However, he is told that if the fullback moves inside the guard area he, the backside linebacker, hangs to prevent a large running lane from opening up. We have corrected the problem with constant drill and recognition. We also have found that our 4-3 defense is most effective versus this play because the running alley is extremely small and our backside linebacker can more easily keep his lag. Finally, no matter what defense we are in our tackles are expected to squeeze the running alley. The reason this play may be effective is the extremely quick-hitting nature of this misdirection play and the overemphasis we put on the linebackers to pursue.

Tight End Directly to Linebacker

On occasion, teams send their tight end down directly on our scrape linebacker. If the linebacker scrapes properly and our defensive end does his job, there is little problem. We immediately call "Step out" when we see this maneuver by the offense, and generally our tackle is standing unblocked in the hole.

Tackles Being Influenced

As soon as we cover our opponent's guards with our defensive tackles, many teams attempt to influence our tackles with a false pull. This is especially true with teams that run the Delaware Wing "T". The trap block is set up because our defensive tackle is getting on the hip of their pulling guard (see Diagram 13-5). We don't feel this maneuver will defeat us, so we don't drill our tackles to look inside when getting on the hip of an offensive guard pulling outside because it slows our tackle down. Also, if our tackle is in a basic technique from the 4-3 alignment, his initial movement doesn't allow for quick movement outside. Finally, we can usually prevent any long gains with a three-linebacker defense.

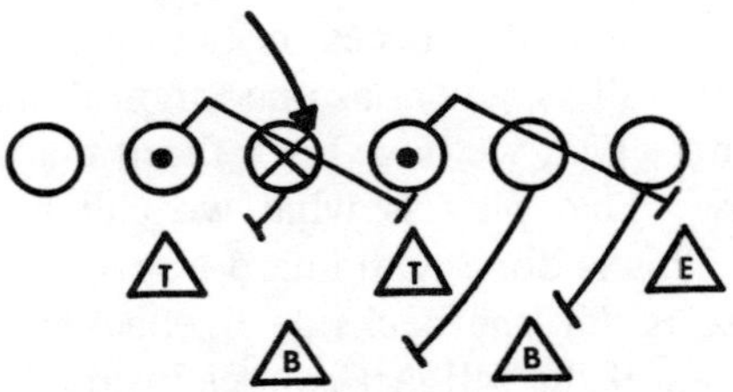

Guard pull to influence tackles on trap.

DIAGRAM 13-5

Corner to the Split End's Side

Anytime a defender is split wide with a receiver, yet is still responsible for aggressive contain, he has a difficult task. This occurs to our split end's side since we do not invert our free safety. (We don't want the safety responsible for aggressive contain because we don't want to lose his deep help, nor is he usually the type of boy who does a great job in aggressive containment.) The defensive halfback away from the rover is always responsible for aggressive contain, as explained earlier. We are always concerned about corner support to the split end's side, but our opponents have not exploited that area with run. We are also over-conscious of the problem and practice contain from the wide alignment a great deal. Finally, if a team is continually trying to hurt us outside away from the rover, we call a weak rotate which is executed on the snap of the ball regardless of flow.

Never Align on the Same Plane and Crossing Receivers

When in a man-to-man pass defense it is important to be sure that the defensive backs (rover and halfbacks) never align on the same plane (see Diagram 13-6). The reason is obvious—we don't want a collision. This is most important versus a twin set where the receivers are in such close proximity. Along the same lines, we must always be prepared for crossing receivers who are trying to force our defenders to bump into each other. We handle this by alignment, as mentioned earlier, and by assigning the rule that the rover, who is moving outside to cover his man, has preference over the defensive halfback moving inside to cover his man. That is to say, the defensive halfback moving inside must get deeper to give the rover room. The halfback must adjust to the rover. Obviously, we do this because we have help in the middle (linebacker and safety) and none to the outside.

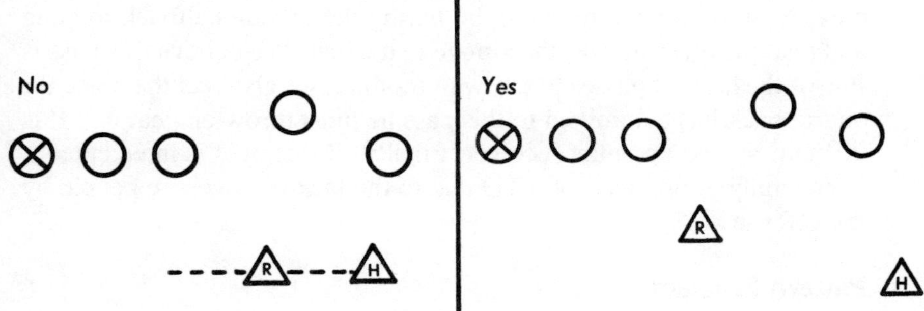

Never align on same plan.

DIAGRAM 13-6

Crossing Receiver Against Flow

The receiver that crosses into the area of the backside flat has given us some problems because the defensive end in our defense does not drop to the flat on flow-away (see Diagram 13-7). The linebackers

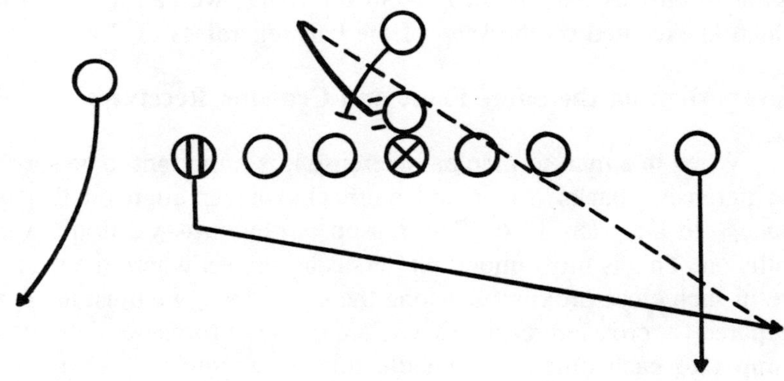

DIAGRAM 13-7

are constantly told never to allow a receiver to cross their face, but this crossing receiver is difficult to see, especially if there is a play-action fake. When in a man-to-man this receiver is also difficult to cover because the defender is about five steps behind the receiver. We handle this by going zone and making our offside halfback conscious of the play. Now we are taking a risk by telling the offside halfback to hang and read the quarterback, then move to the ball. We believe this pass is one of the hardest passes to throw in football; we also feel that once the quarterback has committed to this pass he must throw or "eat it." It is difficult to find an outlet receiver. Finally, if this pass is intercepted it is generally a long gain or a TD due to the lack of coverage people by the offense.

Pattern Problem

We have seen all possible routes to beat a rover secondary. Our defensive secondary has no more weaknesses than any other pass defense when in a zone (seams, etc.). However, when in a man-to-man in a rover secondary and not wanting to go to an automatic call versus two quick receivers to both sides (four quick receivers), it can be a problem. The safety must go man-to-man opposite the rover, yet we want him to stay deep to give deep help. The darkened receivers in Diagram 13-8 (A and B) are the men who will be open short. We generally are automatic to these circumstances, depending on the opponent's tendencies.

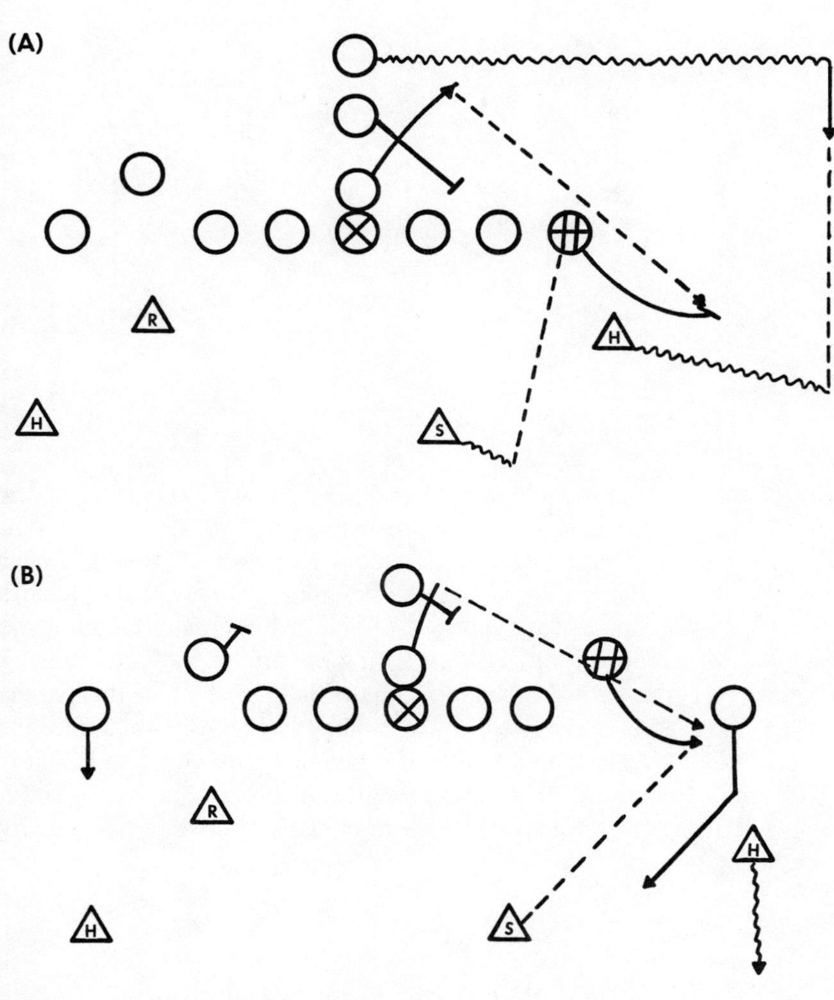

DIAGRAM 13-8

14

Team Defenses

Now we must put everything that has been discussed earlier into a complete package. All details have been discussed and keys have been previously assigned. Alignments may be illustrated to both sides, but an alignment can be assigned to only one side and another alignment to the other side. Because the front seven are separate, in regard to alignment, from the rover secondary the front seven will be illustrated separately from the secondary. Also, remember that alignments may change but technique seldom, if ever, is affected.

Included in this section are some very broad reasons why we like to use these defenses.

1. Alignment of Front Seven

a. Regular 5-2 defense—Diagram 14-1

b. 4-3 Defense—Diagram 14-2

c. 40-Contain—Diagram 14-3

d. Eagle—Diagram 14-4

e. Over calls—Diagram 14-5 and 14-6

f. 50 Tight—Diagram 14-7

g. Gap stacks—Diagrams 14-8 and 14-9

h. Stack—Diagram 14-10

i. Split end adjustment—Diagram 14-11

j. Goal line defense (6-5)—Diagram 14-12

k. Prevent—Diagram 14-13

2. Defensive Secondary Alignments, Calls and Duties

a. Hawk (man for man)—Diagram 14-14

b. Keying secondary—Diagrams 14-15a, 14-15b, and 14-15c

c. Invert—Diagram 14-16. This zone movement is made on the snap of the ball regardless of flow. We will also execute this with the rover on the line (on the line invert).

d. Weak rotate (level)—Diagram 14-17. This zone movement is made on the snap of the ball regardless of flow.

e. Double rover (hawk—man-to-man)—Diagram 14-18

f. Goal line and bump/run—Daigram 14-19

g. 4 Across—Diagram 14-20. Each defensive back protects deep ¼ of the field.

h. Rover free—Diagram 14-21

i. Prevent—Diagram 14-22. Nutcracker comes out and another defensive back comes in.

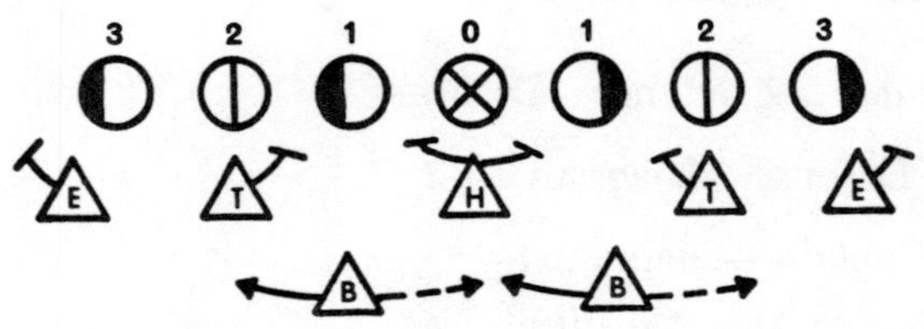

DIAGRAM 14-1

Ends:	Inside eye to outside eye of No. 3.
Tackles:	Head up on No. 2.
Nutcracker:	Head up on zero man.
Linebacker:	Inside eye to outside eye of No. 1.

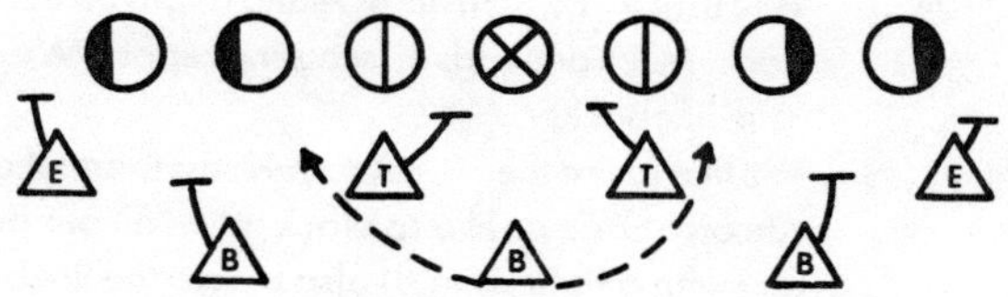

DIAGRAM 14-2

Ends:	Regular.
Tackles:	Head up on No. 1, regular technique.
Nutcracker:	Up technique—may put in linebacker—protect guard tackle gap to either side.
Outside Linebackers:	Regular, align on No. 2.
Comments:	We like to use this on passing downs and versus teams that try to pull guards a lot or that have based their attacks against the guard area of our base 5-2 defense. Finally, we like to use this versus teams that like to run option a great deal.

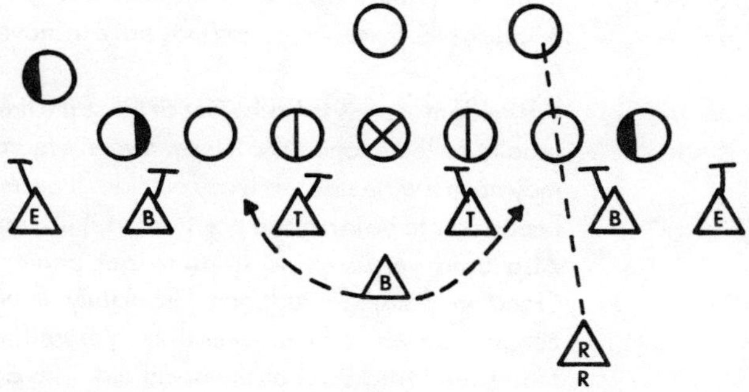

DIAGRAM 14-3

Ends:	Use the wide alignment, aggressive contain.
Tackles:	Regular 4-3.
Nutcracker:	Up technique regular 4-3.
Outside Linebacker:	Inside shoulder of tight end, delivers blow and plays regular.

Rover: Will usually be in rover free and aligns on the running back. Much depends on scouting report. We may put in a linebacker.

Comments: We like to use the 40-contain versus teams that like to run off-tackle or like to block down on our defensive end with a tight wing. It also places the linebacker in position to be pre-aligned in his responsibility. It has all the advantages internally of the 4-3 defense. Very effective versus option and bootleg teams.

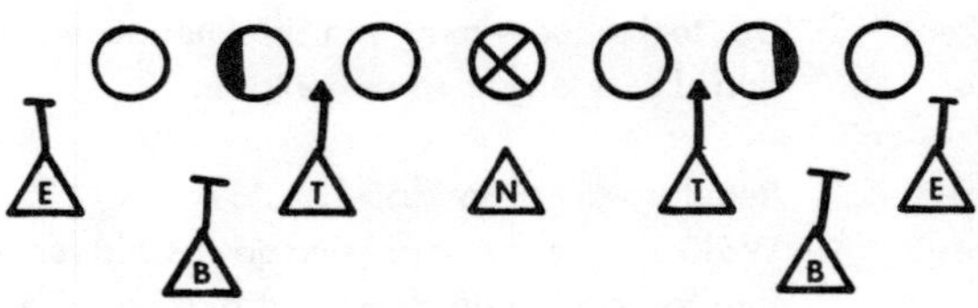

DIAGRAM 14-4

Ends: Regular.

Tackles: Gap.

Nutcracker: Regular (he may be a little deeper in alignment).

Linebacker: Align on No. 2, play regular (may have to move close to end).

Comments: We seldom use this to both sides at the same time. It is usually called to one side. It is used versus teams that may have a wide side tendency outside. It permits the linebacker to be in a good position to fulfill his duties. Also used versus large splits to get penetration. Good in passing situations, especially if used in conjunction with a linebacker blitz. Very effective if teams send backs out of the backfield. This defense usually forces a double team on the tackle, in which case a linebacker may be free. Also good if linebacker is having trouble scraping for one reason or another.

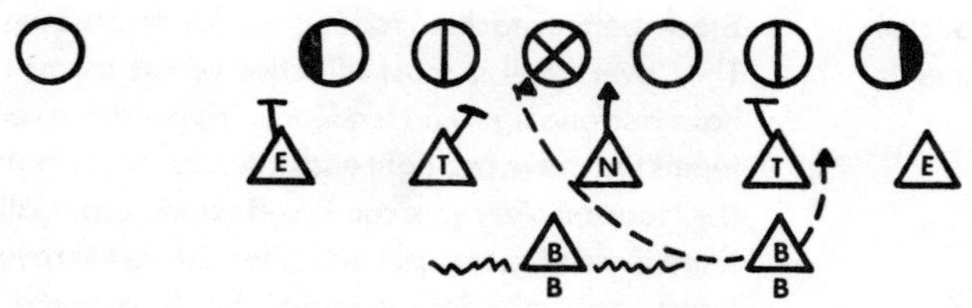

DIAGRAM 14-5
Over right

Note: This is usually called to tight end side.

Ends:	Regular.
Right Tackle:	Regular.
Left Tackle:	Regular from head-up on No. 1 (guard).
Nutcracker:	Gap technique—aligns on call side gap.
Right Linebacker:	Stacks behind tackle, follows regular techniques.
Left Linebacker:	Aligns head up on zero and plays football.

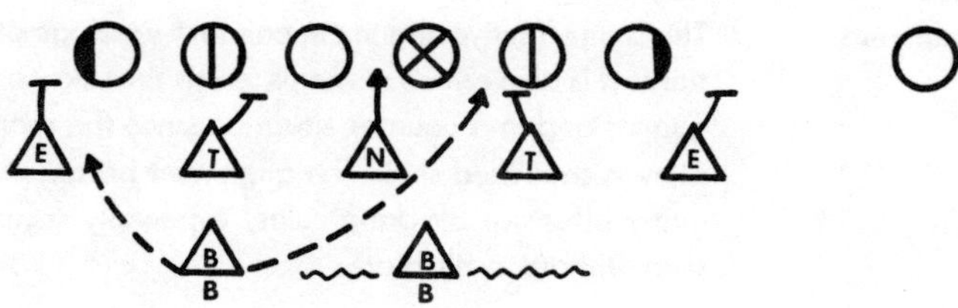

DIAGRAM 14-6
Over left

Ends:	Regular.
Right Tackle:	Regular from head up on No. 1 (guard).
Left Tackle:	Regular.
Nutcracker:	Gap technique, aligns in call side gap.
Right Linebacker:	Aligns head-up on zero and plays football.

Left
Linebacker: Stack behind tackle, follow regular techniques.

Comments: The "over" call is most effective versus teams that have a strong tight end tendency. It is not great versus teams that have two tight ends. Versus teams that run the Houston Veer this can be effective, especially if there is a slot to the split end side putting the rover in good position to defend option. We have had great success with this defense.

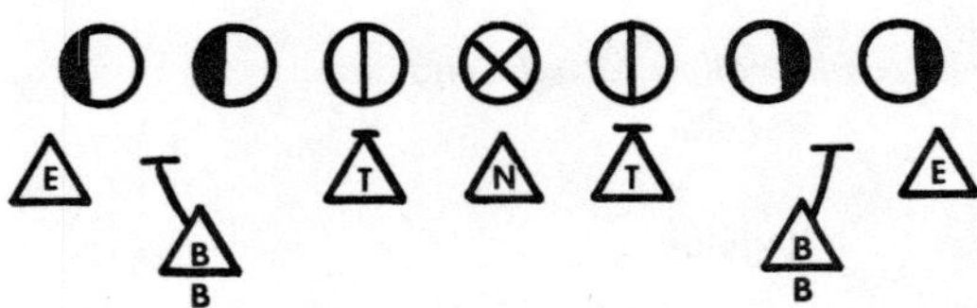

DIAGRAM 14-7

Ends: Regular.

Tackles: Regular, 4-3 alignment (almost always we will be in a "lock-up" or step-out call (never regular technique).

Nutcracker: Regular.

Linebacker: Eagle alignment.

Comments: This is an effective alignment on short-yardage situations. It is also effective versus teams that like to pull guards and in a counter situation since the running alley is squeezed shut. The alignment breaks down many offensive blocking rules, especially a guard trap without a fill block.

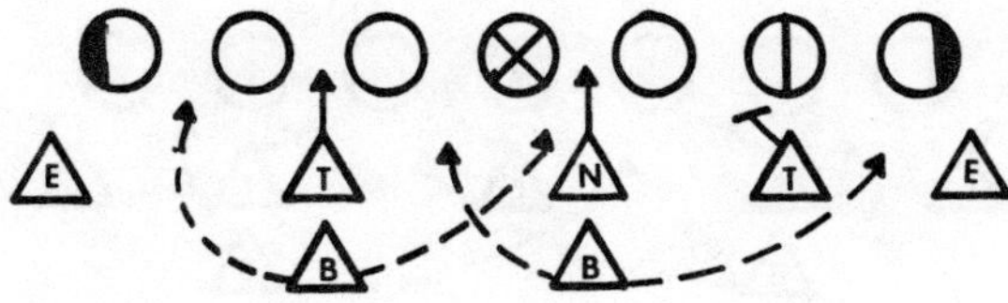

DIAGRAM 14-8
Gap stack right

Ends:	Regular.
Backside Tackle (lt):	Gap.
Callside Tackle (rt):	Regular.
Nutcracker:	Gap rt.
Linebacker:	Stacks behind men in gaps, all duties the same.

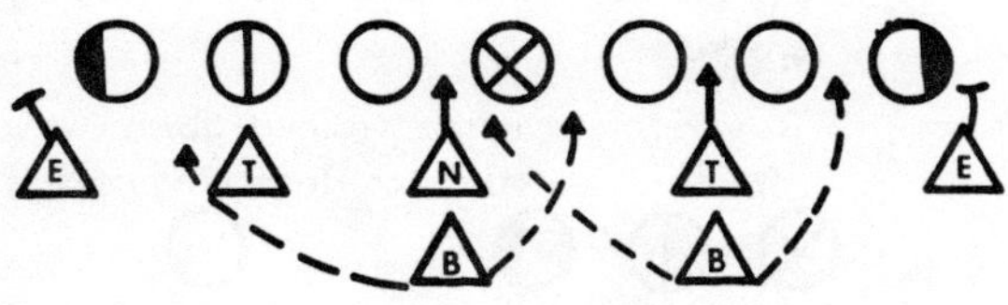

DIAGRAM 14-9
Gap stack left

Ends:	Regular.
Backside Tackle (rt):	Gap.
Callside Tackle (lt):	Regular.
Nutcracker:	Gap lt.
Linebacker:	Stacks behind men in gap, all duties the same.
Comments:	Effective versus large splits. It almost always assures a free linebacker and sometimes two because there is usually a double team forced on the gap defenders. In theory, this can hurt the inside running game. We don't like this on short yardage due to large gaps and most of all we *never* use this on first down; quarterback sneak "kills" us on early down.

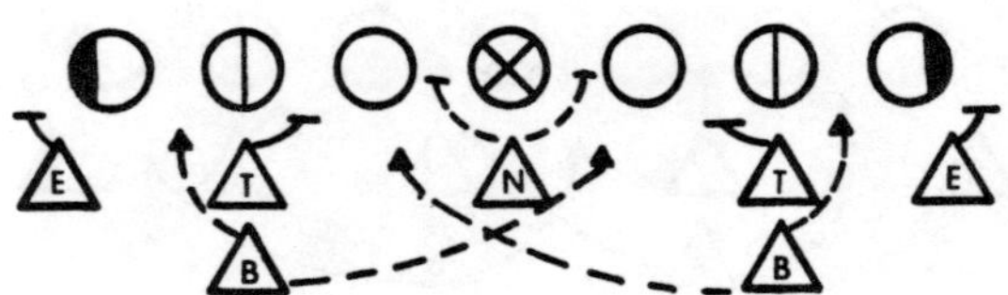

DIAGRAM 14-10

Ends: Regular.

Tackle: Regular.

Nutcracker: Regular.

Linebacker: Stacks behind tackles, play regular.

Comments: We seldom use this to both sides. It is most effective if the tight end has been able to down block on the linebacker in his scrape. The alignment allows a quicker scrape. Also effective for stunting purposes. Finally, it is used in conjunction with a rover free if we put the rover in a stack position behind the nutcracker.

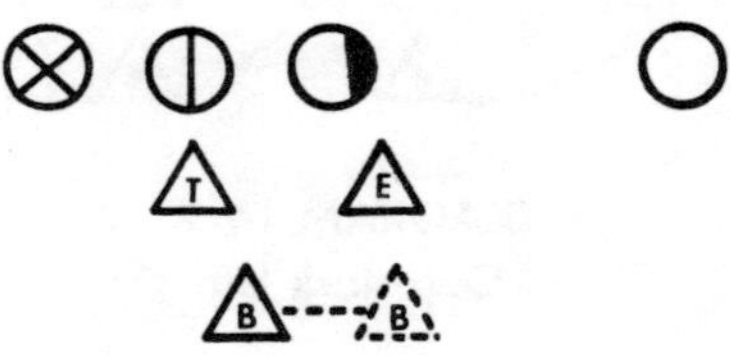

DIAGRAM 14-11

(This adjustment used only to split end's side.)

Tackle: Head up on No. 1 (guard) regular technique.

End: Moves to normal position on No. 2 (tackle), plays regular.

Linebacker: He may play anywhere from a regular to outside our defensive end, depending on offensive back's alignment and scouting report.

Comments: This is most effective versus teams that seldom run outside to the split end's side. Also effective versus teams that like to pull the backside guard on plays to the tight end.

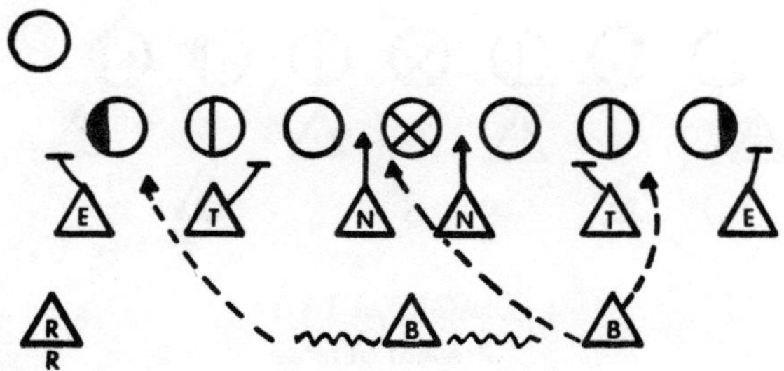

DIAGRAM 14-12

Note: Safety out, another down man comes in.

End:	Regular.
Tackle:	Regular.
2 Nut-crackers:	Gap (they must keep relation to each other, almost touch hands).
Middle Linebacker:	Must protect every hole, must make tackle.
Linebacker:	Line up opposite rover.
Comments:	We use this on the goal line, usually inside the ten-yard line. We are attempting to get penetration and to stop the run and force the opponent to throw. We also use this on extremely short yardage anywhere on the field.

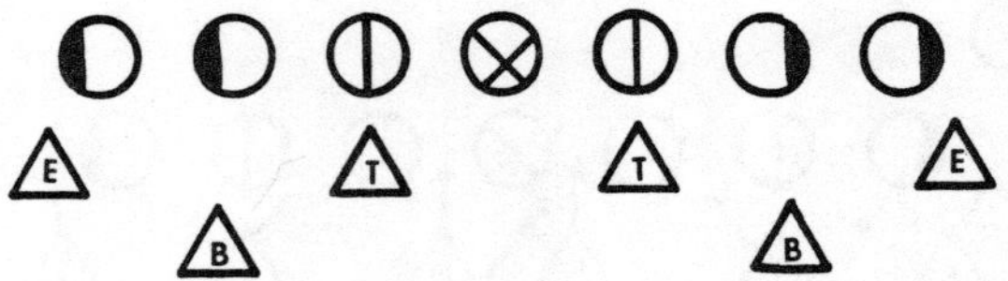

DIAGRAM 14-13
Prevent defense

Ends:	Regular.
Tackle:	4-3 alignment, aligns on No. 1 regular (usually lock up).
Nutcracker:	Comes out of game, another defensive back in.
Linebacker:	Aligns on No. 2 (4-3 alignment), plays regular.
Comments:	Used near end of half or end of game when we are ahead.

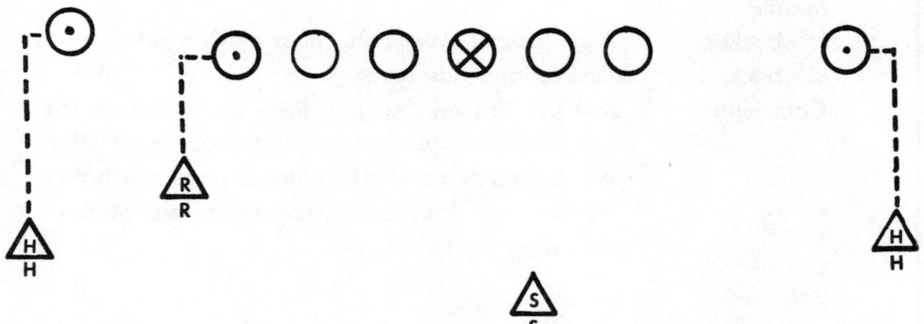

DIAGRAM 14-14

Rover:	(From outside) second eligible quick receiver, play man-to-man.
Halfbacks:	Man-to-man on first outside quick receiver.
Safety:	Free.
Comments:	We use this anytime and especially when blitzing. Also used versus two wide-outs.

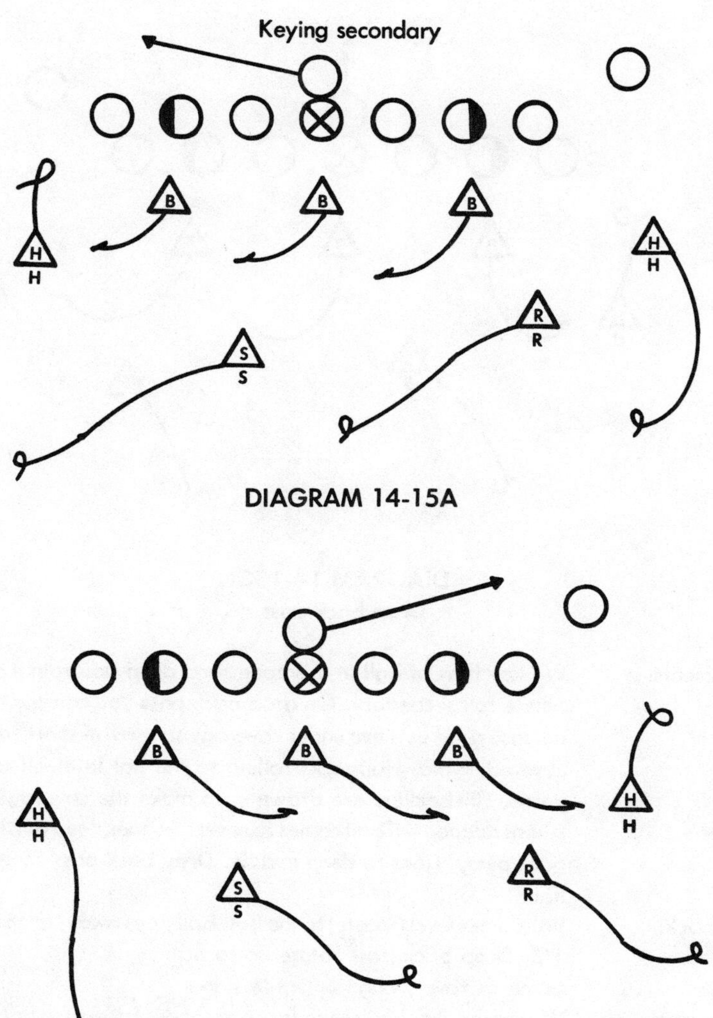

DIAGRAM 14-15A

DIAGRAM 14-15B

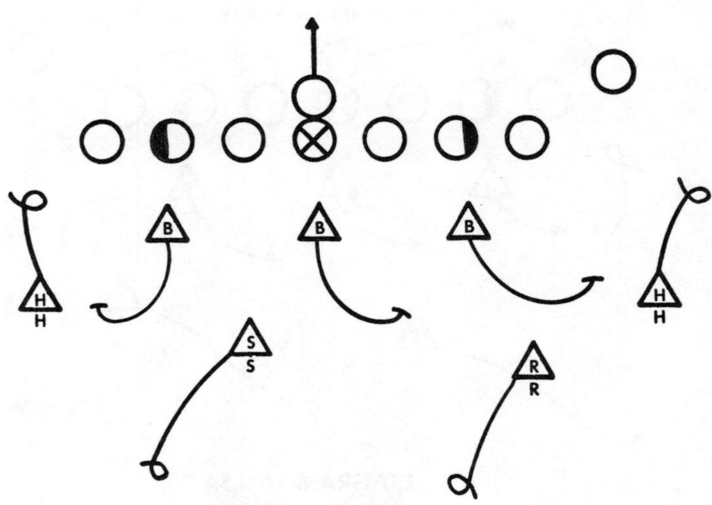

DIAGRAM 14-15C
Drop back pass

Comments: We key flow of ball in this zone, and drop accordingly. It is a simple roll secondary. On drop back pass you can see that this defense gives us a five under coverage so our five short zones are covered. *Note*: Halfbacks rolling to the flat level off at seven yards. Linebackers are drawn in to make the coverage clear.

Rover: Aligns deeper—if ball comes to rover, he goes deep outside, ball goes away, goes to deep middle. Drop back pass covers deep half.

Halfback: Ball comes level (rotate) to the flat, ball goes away, drop to deep 1/3. Drop back pass rotate up to flat.

Safety: Same as rover, align opposite side.

Comments: We use the "keying" secondary a great deal. Versus a tight wing it gives great corner support. Most used on obvious pass downs.

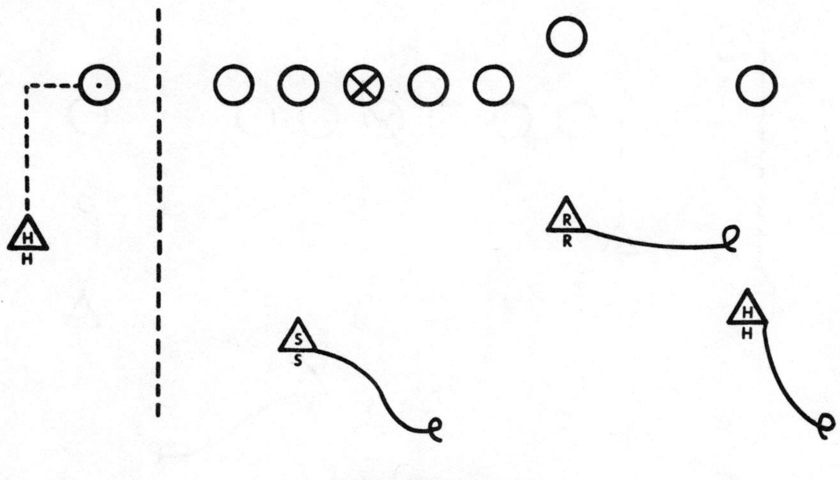

DIAGRAM 14-16

Rover:	Protect flat area.
Halfback to side of rover:	Deep outside.
Free Safety:	Still free, but protects deep middle.
Halfback away from rover:	Lane coverage or man-to-man (depending on team).
Comments:	We especially like this versus the slot formation. Also effective versus sprint out pass. Finally, we like it versus a team that likes to throw to a receiver going against flow (see Diagram 13-7). We tell the defensive halfback to hang on flow away and take a chance.

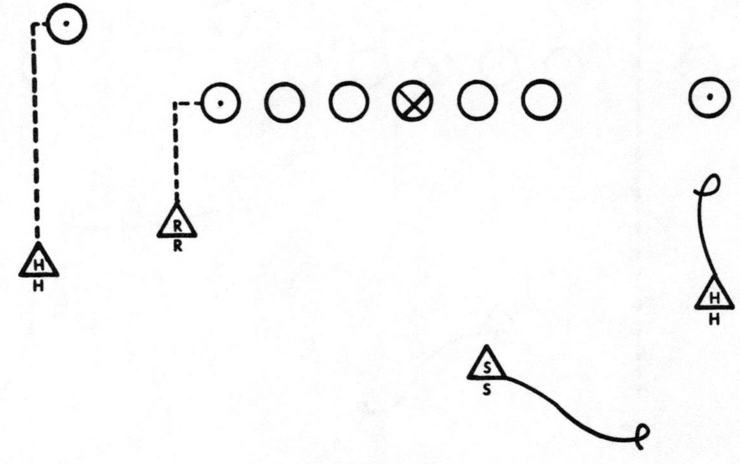

DIAGRAM 14-17

Rover:	Regular - hawk (man-to-man).
HB to side of rover:	Regular - hawk (man-to-man).
HB away from rover:	Levels to flat on snap.
Free safety:	Protects weak side halfback - cover deep half.
Comments:	We use weak rotate versus teams that try to base their offensive attack away from our rover.

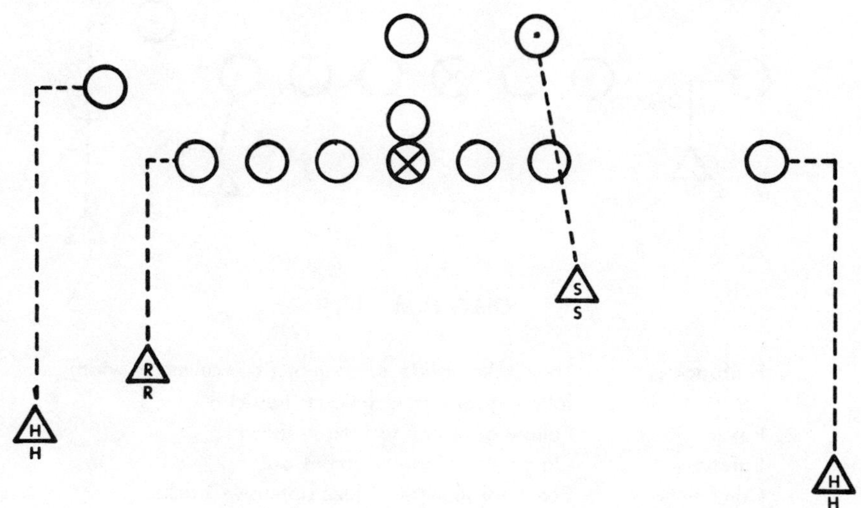

DIAGRAM 14-18

Rover:	Regular hawk.
Halfback:	Regular hawk.
Safety:	Follows rover technique, keys second receiver, may be a back; if action goes away he goes deep middle. We may put in another rover.
Comments:	We use this versus teams that throw very little. It is also effective versus teams that try to base their running attack away from our rover. It is also effective versus teams that like to throw to backs out of the backfield.
Note:	On occasion we will call a zone from this alignment and ask everyone to execute his zone technique.

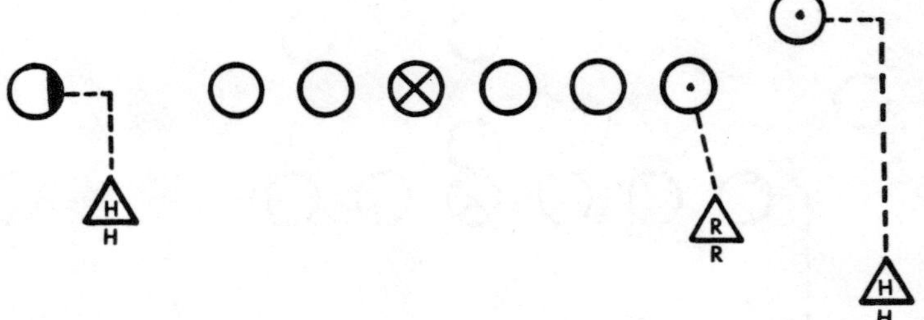

DIAGRAM 14-19

Halfbacks:	They take inside alignment (if receiver is wide), follow goal line technique (hawk).
Rover:	Follow goal line technique (hawk).
Safety:	On goal line safety comes out.
Comments:	See goal line techniques defensive backs.

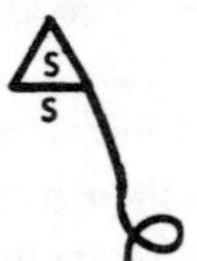

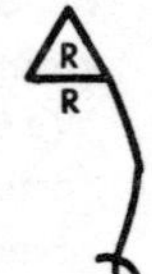

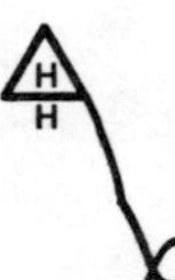

DIAGRAM 14-20
4 Across

Rover:	Aligns deeper, on snap gets depth, protects deep area.
Halfback:	Drops deep and protects deep area.
Safety:	Drops and protects deep area.
Comments:	We use this when there is an expected deep pass, near the end of half or near end of game, but too soon to use a prevent.

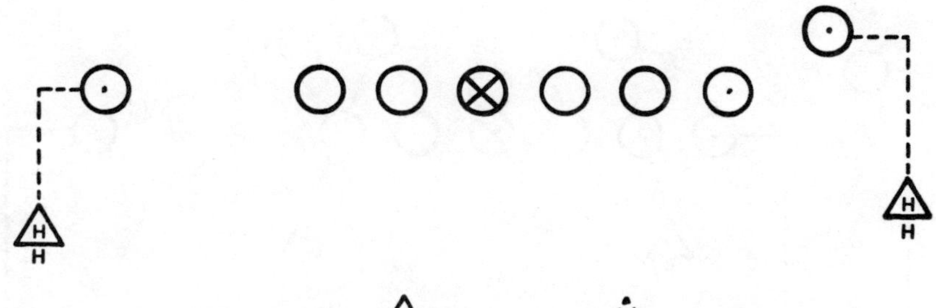

DIAGRAM 14-21

Rover:	May be placed anywhere according to scouting report.
Halfback:	Regular.
Safety:	Covers rover's man, cheats to rover's man in alignment.
Comments:	This is used to stop an opponent by putting an extra defender at the point of attack (wherever it may be). Also used to establish double coverage on particular receivers. Rover free can be used for a multitude of reasons.

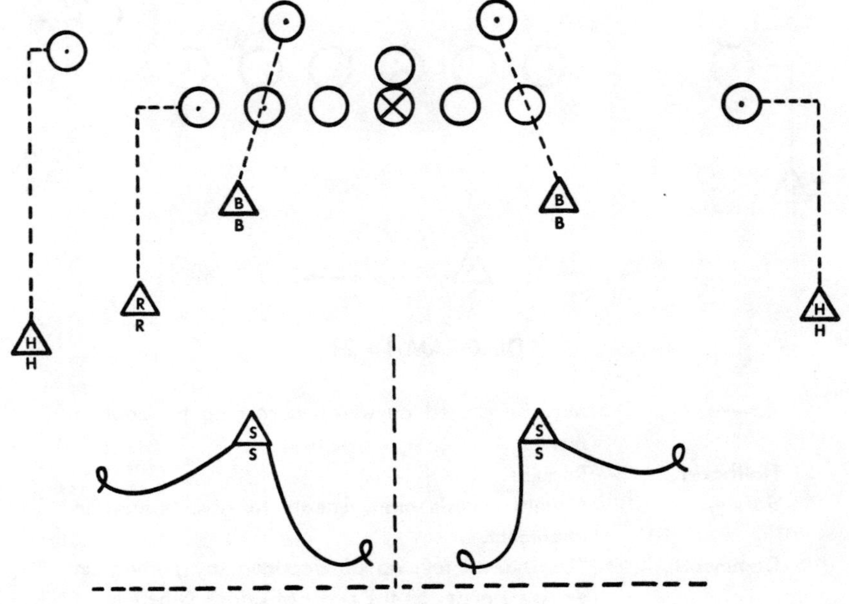

DIAGRAM 14-22

Rover: Regular (hawk), aligns deeper than normally.
Halfback: Regular (hawk), aligns deeper than normally.
Safetys: Cover deep halves of the field.
Comments: This is used when we are ahead towards the end of the half or towards the end of game.

15

Skill Drills for the Gap-Control Rover Defense

The drills that follow are by no means all-inclusive. We use several other drills, i.e., agility, individual, half-line, etc. The following drills are game situation drills. We believe that the best way to teach something to the the point where the player will use it without thinking is to simulate what will occur in the game and repeat it until the player reacts to it automatically. If a drill is to be worthwhile it must serve a purpose.

Implementing and constantly using a drill without giving its purpose to the players tends to make the drill wasted effort, and much interest may be lost.

If a particular drill is to be used every day there is a tendency to become complacent. Not just the players become complacent —coaches may become complacent too. If drills are not constantly done with enthusiasm and with all-out effort, there is no sense doing them. Correction of the technical skills of the players during the drill must occur constantly especially if a drill is used every day. *Correct* repetition is the mother of learning!

We have a drill for every technical skill that is taught. We like to think that every time a player is taught something it is actually drilled about 100 times.

Note: All techniques were given earlier.

1. Nutcracker

These drills are just a few of the drills that are used by our nutcracker.

a. Center 1-on-1 Drill: The nutcracker is placed on the center and on the snap goes through his (the nutcracker's) initial movement. He will react to the center's head (see Chapter 6). This drill has our first two or three nutcrackers working at the same time. The players in the center position need not be offensive centers. (See Diagram 15-1.)

Center One-on-One
DIAGRAM 15-1

b. 3-on-1 Drill: The purpose of this drill is to simulate the 3-on-1 situation the nutcracker will face in the game. He will work on the double team of the center and guard. He will also work on reading the guard pull and trap. Finally, from this drill the nutcracker will work on pass rush. (See Diagram 15-2—A and B.)

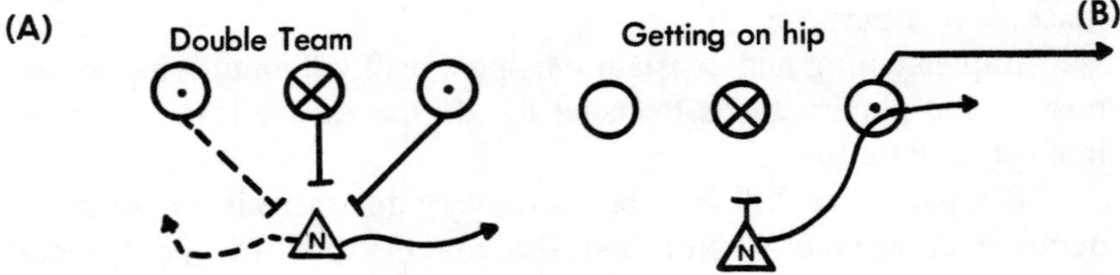

DIAGRAM 15-2

Note: In all these drills the coach may use dummies for reaction but we have found it to be preferable, whenever possible, to use players.

2. Tackles

a. Step-and-Blow Drill: This drill may be performed on a seven-man sled. The tackle will take his initial step, and as he is stepping he will deliver his forearm blow. We will on occasion use other players as offensive lineman. For exact technique see Chapter 5. The step-out technique is also executed by the tackles in this drill. The tackle just reverses the initial movement from the normal stance. (See Diagram 15-3.)

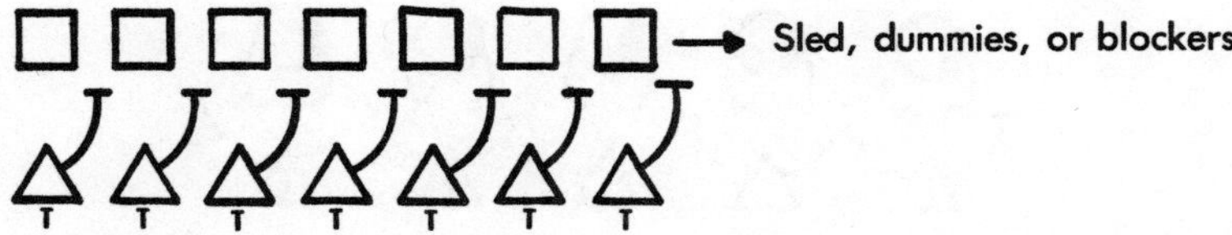

Step and Blow

DIAGRAM 15-3

b. 5-on-2 Drill: This drill is used a great deal in our group period. The five interior offensive linemen are used (they need not be offensive linemen; any players may serve the purpose) and our defensive tackles will take their normal alignments—head-up on the offensive tackles or offensive guards. The coach will stand behind the defensive tackles and give the blocking schemes that the offensive linemen will use against the tackles. They will pull, trap, fold, and man block. (See Diagram 15-4.)

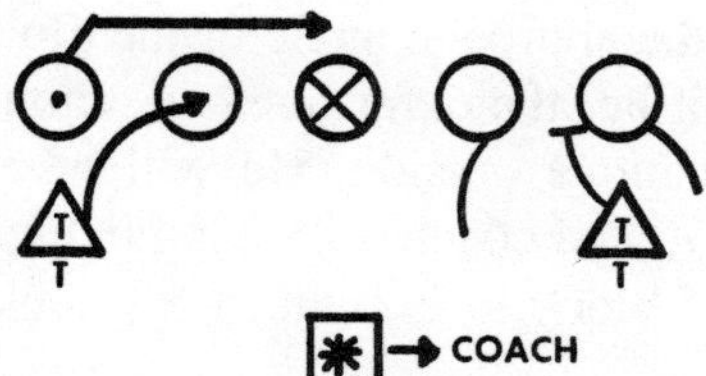

5 on 2—Facing various blocking schemes

DIAGRAM 15-4

Note: We also use a great deal of individual work with our tackles to go through the actual technique of getting on hip, reading, trap, beating the guard up block. See Chapter 5.

3. Ends

a. 1-on-1 Drill: The offensive blocker over the defensive end will fire—off the ball. The defensive end will deliver the blow on the offensive blocker. The blocker will attempt to turn out, hook, or just drive the end off the ball. The end will react accordingly. (See Chapter 7. Also see Diagram 15-5.) The coach will stand behind the defensive ends and give the signal to the blockers to execute the type of block.

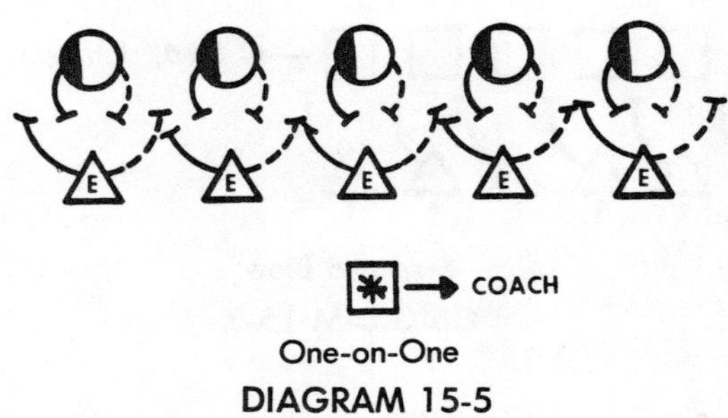

One-on-One

DIAGRAM 15-5

Note: We also drill the wing down block in this drill.

b. Take-on Drill: Once the blocker over the defensive end is no longer a threat (usually releasing inside), the end is ready to take on blockers from inside either a back or lineman (techniques have been discussed). We will have two lines, one simulating a lineman approaching the end and one simulating a back coming to block the end. The end must read the approach angle of the blocker or blockers in an effort to determine if he, the defensive end, should stop squeezing the off-tackle hole and move outside. He will take on blockers, as described in Chapter 7. The coach will stand behind the end and tell the blockers the type of block to execute, i.e., hook, kick-out, etc. (See Diagram 15-6.)

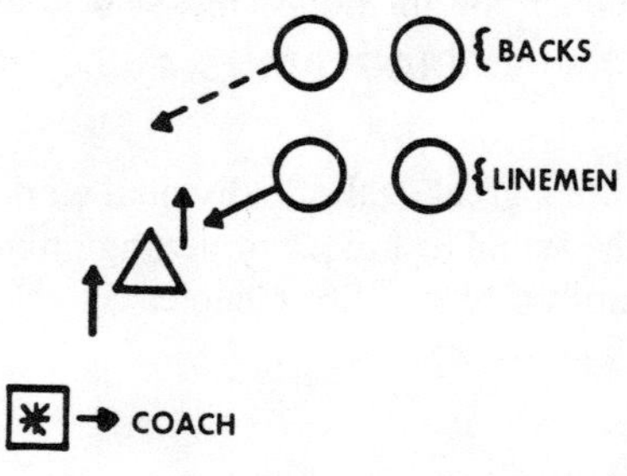

Take-on Drill

DIAGRAM 15-6

Note: We put ends on both sides, and when the play is away the end away from the play will execute his technique on plays away. See Chapter 7.

4. Linebackers

a. Scrape Drill: The linebacker will scrape up to his tackle-end gap if his keys so determine it. The linebacker will take on or tackle the blocker or ball carrier. The backs in the backfield will flow either way; on occasion they will cross key. This is not done too often in this drill, which is primarily for repetition; for coaching points see Chapter 8. In this drill the coach will stand behind the linebackers and give direction to the backs. (See Diagram 15-7.)

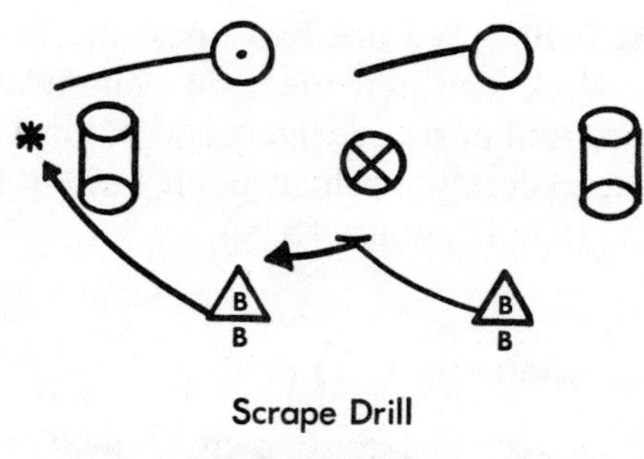

Scrape Drill
DIAGRAM 15-7

b. Read Drill: This drill is set up exactly like the scrape drill except that offensive linemen may be added, especially guards and tight ends. The linebackers are now faced with linemen attempting to block them while reading their keys.

5. Rover and Halfbacks

In these drills the safety is also included in most instances.

a. Wave Drill: This drill is the common drill used by most teams. The defenders are in their positions, and on the movement of the ball the defenders take their initial movement and on the second move of the ball they start their drops (see Chapters 9 and 10). They constantly change direction on movement of the ball (see Diagram

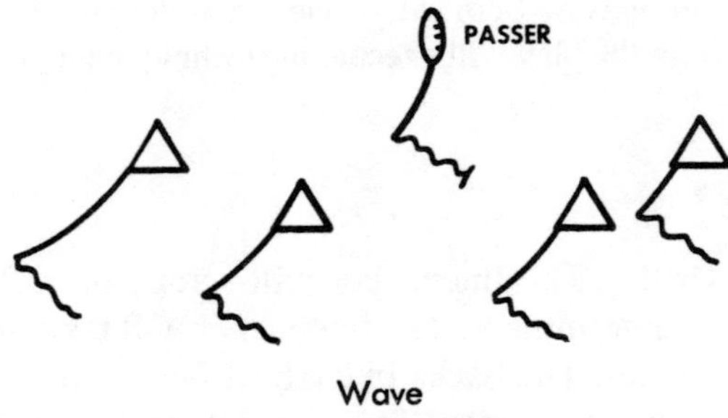

Wave

DIAGRAM 15-8

15-8). Coaching points are explained in Chapters 9 and 10. (Drops may depend on secondary call.)

b. High Point Drill: We use two lines: the front line simulates the receivers; the back line defenders on command move forward, getting their hips in front of the receivers and going as high as possible for the ball. All defenders jump high point but the ball is thrown to only one defender. (See Diagram 15-9.)

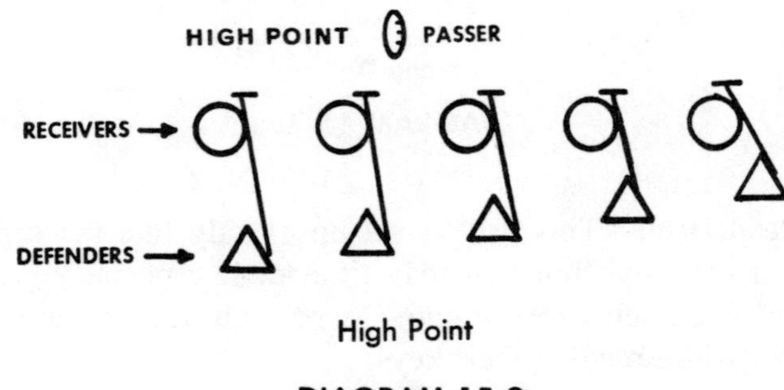

High Point

DIAGRAM 15-9

Note: This drill eliminates the lines that are common to high point drills.

c. Contain Drill: This drill is to improve the run support of our defensive backs. There are four defenders lined up in their respective positions and when the secondary call is made, the defenders on movement of the ball take their contain responsibilities. There are

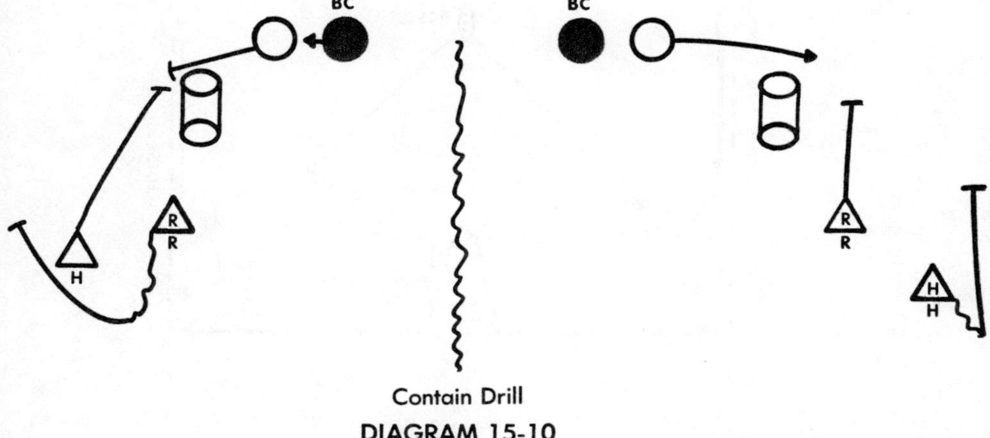

Contain Drill
DIAGRAM 15-10

offensive backs in the backfield and the defensive back who has aggressive contain takes on the lead blocker. They follow all techniques given earlier. (See Diagram 15-10.)

6. Safety

The safety will execute all drills of the rover and halfbacks.

a. Deep Drill: This drill is done for the safety to assure that he will always take his drop steps and to assure constant work in covering deep routes. The safety is placed in the middle of the field; there are two receivers placed on the hash marks. They are told to sprint downfield; the passer is told not to look to a receiver until the safety has taken his drop steps. Then the safety moves to the receiver that the passer is "eyeing." The receivers will either streak straight downfield or run a post route. The safety will follow all techniques given in Chapter 11. (See Diagram 15-11.)

7. Notes on Defensive Team Pursuit Drills

The use of team pursuit drills is easily devised by the coach. We do nothing unusual in the use of team pursuit drills. We always put a clock on our pursuit, or we use a pre-set timer. Usually we ask our defenders just to break down around the ball carrier, and the clock

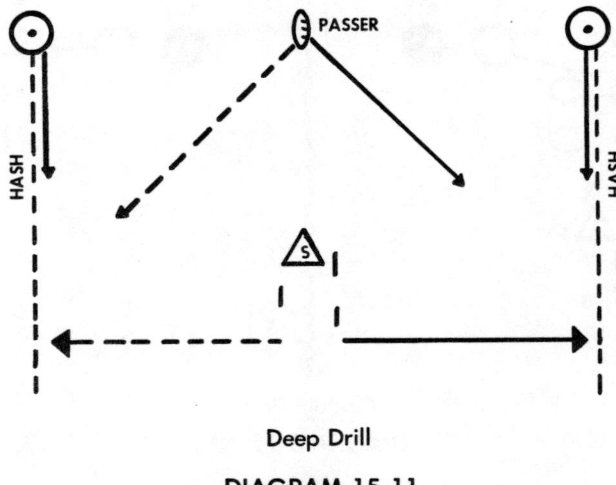

Deep Drill

DIAGRAM 15-11

stops when all defenders are to the ball carrier, with the exception of the off-side end and halfback.

On occasion we will spread four dummies all over the field and, on movement, point to a dummy and ask all defenders to sprint to the designated dummy and break down. There is a time limit placed on the time it takes to get to the dummy and also on the time it takes to return to the original alignment.

The coach can never overemphasize pursuit. He must "go nuts" over good pursuit.

8. Pass Rush Drills

Since we face a great deal of play-action passing, our pass rush drills are geared to that aspect of the game. In every pass rush drill we emphasize constantly moving to the passer, and the playside rushers are told to get into the throwing path of the passer. Backside rushers just keep rushing.

Versus drop-back and semi-roll (with no play fake) passers, the defenders are able to use all techniques given earlier. Versus play-action fake with aggressive blocking, the key coaching point is acceleration away from the blocker. We don't enforce a rigid rule of staying in lanes for our defensive downmen when confronted with a play-action fake. They can take any opening and get to the passer. It is easier for a pass rusher to break clean versus an aggressive pass blocker than a passive blocker. This is especially true if the rushers read their keys properly.

Naturally our ends are responsible for containment of the passer, and they must keep their feet at all costs. They also have the best chance to get into the passer's face.

Drills for our defensive downmen begin with a one-on-one drill. The defender faces the offensive blocker and executes his initial technique or "called" technique, then rushes the passer. He attempts to knock over the dummy that is set at various points behind the blocker. The dummy may be moved on the snap of the ball to simulate various set-up areas for the passer. The rushers must use any technique to get to the passer. He will have anywhere from 2.5 seconds to 4.0 seconds. (See diagram 15-12.) All coaching points of the pass rush which were discussed earlier may be emphasized according to who the defender is and what he needs the most in regard to his weak areas. Obviously more than one rusher at a time may be used.

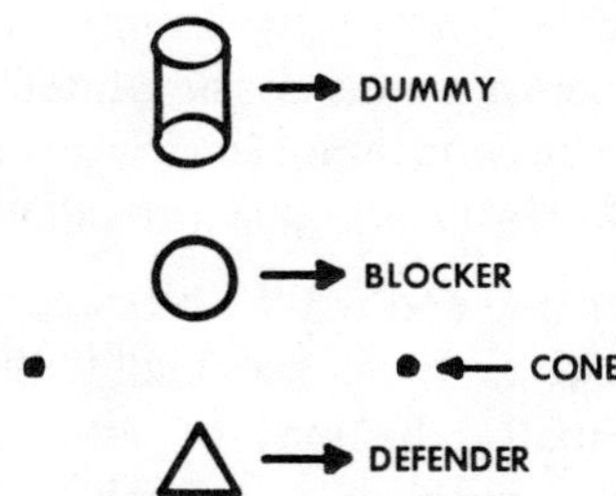

Dummy may be moved anywhere after snap.

DIAGRAM 15-12

Note: The blocker may use a variety of techniques to block the defender, depending on the opponent for that week.

Another drill that the downmen use for pass rush is a three-on-three drill. We use a center, quarterback, and back, along with three offensive linemen. The back is faked to by the quarterback in one direction or the other. The playside blockers will attack the defenders low and aggressively, while the backside blockers may cup protect.

The object is to get to the passer: the whistle will not blow if the defender can get to him in less than 4.0 seconds. You can see that if we ask a player to give 100% on a rush and then blow the whistle when he is about to obtain the rewards for his work, we don't think he will continue with the same effort. On occasion we will give the ball to the back to keep the defenders honest. (See Diagram 15-13.)

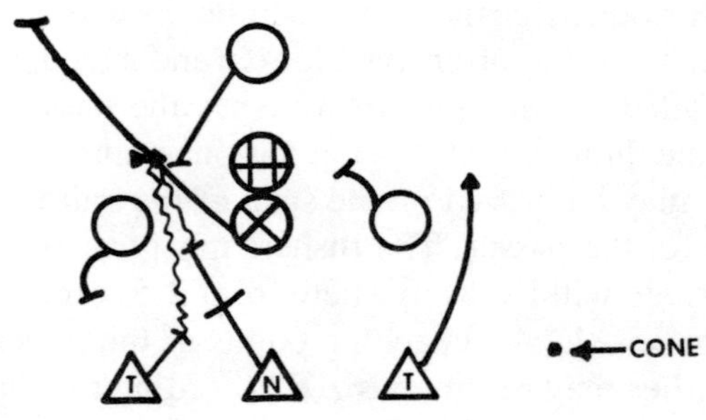

Play-action pass rush.

DIAGRAM 15-13

> *Reminder*: Remember we are discussing game situation drills. We have a drill for every technique. These drills are for the individual's repetitive work and skill correction.

Basically the defensive end will be blocked passively by an offensive back on drop-back, or he is blocked with cup blocking by an uncovered lineman. Finally, he may be attacked aggressively by a lineman (i.e., on bootleg pass) or by a back (i.e., sprint pass).

Before discussing the pass-rush drills of our defensive ends, it would be appropriate to emphasize the fact that our backside end (if flow or action is away) gives us a very poor pass rush. He is first checking for guards pulling as on bootleg. Then he is checking for any garbage, or backs sneaking backside for screen. We don't want to give the big play to the offense. As mentioned earlier, we tell him to check for faces. Therefore it is easy to see his pass rush is delayed. Remember this is just on flow-away; on drop-back pass he rushes all out unless a back crosses his face laterally for screen.

The first drill that is used is the one-on-one attack; this is done by a back or backs on sprint pass. The drill is set to both sides. The back is told to attack the end's outside knee. The defensive end follows all the

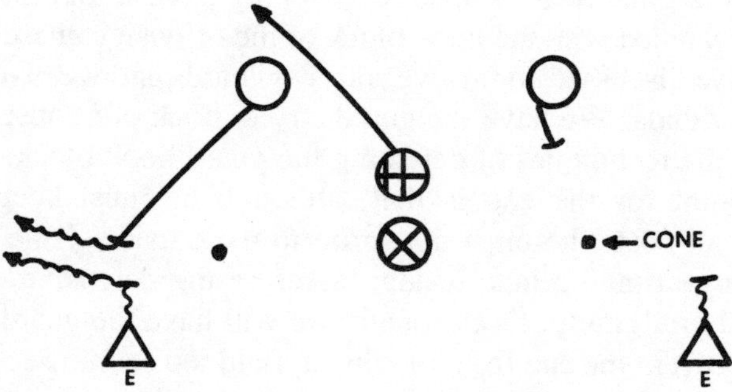

Sprint Pass—attacking the end's outside knee.

DIAGRAM 15-14

techniques discussed earlier for defeating the hook block. The quarterback attempts to get outside. Occasionally we have the back kick out our defensive end if the end is moving upfield and forcing the play too soon. (See Diagram 15-14.) The key coaching point is that the end must protect his outside leg at all costs, thereby allowing him to keep his feet. Along with this drill we will have the quarterback drop straight back and the end is to attack the offensive back (following pass rush principles that were given earlier). The key coaching point we stress to the end versus drop-back pass is to move straight upfield and get even with the passer. Then move to the passer; this allows the defensive end to get into the quarterback's face and it gives the impression to the passer that he is in trouble. (See Diagram 15-15.)

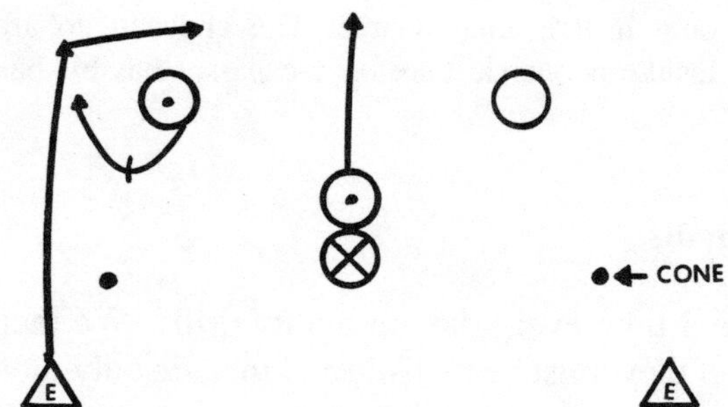

End moves upfield—then to the passer.

DIAGRAM 15-15

We see a great deal of misdirection play passes, and thereby our ends are threatened with the hook block of the offensive guards. To the drills we have discussed so far, we add two guards and we give bootleg action to our ends. We have the guards try to hook our ends; the ends will follow the techniques of defeating the guard hook block. The key coaching point for the end is that, although he must keep outside leverage at all costs, he must not sprint to the outside. If he does, he creates a large running lane inside; therefore the defensive end must give ground grudgingly. Occasionally we will have the guard kick out the end to prevent the end from moving upfield too soon. (See Diagram 15-16.)

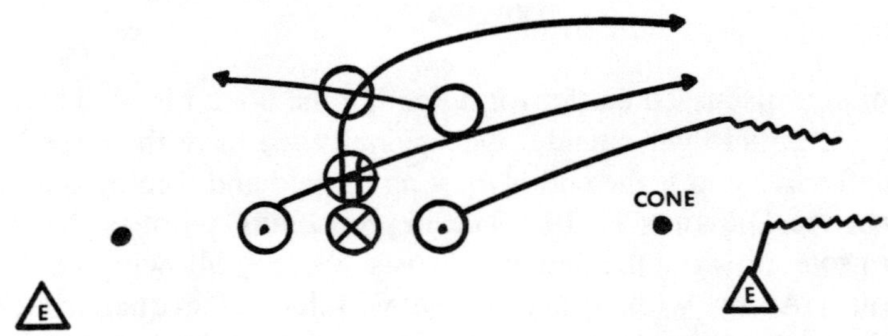

Bootleg Drill—End keeps outside leverage but doesn't create a large running lane.

DIAGRAM 15-16

Note: On occasion the end is confronted with the block of a lineman on backside cup protection. We ask the end to make contact only if it is unavoidable. The end can go around the blocker inside or outside because the passer has his back to the end.

9. Agility Drills

We spend time every day on agility drills. We feel that they are important, yet they must be realistic and include only those actions that are used or needed in a game situation.

We have four stations with a group at each station. Each group will go through the required agility drills for that station, then each group will proceed to the next station. On the way to the next station every group will use a high knee run. The stations are basically set in a square (see Diagram 15-17). Some general points: the coach should constantly be sure that the team executes the proper high knee running form between each station. Also, we always keep a close watch for proper football position (breakdown position) in all drills.

AGILITY CIRCUIT

a. Square Drills: The standard carioca drill is used, right over left and left over right. Then the player reaches the cone and immediately starts a back pedal; emphasis is placed on keeping the shoulders in front of the knees. Then the player comes to the next cone where he will repeat the carioca drill, still facing the coach. Finally he comes to the next cone in which he will jump and spin in the air, then land facing the starting position. The square drills are repeated until the bell sounds for the next section of the circuit. The group will proceed, with a high knee lift, to the ground drills.

b. Ground Drills: The coach can use any set-up of lines he desires. The group will immediately break down; on a signal from the coach they will get their feet moving, turn their feet quickly to a side and then back to the original position. This is all done on the coach's signal. Emphasis is on quick feet, short and chopping steps. Then on the coach's signal they will get in a four-point stance and crab quickly from side to side. On occasion they will be asked to spin while in their crab and return to their original position. On the command of the coach they will sprint to the manager and break down, while the next line comes up and starts their work from a four-point stance. On the bell the groups again rotate. The ground drill group proceeds to the shuffle drills.

c. Shuffle Drills: Facing the coach, the players, in a low breakdown position, shuffle over the dummies, being sure they don't cross their feet. Emphasis is placed on getting the feet back on the ground as soon as possible—that means just clearing the dummy but not hitting the dummy. When the cone is reached they will backpedal and begin the shuffle, still facing the coach, over the next set of dummies. On the bell they go to the next station.

d. Rope Drills: It should be pointed out that while we call this the rope drill we don't have ropes, so we use dummies. (We would prefer ropes, but when we tried them we found that it took approxi-

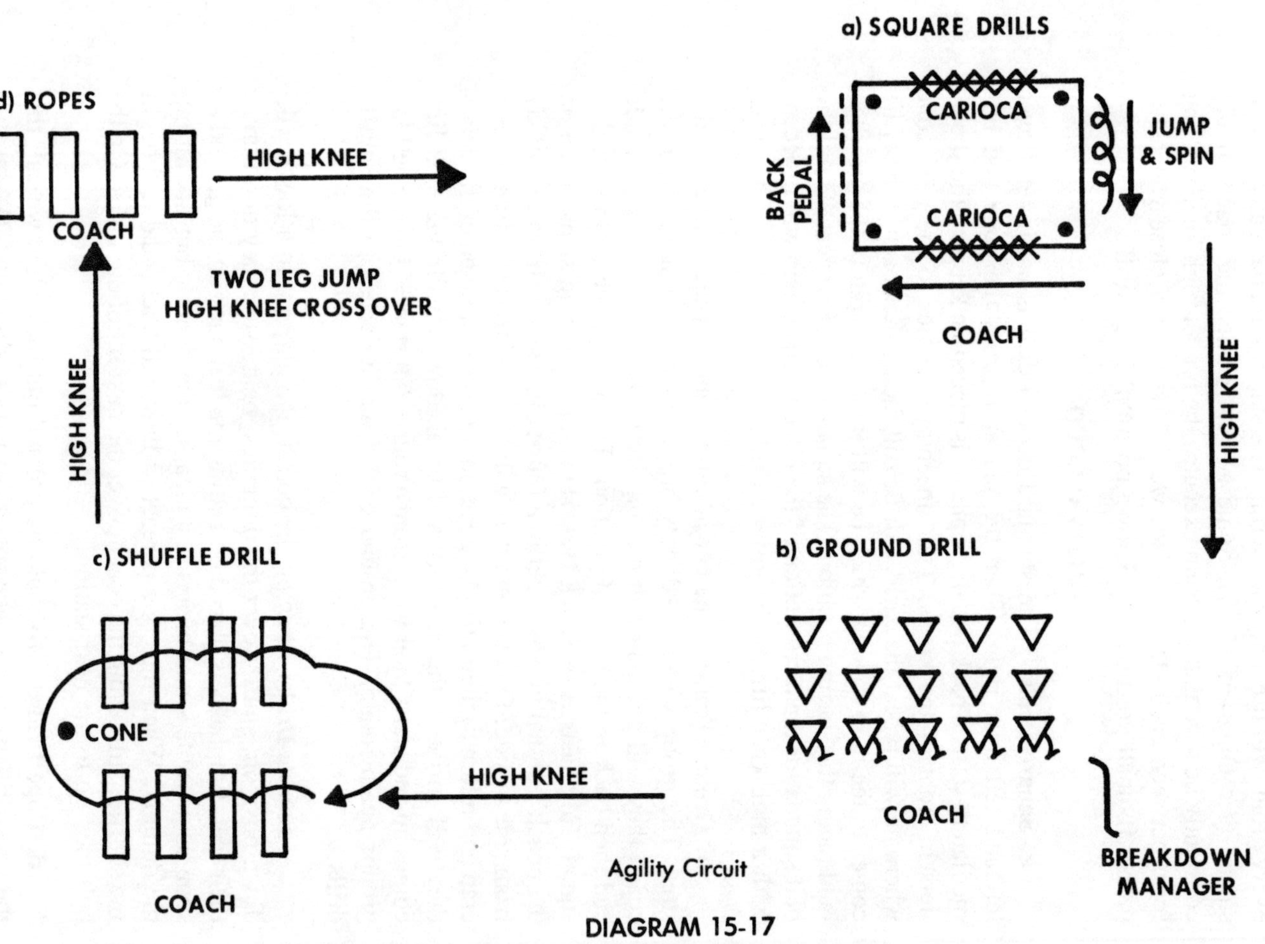

Agility Circuit

DIAGRAM 15-17

mately two days for the permanent non-removable ropes to be removed.) The first time over the dummies the players will jump with both legs, not only to increase agility but also to increase explosive power. The next time through the players do a high knee cross-over. These are repeated until the bell sounds.

Agility drills in this circuit during the season take four minutes. During pre-season more time may be spent on them. They are done every day.

10. Key Points About Drills

Rather than give a multitude of drills, which any coach can make up by simply doing a "job analysis" of each position and what is needed for it, it might be helpful to discuss drills on a general basis.

a. Types of Drills: Basically there are four types of drills: agility drills, skill (technique) drills, reaction/quickness drills, and conditioning/contact drills. Every drill must be defined and, contrary to the belief of many, we feel it is acceptable for a drill to serve more than one purpose as long as the primary purpose of the drill is not forgotten.

b. Drill Objectives and Thoughts: We believe that the objective and the purpose of every drill should be given to the players. For players to work hard in drill they must believe that the drills are an asset to them and will help them to improve their game performance.

In order for the player to succeed he must be drilled on every major skill that he will use in a game. It means the coach must have a drill for every skill. The primary objective of repetitive drilling is to make sure that the player will have reactions that are instinctive in given situations rather than having to think before reacting. The instinctive reaction must be perfect if the player is to succeed against the best competition, therefore the coach must insist on perfection in all drills—especially daily drills. This leads us to another problem—complacency on the part of the coach in his daily drills. This will lead to player complacency in drills. The result of this non-perfect repetition is wasted time. For repetitive drills to be successful they must be constantly observed and corrected.

Although a drill can possibly serve more than one purpose, the coach must constantly be sure that the drill is serving the purpose for which it was intended. The coach must constantly evaluate the drills. Important skills, most used skills, and most difficult skills should be the most used drills. This is common sense, but how many times have you seen waste of time drills? We call them "alumni drills"; they are used to impress the alumni because they look nice. It should be obvious that we believe strongly in repetitive game-situation drills that are broken down to individual skill development.

It is important to develop confidence early in the players, so our drills are not difficult. It might be said that they are stacked so the players will experience success early. However, to prolong this false success is to invite trouble.

c. Drill Description and Set-up: The drill must have a limit to the number of words that define it. This will save time and will also allow the players easy recall to a drill. We are not saying that every drill a coach does should be done every day (daily drills are done every day). The coach should not have a hodge-podge of drills, yet different drills may be used to accomplish the same results as long as the drill is not too complex. Drills that are to be used should be explained before going on the field, to save time and prevent boredom. Along the same line, the managers or injured players must be taught to set up drills so there is no wasted time. The coach can move from one drill to the next with a minimum of lost time. Managers are most important to our program, and we can't seem to get enough of them except on game day. Also, having injured players assist in drill set-up seems to motivate them to heal faster.

The drills should be done on the same areas of the field each day. If a change is made to break the monotony, then the coach should remain at the new spot for a period of time. I really don't believe in changing areas of the field because our players (and coaches) have trouble getting reoriented. Our players are very smart young men and they aren't excited about change for the sake of change.

d. Whom to Drill: Naturally, time is given to all, but emphasis is given in drills to those who will play. We avoid long lines and attempt to get as many people as possible in the drill without the loss of the teaching and learning process. What that means is that many may participate in a drill, but only those who play can really be observed by the coach. It is better to have players moving than standing around.

This may seen to be in contradiction to the principle of perfect repetitive drill with constant correction, but actually it isn't because prime time must be given to those starters and their immediate back-up players. We try to coach the other players the best we can without sacrificing the winning edge. Since we do not cut players we have boys who may not help us to win in an actual game but who certainly have the right to participate in our program. We want a lot of people involved in our program.

e. How to Present the Drill: If a coach can't be positive and enthusiastic about a drill, then he had better not use it, because it will probably be executed poorly. The coach must know the drill thoroughly, not just the mechanics of it. He must know the important coaching points, the important points of emphasis, and most of all, he must know how to correct errors. This means he must know why an error is occurring. Anyone can read how something should be done and read it to his players, but can the coach tell his players why things aren't being done properly in understandable details?

Have you ever been asked, "Coach, it works the way I'm doing it now, why do I have to do it your way?" Possibly, if the player can be successful consistently and it isn't harmful to the rest of the defensive theory and structure, the coach may have to re-evaluate what he is doing and consider the wishes of his player. However, when we present a drill to our players, we tell them it must be done properly because we are coaching to beat the best teams on our schedule. Although they may be successful against an inferior opponent, the same procedure against a good opponent may be disastrous, therefore we lose consistency in our defense. That is the answer we give to the above question.

When we present a drill to our players, we never say anything negative about the drill. In the correction of errors we attempt to be positive. The only thing that will not be tolerated is a lack of effort. Then we become very negative. Fortunately this seldom occurs.

f. Why Drill: I know coaches who seldom drill for specific technique and they are very successful. They are constantly working in team work. In football there seems to be no right or wrong way to do things. All there is is "my way or your way." We believe specific drills are a must for the reasons mentioned earlier, i.e., to make reactions instinctive rather than a thought process. Specific drills are also necessary to correct errors from a previous game, to prepare for a future opponent, and, naturally, for improvement. These things are obvious, yet must be stated to justify constant drilling.

16

Coaching Practices, Principles and Theory

In coaching, the most important aspect is the ability of the coach to teach and to correct errors. The difference in a coaching staff is not necessarily drills, time, or even the initial teaching that is done (everyone teaches initially). The difference is in the fact that a good staff never becomes complacent. They are always enthusiastic, always seeking perfection, always recognizing errors and correcting those errors. All have a common goal—to win.

1. Some General Points and Principles

The most important teaching point is this: no matter how much knowledge a coach is giving out, if the pupil is not learning then the coach is not teaching. For example, if there are 22 key players on a team and only half of the team clearly understands what is going on, then the coach is doing a poor job in communications. This is why we believe strategy plays only a small role in the overall success of a team. The real success is in the learning process.

When errors are made on the field, the coach should first question himself before yelling at the player. The coach must ask himself how much time was spent practicing this skill and how well he got the point across. We have found that on occasion a loss is the result of a teaching error during the week. You can see that we feel great coaches are great teachers and not necessarily great strategists. If in doubt, ask yourself when was the last time you lost a game on paper. Seldom do we lose on paper!

We don't want players or coaches to shoot off their mouths. We believe in being humble—but the coach must also be positive and confident. Everyone must believe we can win. Being positive yet humble is a difficult task, but it can be accomplished.

The football program must be the most organized and the best taught subject in the school. It must be more complete than any other subject. Players must get more out of the program then just winning—obviously this is an important objective. We try to make football as academic and as valuable a subject as are English, music, etc.

Our program is based on pride and 100% effort. If it were based on wins and losses, it would fall apart when a loss occurs. A football program is really not tested when the team is winning. On the contrary, the program is tested when there is defeat. How does the team handle defeat? Will they come back? Our program is blessed with players who have great pride and dedication. Losing is terrible, but it must be handled as a learning experience. The coach and the team must come back stronger from a defeat—and must improve. In other words, the team must move forward two steps after a defeat instead of one step. I am not saying that losing must be accepted—there is no worse feeling, initially, than losing a football game, for everyone concerned. The sadness must occur but it must be short lived. One quote from Lou Holtz holds very true: "Nothing is ever as bad as it seems, nor is anything as good as it seems." You can get over anything that happens.

It is important to note that players will respect coaches for basically two things: how the coach teaches, and the knowledge they can use that is given to them by the coach. Players want coaches to teach them things they couldn't learn without the coach's tutoring.

One of the general points we want in our program is position competition. We realize that some players don't need it to be great, but those players don't mind competition, they like it. Competition in a position forces a player to improve and puts him in a pressure situation in practice. This is good, it simulates a game feeling. Finally, competition keeps everyone humble. The competition a player faces in a game is the big test. The player is tested by the opponent; the player's objective is to win the play. His success or failure is determined by the grade he receives for that play. His overall performance is the efficiency score he receives after every play is graded. Players must learn to like competition and not fear it. They must realize that winning every play—every battle—will win the game.

2. The Process of Learning

There are many theories on the proper learning and teaching process. The human mind can learn almost anything if it is taught properly and organized in a well-structured manner. Of course, the coach cannot go overboard, because learning something is a lot easier than executing something to near perfection. This is why simplicity is a must.

The whole-part method of teaching is one way to reach an end. That is, the player is shown the whole picture, then given the respective parts and sections of that total picture. Whether we agree or not is unimportant; what is important is that the player must be exposed to what he is trying to learn initially, then break it down into parts. He must see where he is going.

These three points in teaching are most important: tell him; show him; and drill him, drill him, drill him! When you think he knows it, test him. Repetition and drilling do not mean the learning process is occurring. On the contrary, if things aren't being done properly, then time is wasted. Remember, *correct* repetition is the mother of learning.

In the learning process it is important to have the attention of the players; this is accomplished many ways (see teaching technique). This is why presenting the same information in several different ways has some advantages. The player may be interested in a particular technique of teaching. Of course, the coach can get a player's attention by getting nose to nose with him.

Getting a mental picture of what should occur is most advantageous. The use of films is a must, especially in football. Our films are the best teaching aid we have in our program, not just to achieve consistency, but to show our younger players how we want things done.

In the learning process we have found that insisting on perfection and detail is a must, but we have also found that we achieve more success by praising a young man than by criticizing him. If correcting an error in a positive way helps the learning process we want to use it. One thing is certain—sarcasm is disastrous.

Learning in football is different from learning in the classroom in regard to time. In football there is a deadline; things must be learned "now"! Nonsense can't be tolerated; however, that doesn't mean a player can't have fun. Pepper Rogers refers to the fact that because of the time element and because most young men stop short of mastering something, they must be disciplined to learn. Since players may mentally stop short of perfecting something the coach should bring them over "the hump." The coach must maintain the learning process.

It is amazing what a young high school player can learn. Many boys can learn to hit and be quick. It is just a matter of the coach overemphasizing these points. Many high school players must think constantly of quickness and hitting in order to do it expertly—training them to do this is the coaches' job.

3. Coaching (Teaching) Technique on and off the Field

Every coach has heard the statement, "Be yourself—be your own personality." We agree with this statement because players can see through a phony. However, we also believe that a coach can use certain techniques to fit into his personality or to improve his coaching technique.

The coach must coach to beat the best opponent on the schedule. Therefore, insist on proper techniques by players. Even though a player is successful doing things his own way versus an inferior team, a coach should not allow it. Against a good opponent the player may cost the team a game if he uses his own techniques. Poor execution will not work versus good opponents.

On the field coaching is a race against time. Therefore, the coach must "coach on the run." Players must be corrected between the drills, the plays, or off to the side of the field. An entire group should not be held up for one boy. However, the group may be stopped if it is a major point of emphasis and many players will profit. We limit "stand still" time on the field. Don't counsel a player on the field; handle problems off the field after practice if a player wants help other than football.

Since the coach must talk to be heard, speak with enthusiasm if it fits your personality. Above all don't whisper; a player will "turn you off." Remember, enthusiasm is contagious.

In coaching, organizational structure of the material being taught is a must, especially because of the time limitations. A coach cannot start organizing himself on the field. It is best to memorize the material and only refer to notes to be sure everything has been covered. If a coach is organized he will get directly to the point he is trying to teach.

Insist on second effort in everything—loafing will not be tolerated. There is no excuse for loafing. We make it a point never to joke about rule infractions such as offsides, illegal movement, etc. These are errors of discipline; however we don't stop errors of legal aggression.

It is important to use key words to emphasize important points and to correct errors. One or two words are ideal. Use of key words will save time on the field by elimination of unnecessary words. However, this doesn't mean that details and perfection will be sacrificed.

The coach must be sure that all players are reached by his teaching. A starter who doesn't understand a point covered earlier must be taught again. However, this should not be considered extra work, as it would be in the classroom. It is the minimum that is done since there can be no "B" or "C" players—they might cost a defeat. All players must be "A" students in football—at least mentally. To obtain this consistency of coaching the coach must put forth 100%. That means that the coach must coach at 100% at all times. If a day comes along and the coach has the "slows," he must not transfer that feeling to his players. The coach must coach over the slows. If a coach expects 100% effort and consistency from his players, he must be willing to give the same 100% effort and consistency.

One problem that may occur is in teamwork. Because of the situation, teaching seems to taper off during teamwork. This should not be allowed. If every coach is given an assignment or group of players that he is responsible for, then teamwork should allow the continuance of enthusiasm. If an assistant coach is not given responsibility he will generally do a poor job of coaching because he really isn't given the opportunity to teach. Of course, it is the head coach's responsibility to teach his staff how to coach/teach.

4. Coaching Relationships to Others

a. Relationships to Head Coach: Any disagreement an assistant coach has with the head coach should be made in private. This is common sense. An assistant does not have to agree with everything but he must be loyal to the head coach and to the program. He can't be a "whisperer." Nothing hurts a program more than an undedicated and moaning coach. There will be times when an assistant will be frustrated; it is suggested that before anything is said the assistant should sleep on it. If it is something that can't be resolved the assistant will have to coach over the problem.

By the same token, the head coach should never embarrass his assistants in front of the players. Along these lines the assistant should not take the correction of his players by the head coach personally. If the head coach sees an error by any player he has the right to correct that error. Remember, when there is a loss the head coach must take the full responsibility.

b. Coaches' Relationships to Each Other: All coaches should respect each other and prefix each other's name with "Coach." Never should assistants talk poorly about each other; things can get blown out of proportion. Each coach has his own personality, and although a coach doesn't agree with another coach's coaching or coaching methods that doesn't make it wrong or unsuccessful. Only one person should have a say in another coach's teaching—that's the head coach. Loyalty to each other is a must for success.

Assistants should not allow a player to be disrespectful in talking about another coach. They should insist he be called by his proper title.

When a coach is talking, other coaches should be sure that the players are paying attention.

c. Coaches' Relationships to Players: Always be honest with the players; be fair and let players see that you are fair in your dealings.

No coach should embarrass a player or hit a player. We want proud players, and to embarrass them is not the way to get pride. However, lack of effort or intentional loafing warrants some drastic action by a coach because loafing by one player is not fair to the entire team.

Every coach is told not to challenge players too early. The players must be given a chance to gain confidence, especially young players. If tested too early by a coach a good future player may be lost.

We don't especially want the players to love their coaches. There will be times when the player will dislike his coach. The only thing a coach really needs for a good relationship is the respect of his players. This may sound terrible, but everything follows respect—and if a coach is not respected by his players he probably will not succeed. Everything else will follow once respect is established.

Substitutes must be treated with respect. Everyone likes a great player but a coach is judged on how he treats his "subs." These players can be the key to success by the end of the season.

d. Relationship to Faculty and Public: We never talk about a player, other than in the coach's office. Not talking in a positive way about a player is not fair to the player. As a matter of fact we strongly suggest that a coach avoid arguing about football. Many spectators feel they are experts and there is no way an argument can be won with this type of person. However, all coaches should be friendly. Also remember there is no simple explanation for the outcome of a football game. Yet the public wants a simple answer and really doesn't care about a team's improvement or that a team effort will insure success. Most spectators only care about the score. Their view is very different from that of a coach. Therefore, an explanation of the game may be worthless.

e. Relationship to Officials: The coach should respect officials, at least to the degree that he doesn't yell at them, because when the coach yells, the players yell and then the players forget the main objective of the game—to win.

Also, if you use officials as an excuse for a loss, the players will tend to use that as an excuse and the team could possibly give up when a bad call is made because the players know you will put the blame on the officials and not on the other factors.

Finally, going crazy over a call or an official can cause loss of respect for the coach by the players.

5. Mental Approach

Mental readiness of a team is a most controversial subject. Every coach feels he can do a better job of "psyching" a team up for the game than his opponent. However, I firmly believe that mental preparation does not come the day of the game. A coach's work, enthusiasm, and preparation during the week can determine the mental readiness of a team. There is no way to determine *wholesale* mental readiness for a team. As a matter of fact, only a player knows if he is mentally ready for a game. The dedication of the coach is important to mental readiness. When there is an upset, too many coaches use the excuse that the team wasn't mentally ready. Then the fault falls on the pre-game talk, when in reality it was the lack of "psych" during the week. I really believe that the pre-game and half-time talks are the most overrated parts of football. I'm not saying they aren't needed: they are. They are the summation of the week's points of emphasis. I am just saying that a pre-game or half-time talk doesn't win the game; the players may make up their minds to play up to potential and the coach may speak at that time. Everything is then attributed to the talk if there is success.

Another problem a coach must watch out for in deciding if his team is mentally ready is that he, the coach, may not be mentally ready so he automatically feels his team is not ready. This reflection of a coach's mental attitude does not necessarily reflect the team's readiness, and it isn't fair for the coach to accuse his team of not being ready.

Psychological analysis of situations and players is overdone. Most of us are generally not psychologists and don't know enough about it to properly determine things. In our program we evaluate a player's physical performance; we worry about his "head" after practice.

Remember, pride is basic to emotion, so we try to develop pride in our players.

6. Deciding Who Plays

Naturally we want only the best football players on the field. We don't care about their personality, hair, religion, etc. The decision on who plays is based completely on physical performance. It is not based on potential, or character, or looks. If a player performs the best in game conditions, he deserves to play. The reason we use ability as a basic criterion for playing is that it is too difficult to determine if a boy is a "winner" or a "loser." On occasion a boy is tagged a loser because his personality is in conflict with the coach's personality. I am not saying that there shouldn't be discipline. I strongly believe a team must have discipline to win. But disciplining a player by a coach and having a personality conflict are different.

The coach must also be aware of fake "rah-rah" on the part of a player. We are concerned about maximum effort in game conditions, not necessarily with how loud a boy yells. Yelling is fine but a coach shouldn't be influenced by the yelling in his decision of who will play; this is why we say watch the fake "rah-rah." Many times players yell and scream but they don't hit anyone.

A boy should continue to play if he remains consistently good, but all players must realize that he is only as good as their last play. This is why we grade films. If consistency of play is expected, then the player should be graded on every play.

Finally, a boy should know why he isn't playing. A second stringer shouldn't be happy about it but he shouldn't moan, he should just work to move up.

7. Details for the Champions

Everything must be considered when developing a team—every detail in the coaching aspect and every non-technical detail. Minor things and little details sometimes can give a team that extra class it may need to be a champion.

In appearance, everyone should be neat. The coaches should also look neat on and off the field. Everyone (including coaches) should be prompt for all meetings. Things like huddle discipline, time-out alignments, pre-game warm-up, etc., are all details that should not be neglected. These little details give a team that extra pride that is needed.

8. Game Day

The coach must keep his composure. No coach, especially under pressure conditions, should raise his voice to another coach. Also under game conditions, the coach shouldn't put extra pressure on a player (i.e., saying to a P.A.T. kicker, ''Well, the entire game rests on you'').

Be respectful to opposing coaches and players. The coach doesn't have to be ''Mr. Wonderful,'' especially if it doesn't fit his personality, but he must be respectful.

Finally, never get involved with fans the day of the game. They can be very brutal. The smart coach will shut off everything except the game.

Index